Interdependency and Care over the Lifecourse

Interdependency and Care over the Lifecourse draws upon theories of time and space to consider how informal care is woven into the fabric of everyday lives and is shaped by social and economic inequalities and opportunities.

The book comprises three parts. The first explores contrasting social and economic contexts of informal care in different parts of the world. The second looks at different themes and dynamics of caring, using fictional vignettes of illness and health, childcare, elderly care and communities of care. The book examines the significance to practices of care throughout the lifecourse of:

- understandings and expectations of care
- emotional exchanges involved in care
- memories and anticipations of giving and receiving care
- the social nature of the spaces and places in which care is carried out
- the practical time–space scheduling necessary to caring activities.

Finally, the authors critically examine how the frameworks of *caringscapes* and *carescapes* might be used in research, policy and practice. A working example is provided.

This book will be of interest to students and researchers of care work, health and social care, geography, sociology of the family and social policy, as well as those in business and policy communities trying to gain an understanding of how work and informal care interweave.

Sophia Bowlby is Senior Lecturer in Human Geography at the University of Reading, UK.

Linda McKie is Research Professor in Sociology at Glasgow Caledonian University and Associate Director at the Centre for Research on Families and Relationships at the University of Edinburgh, UK.

Susan Gregory was Research Fellow at the Research Unit in Health, Behaviour and Change and, following her recent retirement, is an Honorary Fellow in Public Health Sciences, both at the University of Edinburgh, UK.

Isobel MacPherson runs her own business, Community Health Research and Evaluation, and was previously a Senior Research Fellow at Glasgow Caledonian University, UK.

Relationships and Resources
Series Editors: Janet Holland and Rosalind Edwards
London South Bank University

A key contemporary political and intellectual issue is the link between the relationships that people have and the resources to which they have access. When people share a sense of identity, hold similar values, trust each other and reciprocally do things for each other, this has an impact on the social, political and economic cohesion of the society in which they live. So, are changes in contemporary society leading to deterioration in the link between relationships and resources, or new and innovative forms of linking, or merely the reproduction of enduring inequalities? Consideration of relationships and resources raises key theoretical and empirical issues around change and continuity over time, as well as time use, the consequences of globalisation and individualisation for intimate and broader social relations, and location and space in terms of communities and neighbourhoods. The books in this series are concerned with elaborating these issues and will form a body of work that will contribute to academic and political debate.

Interdependency and Care over the Lifecourse

Sophia Bowlby, Linda McKie, Susan Gregory and Isobel MacPherson

Routledge
Taylor & Francis Group

LONDON AND NEW YORK

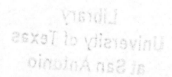

First published 2010
by Routledge
2 Park Square, Milton Park, Abingdon, Oxon, OX14 4RN

Simultaneously published in the USA and Canada
by Routledge
270 Madison Avenue, New York, NY 10016

Routledge is an imprint of the Taylor & Francis Group, an informa business

© 2010 Sophia Bowlby, Linda McKie, Susan Gregory and Isobel MacPherson

Typeset in Times New Roman by Pindar NZ, Auckland, New Zealand
Printed and bound in Great Britain by TJ International Ltd, Padstow, Cornwall

British Library Cataloguing in Publication Data
A catalogue record for this book is available from the British Library

Library of Congress Cataloging in Publication Data
Interdependency and care over the lifecourse / Sophia Bowlby ... [et al.].
    p. ; cm.
    Includes bibliographical references.
    1. Social medicine. 2. Continuum of care. 3. Human services. 4. Caring.
    5. Medical care. I. Bowlby, S. R. (Sophie R.)
    [DNLM: 1. Delivery of Health Care. 2. Age Factors.
    3. Community Networks. 4. Cross-Cultural Comparison.
    5. Home Nursing. 6. Socioeconomic Factors.
    W 84.1 I6085 2010]
    RA418.I5235 2010
    362.1—dc22   2009030561

ISBN10: 0-415-43466-1 (hbk)
ISBN10: 0-415-43467-X (pbk)
ISBN10: 0-203-86007-1 (ebk)

ISBN13: 978-0-415-43466-9 (hbk)
ISBN13: 978-0-415-43467-6 (pbk)
ISBN13: 978-0-203-86007-6 (ebk)

This book is dedicated to:

Peter and Thomas who are at the centre of my 'personal community'
Sophie

The Andersons, Cowies, Houstons, McIlroys and McKies; thanks to one and all!
Linda

Rózia Gregory for her kindness and support
Sue

My late parents, Willie and Mary MacPherson, who taught me the meaning of care, and family and friends who put up with me
Isobel

Contents

Illustrations

Acknowledgements

There are many who have shared their thoughts and ideas, and offered practical help during the writing of this book. Too many to mention, but they know who they are and we thank you all. In recent years, the authors have presented a number of papers and workshops on relevant topics and gained much from the comments and insights offered. Our gratitude and warmest thoughts go to all those who have encouraged, supported, as well as challenged us.

A number of people and networks are noted below as their support went well beyond good humour, interest and ideas; they 'rolled up their sleeves' and got stuck into the book project in notable ways.

Dr Ruth Evans of the Department of Geography, University of Reading, UK, provided invaluable information and comments on the People Scenarios located in Sub-Saharan Africa. Moira Wilkinson, of UNICEF, provided access to their research on schools and commented on our application of the findings and recommendations. The staff of Eurostat, the US Census Bureau and the National Carers Association USA helped us to identify relevant data sources. Charles Breslin, of British Gas, gave valuable time and ideas to comment on Chapter 7. His energy rejuvenated our flagging minds.

Some research networks and groups intertwined with our work. The Gender Research Group of Hanken, School of Economics, Helsinki, offered detailed comments, references and ideas as chapters evolved. Particular thanks to Sanne Bor who read and commented on a draft of the book and to Jeff Hearn, Marjut Jyrkinen and Teemu Tallberg for sharing references, data and ideas. Members of the Economic and Social Research Council (ESRC) project, Organisation Carescapes, Gill Hogg, Heriot-Watt University, Andrew Smith, University of East London and Maria Breslin helped with debates and data. The then Divisions of Social Sciences at Glasgow Caledonian University provided a small grant to fund secondary data analysis for Chapter 1. We acknowledge their financial and collegial support.

On a personal note, we would like to thank academic colleagues Tim May, University of Salford, Debra Hopkins, University of Aberdeen, and Lydia Lewis, Bath Spa University, who kept a look out for information and sources of potential interest to the book.

The series editors, Ros Edwards and Janet Holland, both of the South Bank University, provided insightful comments that helped us to refine and revise the book. Khanam Virjee of Routledge was a tower of strength, guiding us through the final stages.

This book grew out of a comment made by Professor Sara Arber (University of Surrey) over a decade ago. Her suggestion that our seminar paper provided the basis to a book has finally borne fruit. Thank you for the idea!

All errors remain those of the authors, but there would have been many more without the input of colleagues and groups noted above.

Introduction

It's all in the timing ...

Our interest in time–space frameworks of care, and informal care in particular, took shape around the participation of three of the four authors in a conference in 2000, titled *Marking Time, Making Time*.[1] Moving into a new millennium promoted debate on the topic of time in a range of ways, including national, ethnic, family and gendered histories. In tandem with this interest in the past has come speculation about the future, and how we as a society, a people and planet might develop, especially in the face of projected environmental and climate change. As individuals, and academic colleagues, we were part of these events and discussions to varying degrees. Drawing upon our respective backgrounds, as women with a range of caring experiences, employed in academia in the disciplines of geography, sociology and social policy, respectively, we considered what 'time' might mean for the analysis of social change and informal care. Our interest is in informal care, evident in public and private locations, which can involve a range of kin and non-kin individuals, including family members, relatives, friends, neighbours and work colleagues. The work of Melucci (1996) provided a starting point in our analysis. His philosophical and sociological reflections on time take the reader from the everyday regulation of clock time, through the rhythms of time, such as seasons, to the ways in which time moves our thinking and actions through past memories, future anticipations/speculations and the lived experience of each day. As human beings, we are, at any one time, working with many experiences and meanings of time:

> Each and every day we make ritual gestures, we move to the rhythm of external and personal cadences, we cultivate our memories, we plan for the future.
>
> (Melucci 1996: 1)

Philosophers have brought together ideas and literature from across the disciplines to further explore interdependencies and 'human flourishing'. This is a term used by philosophers to denote 'true happiness' in discussions of how people can live a fulfilled and complete human life (Paul and Miller 1999). We start here, from accepting the argument that recognising and promoting caring interdependency is vital to such 'human flourishing' (Groenhout 2004). We focus on informal, unpaid care and explore:

* How we receive, and offer, informal care and how informal care nudges up against formal care. For example, the way in which family members, friends and neighbours work together to support those requiring care and how other types of care provision, such as paid carers and community-based services, link with that informal provision.
* How our understandings, practices and experiences of care change over time and space as we learn about care and caring in families, schools, neighbourhoods, workplaces and through activities such as volunteering, working, and engagement in leisure or sports groups.

Space to consider ...

Hagerstrand's (1978) development of time-geography explores the intersection of not only human trajectories in time–space, but also the trajectories of other biological entities and human artefacts. Hagerstrand's work (1978) draws out the significance of the simple fact that movement between points in space consumes time, in addition to movement through spatial contexts.[2] Giddens extended and developed Hagerstrand's work in his theory of structuration in which he attempts to provide 'an adequate account of human agency' that situates 'action in time and space as a continuous flow of conduct' (Giddens 1979: 2). He introduces the concept of 'locales' to replace Hagerstrand's concept of 'stations', which Giddens considers does not give enough emphasis to human agency and power relations (Giddens 1979, 1984). Giddens explains the term as follows:

> Locales refer to the use of space to provide the *settings* of interaction, the settings of interaction in turn being essential to specifying its *contextuality*. ... Locales may vary from a room in a house, a street corner, the shop floor of a factory, town and cities, to the territorially demarcated areas occupied by nation states.
>
> (1984: 118; original emphasis)

By contextuality, Giddens is referring to not only the physical character of the setting but also to the mix of people present and the forms of communication between them. Thrift (1983, reprinted 1996) explores the importance of locales. He argues that '[i]n any particular organisation of production, certain of these locales will be dominant; that is, time *must* be allocated to them (Thrift 1983 [reprinted 1996: 81], original emphasis). He continues by suggesting that differences in the time allocated to different locales through the lifecourse distinguishes class groups – and, we would add, further distinctions of age, gender and ethnicity. Furthermore, although the quote above from Thrift emphasises the organisation of production, the same point can be made in relation to the organisation of social relationships and social reproduction.

Locales are linked through webs of communication media and social networks to other locales and scales of interaction. Moreover, the scales over which interaction occurs are socially differentiated (Thrift 1983). Here, it is important to recognise that the changing technologies of communication and transport that have recently accelerated the processes of time–space compression and convergence may also change the nature of our social experience of activities. In Giddens' discussions of interaction within locales, he lays great stress on the importance of co-present interaction, although he also implies that interaction within a locale can be mediated by other methods of communication. He also insists on the importance of what he terms the regionalisation of forms of interaction within a locale as in, for example, the zoning of different social practices to front or back regions of everyday life (Giddens 1984, Goffman 1959). In relation to care-giving, the dominance of co-presence is obvious. Although care can be provided 'at a distance' (Silk 1998) through, for example, telephone or e-mail exchanges or the provision of money, certain types of care, especially care for younger children, elderly, sick or severely disabled people, requires the physical presence of a carer in the same location as the person receiving care and offer few possibilities for realising economies of scale or scope. As Hagerstrand remarks, '[i]t is an activity of artisanal rather than industrial character to rear a new individual' (Hagerstrand 1978: 222). This has clear practical implications for the possibilities of combining paid work and care (Palm and Pred 1974) and for the social organisation of the resources for caring.

A further implication of Giddens' emphasis on the significance of the regionalisation of locales and the contextualisation of interaction is the importance of paying attention to the power relations through which the regionalising in time and space of particular social practises within a locale is achieved and maintained. In relation to care, this implies that we should examine critically both the forms of caring encounters within locales dominant in care work (e.g. home, nursery or school), the power relations that are significant to their organization in time–space relative to other locales; for instance, the assumed role of parents in managing homework (Stephens 1999). In addition, Jamieson (1998: 9) points out that notions of caring take on different meanings over time. She cites changing patterns of physical expressions of love and care over the last century in which emotional bonds were expressed in different ways to those accepted today. For example, expressions of emotion through physical affection have become more evident in recent years as family members dilute what is termed the 'stiff upper lip' approach to familial relationships, and now openly hug or kiss each other in ways that were considered to be inappropriate even 30 years ago.

For many social scientists, although the importance of time–space relations may be acknowledged, the major difficulty is to retain the complexity of time–space at both the levels of the theoretical and the empirical. Often, the study of space is ignored and the study of time is conflated with social change (British Social Attitudes 1999) or economic exchange (Balbo and Nowotny 1986). Yet, as Ermath (1998) comments, this apparently neutral medium is a particular construction of industrial culture that has been 'naturalised' and 'universalised'. The challenge is to introduce and work with temporal spatial frameworks 'at multiple levels' (Mills 2000: 121).

Working over time and space

Our development of temporal spatial frameworks of care owes much to the work of Adam (1990; 1995; 1998), who outlined the challenges posed by notions of time for social theory. She contends that the project of keeping time and space explicit in social research and theory is one made problematic by the complexity of social time and the difficulties of disentangling the power relations involved in the construction of conventional times in economic and industrial cultures:

> Not all time is money. Not all human relations are exclusively governed by the rationalized time of the clock. Not all times are equal. That is to say, all work relations touched by clock time are tied up with hegemony and power.
>
> (Adam 1995: 94)

Adam (1995) also noted there is a gendering of time in that there are different valuations of men and women's time and tasks, together with different physical realities of time (most obviously, pregnancy and childbirth). The gendering of time impacts on power and the ability to negotiate everyday and longer term plans. For Adam (2000) and Melucci (1996), the project for social scientists is to move analysis beyond the apparently 'neutral medium' of quantitative time to the rhythms of time; the multi-dimensionality of time and space. For us, this necessitates a gendered exploration of the multi-dimensionality of time and space, which addresses the gendered basis of temporal and spatial frameworks.

Adam proposed the 'temporal gaze' as an approach to analysing social phenomena and concepts that goes beyond the limitations of quantitative time:

> The temporal gaze ... can take many forms. Time may be added to existing approaches without disturbing the *status quo* of theory and methodology. Alternatively, focus may be on the time–space ... or typologies constructed of the complexity of ... time. Finally, phenomena, processes and events may be conceptualized as timescapes.'
>
> (Adam 2000: 125, original emphasis)

Adams (2000) proposes four dimensions to the temporal gaze, moving from the simple notion of *quantitative* time (such as calendars of clocks); through a recognition of *context* (time and space as an 'indivisible unity'); recognising the *multidimensionality* of time (incorporating the dynamic of levels and functions of time); culminating in the notion of the *timescape* perspective (bringing together the previous three to a theorised coherent whole).

Time of life, living life

The 'life cycle', 'life stages' and the 'lifecourse' are all terms that attempt to encapsulate the passage of time between birth and death that people progress through, encountering largely predictable life events along the way. Because these events, certainly over the course of the twentieth and now the twenty-first centuries, have become less predictable in terms of when, where and whether they will take place in the majority of people's lives, the term *lifecourse* has become the preferred term used to sum up this process. Dewilde (2003) sees the lifecourse as multidimensional, '.. an amalgam ... of the multiple, interdependent trajectories relating to different institutional spheres in society' (118). In particular, she identifies the institutional spheres of the family, of education and of the labour market. She distinguishes between 'transitions' – 'changes in the lives of individuals that are in accordance with the socially constructed life course' (Dewilde 2003: 118) and which are linked to age (for example, leaving school or having children) – and 'events', which may or may not be predictable and which are not *a priori* linked to age (for example, war or redundancy). The lifecourse is influenced by the actions of the state, particularly in countries in which the state is able to provide a range of welfare services, as these are often structured in relation to age or lifecourse stage – for example, support for parents with children or for the retired. Between them, the state, the market and the family influence the individual lifecourse and create inequalities between different social groups (for example, men and women or social classes) and may also create cumulative advantages and disadvantages between different groups.

Different lifecourse transitions and events bring with them a need for the exchange of care. For example, transitions to do with bodily growth and ageing involve care between adults and children and between younger and older adults; the path through family relationships involves care between partners, between family members and friends, and again childcare and eldercare; the path through education to providing a livelihood to no longer actively working involves care exchanged between workmates and friends. We suggest that we should examine the ways in which care at one point in the lifecourse reflects past or affects future caring encounters. Such examination should be alert to both the material aspects and impacts of care, and the influence of ideas of the 'normal' and desirable patterns of care over the lifecourse – ideas shaped through social experience and communication.

Time to evolve: Moving over *caringscapes* and *carescapes*

The journey that the authors took in developing an analytical framework included exploring what we came to see as an active ongoing process, rather than a static framework. Accepting the complexity of spatial–temporal dimensions of care, we found ourselves reflecting on the range of activities, feelings and relationships that might exist in people's mapping and shaping of their routes through life. In refining these ideas, the notion of terrain was one we explored. A terrain is a landscape – mountains, valleys and areas of contrasting vegetation and environments. This image of a terrain envisions the varied landscapes as representing alternative future ways of life – people may plan for, hope for or simply expect to spend time in a particular type of environment; they may fancy a charming, relaxing valley with trees and flowers, or enjoy the idea of a challenging climb to a glorious view.

As a person moves through a terrain, s/he can look ahead and plan a direction and a route across this varied landscape. A traveller may set out on a well-trodden path only to find the way barred or may leave the main route for an interesting byway. Some travellers do not plan their route but follow the main path without thinking or follow a path marked out for them by others. Many plan some sections of their journey but leave others to chance.

But this is not a static landscape waiting to be discovered. As in Alice in Wonderland, the view ahead changes with changes in life possibilities – a green valley may become a desert of dead trees, a steep mountain may become a gentle slope. And the traveller may acquire better shoes or a better compass – perhaps a horse or car to make the journey easier. Moreover, travellers are not alone but may spend some or all of the journey with others (a group of friends, a family, work colleagues) who may influence the choice of route and affect the experience of travelling.

Drawing upon the ideas of movement and flows in time and space, we offered the framework of caringscapes (McKie *et al.* 2002). A caringscape perspective should consider the complexity of spatial–temporal frameworks and reflect a range of activities, feelings and reflective positions in people's mapping and shaping of routes through caring and working. It requires the examination of the actualities and possibilities of the social patterning of time–space trajectories through a range of locales significant to caring. It questions the conflation of female biology (such as pregnancy or childbirth) with feminised tasks (such as housework or childcare), which associate naturalness with the caring that women are expected to undertake. This challenges power imbalances between those who can choose to care, usually fathers and other men, and those considered 'natural' or more socially appropriate carers, usually wives, mothers and women in general. Time–space practices that would require empirical and conceptual analysis might incorporate the following dimensions of the processes of caring and working:

> planning, worrying, anticipating, speculation, prioritising, assessing the quality of care, accessing care, controlling care, paying for care, shifting patterns of work, job (in)security, the potential for promotion, moving home, managing family resources, supporting school work, being involved in the school or care group, and so on.

For example, if we consider the process of becoming a parent and taking maternity or paternity leave, speculating and planning about parenting starts many years prior to pregnancy and the actual experience of parenting. Children and young people will speculate about parenthood; they play 'families' in nursery and school, participate in social and personal education classes (Gittins 1997; Prout 2000). Schools and other societal pressures will promote certain notions of family life and locations of family living (the 'home'). Children grow up in 'their family' in a particular locality and within their family's social network and will reflect on parenting and what they might do differently when they grow up. In some families, children and young people may come into contact with social and legal services as a result of parental abuse or divorce (Daniel and Ivatts 1998; Charles 2000). Thinking about these processes over time and in space alerts us to the possible times and spaces in which policies and services might be relevant to these informal care processes.

If caringscapes is about the *doing of care*, with a focus on the interactive, processual experiences of making informal care happen, then carescapes is about the broader lifecourse representation, or map, that constitutes informal care. This opens up analytical possibilities through a broader purview, enabling policy and services to be considered. Over time, our thinking on caringscapes and carescapes has led us to develop different frameworks for investigating care, reflecting the diverse ways in which care impacts on lives, policies and service:

- Caringscapes of the doing of care – informal care, in particular – at the individual level
- Carescapes or policyscapes – these focus on the development, implementation and evaluation of policies affecting care exchanges
- Organisation carescapes – which focus on how 'care' is manifest in relationships, policies and practices in employing organisations

This book allows us to explain and critically review these developments, and to consider global variations in care expectations, experiences and possibilities. Our research and reflection on care is a journey with numerous destinations en route. Our goal is to achieve an awareness of the non-linear nature of care both in its conceptualisation and application. We also want to provide a practical map that links the individual, service and policy levels to create a more realistic approach to facilitating and supporting care over the lifecourse.

Illustrating and illuminating informal care

In the following section, we introduce two key devices that we use through the book: 'People Scenarios' located in the context of 'Geographical Zones'. We offer these devices as vehicles to aid the exploration of the variety of circumstances in which the everyday practices of informal care take place.

Geographical Zones

We have selected these to illuminate and illustrate how changing economic, social and cultural systems impact on informal care. In Chapter 1, we produce a profile of the Zones, with information drawn from available statistical data and reports. When it comes to informal care, much remains unknown, although we can identify the changing political and socio-economic contexts of care. Each zone illustrates enduring divisions of care – divisions of age and gender, as well as ongoing changes in the world, including ageing populations, changing work patterns, migration, the effects of disease, war and conflict. Three Zones provide a framework through which we explore these issues:

European Union Zone (EU)

Here, the dynamic relationship between caring and paid working provokes heated debates about parenting and gender and a growing body of legislation. In this regional zone, we draw a distinction between what we term the 'new' EU (countries that joined as part of the Fifth Enlargement in May 2004 and after) and the 'old' EU (members prior to the Fifth Enlargement), recognising the impact of differing welfare systems and cultures.

USA Zone (USA)

In common with many other post-industrial economies, the USA has an ageing population. There has been a history of migration between certain states as people age, with implications for the giving and receiving of informal care and knock-on effects in terms of formal service provision. More recently, there has been a subtle change in some of the states as more of the population age in situ, increasing the numbers in need of elderly care and support. This care need is largely being met by low-cost migrant workers, many of whom have obligations to family members who live in other states and countries. Indeed, the carer and cared-for share some fundamental similarities, which become apparent through the People Scenarios.

Sub-Saharan Africa (S-SA) Zone

Inter-generational care has moved centre-stage as a result of the impact of conflicts and wars, and diseases such as HIV/AIDs, malaria and TB in Sub-Saharan Africa. In many places services are improving but nevertheless, limited access to health care, medicines, clean water and sanitation continues to exacerbate illness and disease, with a still high resultant death toll. The advent of the child-led households and street-based child families has challenged both governments and non-governmental organisations (NGOs) to provide culturally appropriate care. These trends will continue to have an impact for decades to come, as children grow up experiencing bereavement and grandparents find themselves in the frontline in a manner they never expected.

People Scenarios

Many of the academic debates on care take place at the level of theory and, relevant as theory is, we need to ground explanations and ideas in the real and varying world of caring relationships, service providers and governments. We have chosen to remind our readers of the differing contexts and cultures of care by providing 'People Scenarios' throughout Part II of the book. These are brief vignettes illustrating particular moments of care in the lives of fictional protagonists. Although they are works of fiction, they draw on truths derived from academic research papers and information on social, economic and political trends and issues. The vignettes that make up our People Scenarios help to ground trends and issues in the everyday. They also illustrate how we draw on memories, experiences and anticipations in organising, giving and receiving informal care.

There are four People Scenarios and these represent each of the Geographical Zones – including the subdivision of the EU into 'old' and 'new'. The four People Scenarios are concerned with the following situations:

- Combining caring and paid work for parents and children living in the 'old' EU, The Netherlands (People Scenario 1) and 'new' EU, Czech Republic (People Scenario 2).
- Elderly care for older people who have moved to seek a better life among similar people rather than locating closer to children in the USA (People Scenario 3). This care is often carried out by migrant workers.
- A grandparent in South Africa caring for grandchildren as a consequence of the untimely death or chronic illness of their adult children (People Scenario 4).

The People Scenarios and Geographical Zones allow us to develop and pursue the metaphor of 'terrains' or 'scapes'; the 'lie of the land' for people, relationships, policies and practices. In particular, the People Scenarios illustrate how care pathways across these 'terrains' or 'scapes' are acted out through individuals' choices and negotiations and influenced by a range of trends in, for example, economies, governments, demography and culture.

Situating the authors

The authors are four women who have spent more than 15 years researching and debating care – in particular, care work that is unpaid, everyday and so often treated in a taken-for-granted manner and rendered invisible in policy decisions. A major trigger to collaboration was the organisation in 1995 of the conference 'Gender perspectives on household issues'. After this event, we anticipated a few years of collaborative work publishing and distributing the outputs from that event, but we soon recognised the ways in which care and care issues are all around us but command limited attention in broader debates and resource allocation. How then might we promote debates, and inform policies and services to support the cared-for and carers? This book is our contribution to keeping the debates moving forward and bringing together the worlds of theory and practice, to provide a flexible pathway to understanding the realities of care and how it might be supported.

We draw on a number of disciplines in the social sciences.

- Sophie (Sophia) is the partner of a fellow academic and the mother of a son who is now at University. She has and still does spend time visiting older relatives who are living independently elsewhere and feels that she has received as much care from them as she has given. Her partner's mother gave a lot of time to caring for her son when he was young. She feels part of two networks of kin (her own and her partner's) and a variety of friendships formed through both work and hobbies. As she approaches retirement, she feels the need to strengthen and re-establish some old friendships. She locates herself as a feminist geographer – a researcher concerned with social relationships in space and place, with a particular focus on gender divisions in spaces and relationships. The interactions between access to paid work, inequalities and the home are a large part of Sophie's research. Among roles as mother, teacher and researcher, Sophie is also a Director and Chairperson of ReadiBus, a not-for-profit bus service in Reading for people who cannot use ordinary buses.

- Linda is a mother of a grown-up daughter who now lives and works in The Netherlands. Married twice, with some 10 years as a single parent in between, she is part of a large Irish–Scots family. She sometimes feels that, first and foremost, her family think of her as a daughter, a woman and a carer, with all that this means. She cares for older relatives on a regular basis and she is aware of investing more time in nurturing family relationships and friendships than previously. In her day job, Linda researches the intersections between organisations, work and care. Prior to this, she worked on the topics of violence and violation. She has been a trustee for three non-governmental organisations, and continues as a trustee for one concerned with rural health and another that promotes capacity in evaluation in the public and third sectors. Linda has a keen interest in promoting research skills in academia, especially among early career researchers, as well as in the third and public sectors.

- Sue has been a sociologist of health and illness who changed focus 20 years ago when she left a career in local government administration. Over those 20 years, she has developed work on gender, the family, health, qualitative research methods and research ethics. Although much of Sue's research has involved the active participation of patient, user and third sector groups, she also has an abiding interest in how families provide both a structure and a process for social life, which formed the basis of her PhD. Sue is single and has never been a mother, but now grapples with caring at a distance for an ageing mother whilst coming to terms with the idea of retirement.

- Isobel is a social scientist with a background in health and community services research and evaluation. Her recent focus has been on the evaluation of health and social services, but she started out in the field of care of the elderly both at the formal and informal levels. Isobel is single and part of a large extended Scots family. She has experience, both direct and indirect, of the practicalities and the emotional ups and downs of caring for parents and friends, and appreciates the crucial importance of informal support networks.

For all four of us, debates on the concepts of gender, time and space, and the relationship between paid work and home, have formed the core of collaborative work as well as of our everyday lives.

About the book

The book is divided into three parts. Each part contains distinctive content, but there is also a flow of arguments and ideas that build up to construct and underpin our framework of care. The over-arching aim of **Part I** of the book is to create a foundation from which our discussions of informal care and caring can grow. We start in Chapter 1, *The Care Context*, by mapping out the global context within which trends in informal care are situated. The fact that much informal care remains under-recorded is, in itself, of significance, and largely a result of the ways in which it remains taken for granted. In this chapter, the devices of Geographical Zones and People Scenarios are fleshed out. In Chapter 2, *Care and Interdependency*, ongoing debates on the concept of care and related issues are considered. What do we mean by care and caring? Why do many of us ignore or shy away from the emotions associated with care? Caring about, and caring for, another person requires reciprocity – forms of give and take. In this chapter, we explore these issues, illuminating the interdependencies that are necessary for human flourishing. Over our life time, we require, offer, negotiate and experience care. Growing up and growing older are fundamental processes in the human condition and, at every stage, 'care' is present.

In **Part II** of the book we critically consider how time and space inter-weave and provide a vehicle through which we can understand how the intersectionalities of memories, experiences and anticipations aid the analysis of practices of care. Time is the theoretical focus of Chapter 3, *Living with Care*. How we consider, how we receive, and offer, informal care changes over time. Many factors can provoke or result in change, not least of which are growing up and growing older, and this process can be complicated by political and economic change, conflicts and disasters. We made a decision to address living with care prior to *Learning to Care*, Chapter 4. Learning about care can precede practices of informal care but learning about care is a continuous, lifelong process and not limited to childhood and early adulthood. In mid and later life we develop, review and change practices of informal care – and how we mould formal and informal forms of care – as we care for a partner, relative or workplace friend. So, in Chapter 4, we begin to map out the terrains of care over the lifecourse. Examining the ongoing process of learning to care allows us to reflect on the spaces and places across or in which informal care takes place. Our arguments move on in Chapter 5, *Networks and Chains of Care*, to tackle the assumption that most informal care is provided by members of families, and in and around the location of the home. Whilst recognising the importance of families and home, we consider the importance of friendships and relationships, such as neighbouring, including volunteering, and social networks. In Chapter 6, *Working and Caring*, we consider the relationships between informal care within and beyond the workplace and the organisation of paid or productive labour. Care is evident in the daily and longer term workings of employing organisations. Combing caring and working is an issue for employee and employer, and of growing concern for governments and supranational organisations. How needs and care and related policies and services are defined and resourced is the outcome of keen debates. The association of women and femininities with formal and informal care work raises particular tensions in intimate, familial and work place relations.

In the final section of the book, **Part III**, we present the evolution of our framework from caringscapes to carescapes (from the doing of care, the caring, to an appreciation of how policies, services and practices inter-weave in and around care) reflecting on the implications for research, policy and practice. In Chapter 7, *Visions of Care*, we reflect on the analytical frameworks presented in Part II, and discuss the potential for these to offer conceptual and practical insights to inform research agendas, policy and service development. The fuzzy boundaries between formal and informal care present challenges to researchers and policy-makers alike. In summary, we see informal care and caring as processes that are fundamental to social interaction in *all* settings. The nature of care will be tempered by the embodied experiences of individuals. So it will change and evolve across people's lives and within and between locales.

Across the book, we explore the paradox between the centrality of care for human relationships and the 'invisibility' of that care as a constitutive component of human flourishing. For all of us, care and caring evokes an interdependency, whether between family, friends or strangers, without which social institutions (such as family or employment) could not function and within which social crises (such as war or illness) could not be survived. The overlapping frameworks of caringscapes and carescapes are stages on our analytical journey. Over this journey, we have moved from considering informal care as a descriptive concept (Thomas 1993), to reflecting on the complex and dynamic ways in which experiences and ideas about informal care can be explored through empirical work. We conclude the book by discussing the ways in which our ideas may aid or hinder the exploration of informal care by researchers, policy-makers and service providers.

Notes

1 This was the Annual Conference of the British Sociological Association.
2 Hagerstrand, in fact, explores eight basic conditions, which he claims limit possible organisation of human life and society. These are: 1) the indivisibility of the human being, 2) the limited length of each human life, 3) the limited ability of the human being to take part in more than one task at a time, 4) the fact that every task has a duration, 5) the fact that movement between points in space consumes time, 6) the limited packing capacity of space, 7) the limited size of terrestrial space, 8) the fact that every situation is rooted in past situations (Hagerstrand 1978).

Part I

1 The Care Context

Introduction

In this chapter, we consider the geopolitical context within which contemporary care relationships take place. This context informs our conceptual framework on care and caring, which we have termed caringscapes. Individual care activities and experiences help to shape and are shaped by their socio-economic contexts. Trends in population, household and family composition, work and employment, income and benefits, health and illness and the funding, public policy, and provision of relevant services will have a particular impact on care. The ways in which we experience care reflects our age, gender, ethnicity, health and social status, and will be influenced by our beliefs and values about families and relationships, and hence by where and when we live. Thus, it is important to place the discussion of care and interdependence in the context of socio-economic, demographic and relevant care policy change. Living under different political regimes – in times of peace, unrest or conflict – the impact of natural and human-created disasters are all factors that have an effect on the care we give or experience (or not). Equally, changes and developments, for example, in infectious and chronic diseases, the environment and national economies, scientific knowledge and technological development, have a bearing on the shape and form of the care that we can expect to exchange.

Any framework for the analysis of care and caring must accommodate change because the interdependencies and contexts in which we live are ever-changing. In this chapter, we use statistical data to illustrate the geopolitical contexts of our three Geographical Zones. These are drawn from supranational, national and local sources, including NGOs, governments and academic centres. We are limited by what is recorded and how that is categorised, analysed, reported and debated: we highlight these issues where appropriate.

The intent of this chapter is to illuminate the varied and changing socio-economic and environmental contexts in which care relations take place. The chapter is divided into four main sections. We open with a consideration of continuities, change and context. The foundations of our data, and thus of our exploration of different care contexts, is outlined. In the third section, entitled Geographical Zones, data on our three comparative geopolitical zones is introduced: the European Union (EU) – old (15) and new (25) EU[1]; USA; and Sub-Saharan Africa (S-SA).[2] We follow this with a section entitled 'Care in Action' in which we introduce the imaginary protagonist actors in our four People Scenarios. Each fictitious scenario illustrates care relations that are particularly relevant to a Geographical Zone. The chapter ends with a summary of data and issues that we will return to throughout the book.

Continuities, change and context

Social change is a broad term used to describe differences over time in social institutions, social behaviour and social relations. Change can be gradual, barely noticeable but, ultimately, revolutionary. For example, in Western societies, many people continue to spend much of their adult lives in partnerships but, over the last 100 years, expectations about partnerships have been changing subtly from the notion of 'death do us part' to the acceptance of partnership changes facilitated by separation and divorce, and from the legal arrangements of formal marriage to co-habiting.[3] So, in the twenty-first century in most post-industrial societies, we are no longer surprised if people do not go through a marriage ceremony and, in many societies, there is much less stigma attached to not being married or not having married parents than in the past.

Change also can be relatively sudden with radical impacts, especially in the case of serious and life-threatening illness. For example, HIV/AIDS has resulted in dramatic changes in family and care relationships, particularly in S-SA. The rate of infection and death has taken many governments, non-governmental organisations and commentators by surprise. The implications are stark in countries where treatment is not routinely available, and poverty, limited knowledge, or lack of political will, leads to the early death of many of the adult population. As a consequence, culturally 'normal' care patterns are disrupted within and across families and societies.

Change can even turn the social conventions of caring upside down: for example, in many industrialised countries, a growing number of grandparents are now actively caring for grandchildren in lieu of childcare facilities that are either too expensive or too inconvenient. In Africa, grandparents are extending their caring role in the face of the HIV/AIDS crisis. In both places, grandparents are increasing their involvement at a time of their life when they might have expected to be recipients of care from the family. However, the delivery of care within a family context can also present challenges, create tensions and even lead to abuse. Indeed, for many people, friendships and community ties offer alternative, and sometimes preferred, forms of security and continuity.

Many commentators argue that change in economies, and the ways people live their lives, have never been faster and more complex (Davis and Meyer 1999). There are, however, continuities as well as change. An obvious continuity is the continued and strong association of all forms of care with women and femininities, despite an increase in men taking part in formal and informal types of care in many countries (Himmelweit and Land 2008, Williams 2004). Presumptions about the centrality of family relationships to informal care also remain strong and it is not uncommon for families to provide practical, financial and emotional support. And for many, friendships and community ties offer forms of security and continuity.

Continuity and change are rarely mutually exclusive and, as we progress through the lifecourse, we may well find ourselves dealing with both concurrently. This has created a need to employ coping strategies or 'care contingencies' in which people anticipate and manage care crises and gaps. One obvious example is the need to reconcile child-rearing and paid employment – a process of reconciliation that is both evolving and gendered. Although most children continue to be brought up in a kin-based context, the implications of the need, and desire, for paid work for both women and men, has resulted in parents juggling various methods of caring for (that is, practical activities) and caring about (psychological dimensions) their off-spring. For many people, this involves a combination of informal care by family members and friends and formal, paid nursery, childminders and school care, and the utilisation of fast-growing technologies, such as mobile phones and email. This example of 'care contingencies' is familiar to northern European and post-industrial societies and is becoming a familiar feature of developing economies in Asia. Therefore, in many ways the experiences of combining caring and working presents similar challenges across the world today. Limited resources lead to gendered compromises; women still dominate in formal and informal care, with attempts to involve men moving forward slowly, reflecting different 'care' cultures, care policies and varying economic circumstances.

Different histories of change and continuities in social and economic relationships have led to distinctively different contexts for care in different parts of the world. In particular, the degree to which and the ways in which the state is able or willing to support the welfare of its members through the supply of formal care services and through guaranteeing the physical and social conditions that make care possible, varies. The work of Esping-Andersen (1993) on welfare state regimes has stimulated a wide range of research on the different ways in which market, state and family relate to one another in the provision of welfare in prosperous, capitalist societies. Esping-Andersen's original suggestion of three ideal-types of welfare state regime – liberal, conservative and social-democratic have been modified and extended (Arts and Gelissen 2002).

A vigorous feminist critique of Esping-Andersen's original ideas has drawn attention to the significance of the family to analyses of the provision of welfare and care and the importance of examining the ways in which women from different ethnic groups are or are not incorporated into the labour market. In particular, the critical importance of the gendered division of caring and domestic work has been highlighted and attention drawn to the ways in which the state can facilitate or undermine different routes to improving equality between women and men of different ethnicities in both the labour market and the home (Lewis 1992, Orloff 1996, Lewis 1997). Research by Morrisens and Sainsbury (2005) examined data from the Luxembourg Income Study for the UK, the USA, Germany, France, Denmark and Sweden. Noting that comparative welfare state research has devoted little attention to the social rights of migrants or to ethnic and racial dimensions, the analysis shows that there are major disparities between how migrant and citizen households fare in welfare states. When migrants are incorporated into the analysis, intra-regime variations stand out in the case of the liberal and social-democratic countries. Discrepancies widen still further for migrants of colour. Given the development of migration across the EU, such findings are of concern.

Research on welfare state regimes has largely been concerned with the 'developed' countries of the West. A new literature analysing welfare provision in 'developing' countries offers further insights. For example, Gough et al. (2004) have examined the processes through which welfare and personal and family security are maintained – or not maintained – in the Southern hemisphere. They highlight the role of 'community' as well as family, market and state in these processes and focus on the issue of insecurity in situations in which an established and legitimate state and well-functioning labour and financial markets do not exist. Thus they identify three broad global 'ideal types' of welfare regime – welfare state regimes (characteristic of prosperous capitalist countries); informal security regimes (characteristic of many parts of Latin America and Asia); and insecurity regimes (characteristic of many African countries). In the latter, where the state is weak, they suggest that global actors such as transnational corporations and supranational bodies and NGOs have become highly influential; at the same time, local patrons, for example, local religious leaders, community elders or tribal leaders, are also powerful, resulting in a precarious livelihood and security situation for many people. In such situations, the state will be of limited relevance to the conditions in which care takes place. However, this research makes only limited reference to gendered differences in access to the labour market, and in care access and provision. A wide range of other research on care in the Global South has emphasised the importance of gender, age and ethnicity in structuring labour market access and informal caring practices in different places (Parrenas 2005). For our purposes, the value of the research on welfare regimes is to re-emphasise both the importance of the socio-economic and political contexts in shaping the practices and possibilities of informal care, and the importance of gendered formal and informal care work to welfare regimes. The concept of 'welfare regime' is to be welcomed insofar as it puts both formal and informal care centre-stage and focuses analysis on identifying the situations in which such care work can prosper alongside moves to enhance social equality. In the remaining parts of this chapter, we focus on our three Geographical Zones and draw out the significance of their varied socio-economic and political contexts for informal care. However, before we detail the differences between our Zones, we discuss the problems of finding appropriate data on care and care contexts.

The data foundations

Statistical data can provide evidence of continuities and change in care contexts and practices. Despite limitations in what is collected, commentators and planners concerned with social and economic trends take these data sources seriously. In most countries, the major source of data is the census, generally conducted every decade, and supplemented by regular surveys on particular topics. Governments, supranational organisations and NGOs may influence and debate the contents of such censuses and surveys so that the particular interests of these powerful groups affect their content. When it comes to the documentation of care, a key driving force is the use, and anticipated need for, formal care services. For example, data often are collected on paid care workers (e.g. nurses, teachers, social workers), but collecting direct information on who provides informal care varies. For example, direct questions may be asked within surveys/census (such as, for example the annual household surveys conducted in the nations of the UK) or household com-position is used as a proxy to make presumptions about informal care-giving. The major presumptions are that spouses care for each other, especially in old age and that parents care for children. Thus, much informal care (such as that of friends and neighbours and relatives living outside the home) and unpaid work fails to be documented. Nevertheless, informal care is assumed to be available for many and this presumed resource is taken into account in the resourcing and organisation of policies and formal services. For example, it is assumed that families and friends are available to facilitate convalescence at home, allowing governments and health services to provide limited access to rehabilitation and convalescence services (Sevenhuijsen, 1998).

Box 1.1 shows a résumé of a report on trends in unpaid caring in the UK. Drawing on the census of 2001, the House of Commons Work and Pensions Committee (2008) explored patterns, gaps in data, and implications for future policy and service provision. These trends are not dis-similar to those in many post-industrial countries and illuminate a heavy dependence by formal health and social care services on the provision of informal care. This report also illustrates another key point – namely, that data collection concentrates on informal care provided for those with a recognised illness or disability, be that physical or mental. Childcare is generally documented in analyses of women's participation in labour markets, re-emphasising assumptions about the 'natural' relationship between women and childcare. Further, care that provides support for those experiencing, for example, bereavement, threat of job loss, or financial or relationship breakdown is valued by those who receive it, but rarely documented.

Attempts to compare care between countries are particularly fraught. Definitions of formal and informal care differ across state boundaries, and the use of com-mon questions in national surveys to aid international comparison remains rare. Supra national organisations, including the United Nations, World Bank, Office of Economic Co-operation and Development, and European Union do run cross-national surveys but the content of these reflect particular political and conceptual interests, often how formal and informal care is moulded around paid employment. Translation into different languages adds a conceptual layer to the practical issues of undertaking cross-national comparisons. Furthermore, notions of care and what forms of care are formal or informal varies markedly. For example, in many Nordic countries, state-run services provide much more care for the elderly and sick than in the UK or Germany. These contrasts are born of different histories, cultures and welfare systems.

Our search for national and international data revealed many examples of the ways in which the provision of information can obscure, as well as illustrate,

Box 1.1 Case Study of Care in the UK

Definition

2001 Census "Do you look after or give any help or support to family members, friends or neighbours or others because of: long-term physical or mental ill-health or disability or problems related to old age?"

Characteristics:

- Almost 6 million identified themselves as a carer – that is, 10% of the UK population.
- Approximately 1.25 million people provided 50 or more hours of care per week. Estimated monetary value = £47 billion per year.
- Just under 660,000 people provided 20–49 hours of care. Estimated monetary value = £17.4 billion per year.
- Around 400,000 people provided 1–9 hours of care per week. Estimated monetary value = £22.6 billion per year.

These figures are an under-estimation of informal care as:

- The definition does not include childcare or recognise the role of friendships and networks in communities and workplaces.
- People are unlikely to report what they view as everyday activities linked to being a family member or friend.
- Many care relationships are transitional as the cared-for may grow up, recover, enter formal care or die. Most people are, have been or will be carers at some points in their lives.

Care patterns:

- Differ across *age* groups, with the peak age for caring being 45–69 years. In the 50–59-year age group, 17% of all men and 24% of all women are carers. By 75 years, almost two-thirds of women and close to half of men will have provided one of more periods of care of at least 20 hours per week. There are 165,000 carers aged under 18 years and 85% of these are aged 12–18 years.
- Demonstrate *gender* differences. One in five women aged 60–64 years and 1 in 6 men of this age are carers. In the over-75s, men are more likely to be carers than women. Men are more likely to care for a partner or spouse, whereas women are more likely to care for a range of people, including partners, spouses, children, other relatives and friends. They are also more likely to organise care.
- Have an impact on *employment* status. In 2001, there were 4.27 million carers of working age. Sixty-six per cent of men and 32% of women were in full-time employment. Carers live with or near to the person or people they care for. This limits employment opportunities. There is a strong positive relationship between the hours of caring per week, the length of time spent caring and poverty.
- Differ among *ethnic groups*, with some having higher rates of caring than others. For example, people in Pakistani and Bangladeshi communities are twice as likely to care for someone with a long-term illness as those in white

communities. These trends also reflect religious beliefs and ethnic/regional cultures.

Futures issues:
• With an ageing population and an increased focus on employment for income an increase in carers/cared-for living in poverty is anticipated.
• Support services, aids and adaptations, access to which can vary across the UK. In all localities services will come under strain due to demands that may be partially met or not at all.
• There will be increased isolation, social exclusion of carers and related impact on health and well-being.
• Governments, policies and services continue to assume the availability of unpaid care and thus lead to under-investment in services and support.

See House of Commons Work and Pensions Committee (2008) Valuing and Supporting Carers. London: The Stationery Office Limited.

trends. This may seem a strange comment given the widespread presumption that statistical data will illuminate trends and offer insights for policy and service developments. In data available on HIV/AIDs in South Africa from 1997 to 2002, prevalence figures demonstrate a notable increase, as do data on mortality, but statistics on cause of death show an increase in respiratory and infectious diseases rather than the category of HIV/AIDS. These apparent contradictions result from cultural, religious and political factors that combine to encourage the attribution of deaths from HIV/AIDS to other categories, as well as the style and content of death certification, which may not distinguish immediate and contributing causes.

The UN Expert Group on Sustainable Development Indicators (2002) noted the gaps that exist in the recording of informal care, especially in terms of 'women's work, social integration & health care' and the group called for the development of common country assessment indicators. Part of the problem, noted by the group, resulted from the failure of governments to involve relevant groups and statisticians early on in the design of surveys for data collection. The EU organisation, Eurostat, has also grappled with this issue and worked on developing common methodologies and definitions for collecting data on caring both for dependent adults and for children (Eurostat 2003a). Their work highlighted the definitional and computational issues, as national statistical organisations found it hard to adapt to requests for cross-national data collection due to interpretation and language problems, resources and national priorities. The quality of the dialogue on indicators has improved and, in Britain, the Economic and Social Research Council (ESRC) has successfully put issues of indicators and measurement on the agenda (Atkinson *et al.* 2009). In turn, these debates have heightened awareness of the limited quality of data and the need for high-quality information for policy and service planning.

With these qualifications in mind, we offer an overview of global trends. To avoid a Eurocentric approach, information is provided on our three Geographical Zones of old and new EU, USA and S-SA. Data includes population trends, health and employment. These data allow reflection on global trends and issues, and provide a contextual framework through which we can explore everyday provision of informal care through our People Scenarios.

Geographical Zones

In the introduction to the book, we outlined the idea of Geographical Zones. These were selected to illuminate global contrasts and similarities in care contexts and, as already mentioned, are the EU 25, sub-divided into old EU (15 member states to 2004) and new EU (the 10 members who joined between 2004 and 2007), USA and S-SA. The following resumé of care contexts presents data and commentary on demography and health, employment and growth, migration and mobility and how time is used in our Geographical Zones. The goal is to provide a wider and more comparative context than simply our own experiences and concerns and thus reflect something of the variety of socio-economic and cultural settings within which care takes place.

Rather than consider each zone separately, data are considered through a number of themes and indicators. These are presented in Table 1.1 – namely, population in urban areas, age structure, population growth rate, infant mortality rate, life expectancy, HIV/AIDS rates and labour force figures. Primary data sources are those that provide comparative global overviews of societal development (for example, the Central Intelligence Agency (CIA) World Fact Book and World Bank data), supplemented by specific regional sources (for example, the EU Eurostat databases and reports from the International Labour office).

Demography and health

Growth in the overall world population has slowed down in the last decade. Population growth, however, remains higher in countries that are often termed 'developing' countries. More than 80% of the world's population lives in such countries, and more than half of the world's population lives in urban areas. The contrast between our three Geographical Zones is stark, with S-SA having only one-third (34%) of its population in urban areas. In developed/post-industrial countries, three-quarters of people live in cities. That figure drops to 43% in less developed economies. It should be noted that almost half of those who live in urban areas, regardless of zones, live in cities of 500,000 or fewer inhabitants and cities vary not just in size but in socio-economic composition. Moreover, their history, environment, economic, migration and demographic trends differ. Life for low-income households in California, USA, may share some broad similarities to a family in a shanty town on the outskirts of Durban, South Africa, but the experience of everyday living is quite different. Across the globe, remote and sparsely populated localities face specific pressures related to the costs of transport

Table 1.1 Summary Key Indicators for EU, USA, S-SA

Indicator	EU	USA	S-SA
% Population in Urban Areas	72% (L=South: 66%; H=North: 83%)	80%	34%
Age Structure of Population (2007)			
0–14 years	16%	20%	44%
15–64 years	67%	67%	53%
65+ years	17%	13%	3%
Population Growth Rate (2007)	0.12%	0.88%	2.5%
Infant Mortality per 1,000 Live Births (2007)	5.84	6.3	96
Life Expectancy at Birth (2007)	78.5 (M=75.4; F=81.8)	78.1 (M=74.3; F=81.3)	49.0 (M=48; F=50)
HIV/Aids Rate (2007)	0.3	0.6	6.1
Labour Force (2006)			
Participation Rate	63**	66***	84**
Unemployment Rate	9%	5%	8%***
% Labour Force Female	43 (2006)*	46 (2006)*	42(2006)*

Sources:

    CIA 2008 World Fact Book (www.cia.gov)
*   World Bank Data (www.worldbank.org)
**   Euro Stat (www.ec.europa.eu/eurostat) and US Bureau of Labor (www.bls.gov)
*** ILO (www.ilo.org)

Note: World Bank data sets do not recognize the EU as an entity in their summary tables: the term used is Europe and then subdivided into a geographic split – that is, North, South, East and West Europe.

and communication, which can affect support for individuals, families and social networks, and access to services. In poor urban areas, residents face a range of barriers and pressures not dissimilar to those facing rural populations. They have, for example, limited transport, higher food costs, and limited health and welfare services, but live at higher densities, often among a more diverse population than in the rural areas.

    The impact of HIV/AIDS, and other infectious diseases, combined with subsistence living resources, has placed particular pressures on both young and old in S-SA rural areas (see Table1.1). In many communities, young and old have become mutually dependent when economically active adults become ill or die.

These experiences differ from common expectations, which assume that when a child is born, caring needs are expected to be met through 'natural' and 'normal' social relationships of 'family', 'gender relations' and 'mothering'. As mortality rates (particularly those of infants) have decreased over the last century, we, in post-industrial societies, have made assumptions about common patterns of parenting and childcare responsibilities as well as expected stages of age-related illness. The enlarged European Union has experienced a change in life expectancy rates over time and, overall, the EU can boast positive and improving average life expectancy rates: the estimated average life expectancy for someone born in 2007 is 78.5 years. The USA shows a similar average.

Regional averages, however, do tend to mask variations in life expectancy – for example, in 2005, the highest life expectancy in Europe was in Spain (80.7 years) and Sweden (80.6 years). In contrast, the lowest was in Latvia and Lithuania (65 years for men and 77 years for women). Indeed, the majority of the lowest life expectancies in the EU were to be found within the 12 countries that joined the EU in 2004. Although this variation is significant, the EU is a success story in longevity in all countries. In 2007, S-SA had a life expectancy at birth of 50 years for women and 48 years for men; whereas 5 countries (Swaziland, Botswana, Lesotho, Zimbabwe, Zambia) within the S-SA zone had the lowest life expectancies of any country in the world, with a range of 33–38 years. The differences in life expectancy manifest themselves in the age structures of the populations – the EU and the USA are ageing, whereas S-SA carries a child population (<14 years) twice that of the other two zones (see Table 1.1). Despite evidence of improved survival rates in some S-SA countries, only 3% of the population survive to reach 65 plus years. Although the frequency of dying young affects the care perspectives of those left to cope, so too does prolonged or improving life expectancy, as we will go on to show.

Although the population growth in the EU was 0.12% per annum in 2007, the rate of growth is slowing in some countries to a level that is below that needed for population replacement. By contrast, S-SA's natural rate of increase stands at 2.5% in 2007, with both birth and death rates considerably higher than any other world population zone. However, the infant mortality rate (96 per 1,000 live births in 2007) and an HIV/AIDS infection rate of 6.1 per thousand (2007) are much higher than either the EU or USA, so that deaths from AIDS in S-SA represent 72% of global AIDS deaths. It is, perhaps, important that birth rates in this region are higher than in the rest of the world, but this combination creates very different caring demands for these countries to those of the west.

The implications of these broad trends include:

- Regions with high longevity and an ageing population must find ways to care for the elderly and chronically sick, despite a small economically active population relative to the 'dependent' population.
- Richer, urbanised Zones can use technology (e.g. computers, medicines, food preservation and preparation technologies) to assist care-giving but some care still requires personal, physical and emotional relationships.

• Regions such as S-SA with low life expectancy, a high proportion of children, a low-income population and limited government resources may face a crisis of informal care provision – especially for the young and chronically sick.

Employment and growth

Individuals and families aspire to a standard of living that reflects societal interpretations of a 'good life'. The ability to earn, earn well and continuously, underpins these aspirations. The International Labour Office (ILO) report on Global Employment Trends 2008 pointed to a continuing trend towards a stabilisation of global labour markets. Interestingly, they suggest that any potential slowdown in the developed industrialised economies might not affect other economic regions due to their own internal strength and trading patterns among themselves. For example, they suggest that African countries trade among themselves to a great degree and this provides a foundation for their economies, albeit it limited and fragile. Economic downturn seems likely to worsen the situation of the world's poorest and to slow or stop development of export industries in developing countries.

Prior to the current economic downturn, global net job creation had continued, although the developed economies (including the EU and USA) accounted for only 4%, with S-SA at 17% (ILO 2008). Despite this latter growth, the report highlights a continuing concern that more than half (53%) of workers in S-SA are in 'working poverty' – that is, earning less than US$ 1 per day. In other words, many jobs are low paid and almost three-quarters of workers (72.9%) remain in insecure employment (seasonal, temporary or casual) compared with less than ten per cent (9.2%) in developed economies (ILO 2008). And this is reflected in the Gross National Income (GNI) indicators for 2007.[4] The service sector (42.7%) continues to dominate the global jobs market, with agriculture at just 34.9% and industry at a distant 22.4%. Here is one of the classic differences between our Geographical Zones in which the USA has 0.6% and the EU 4.4% of jobs in agriculture compared to 64.7% in S-SA, which has only 25.7% in services (CIA World Fact Book 2008; ILO 2008).

In terms of labour force participation, the highest rate occurred in S-SA at 83% (World Bank Statistics Africa), but this is not as positive as it might seem because poverty and lack of educational opportunities generally result in more people having to take whatever work is available regardless of the pay and conditions of the work. The percentage of females in each of our region's labour forces is not vastly different. However, the global employment gender gap remains with just under a half (49.1%) of working-age women in paid employment compared with nearly three-quarters of men (ILO 2008). When looked at across our regions we can see a considerable contrast in the position of women in the labour market. In S-SA, '... *less than two out of ten women have a job with a regular income and a lower economic risk ...* ' and 34.7% are '*trapped as unpaid contributing family workers with no income at all.* ' (ILO 2008). In the developed economies, we find 88% of women in a regular waged/salaried job and, not only that, but 84% (1.6 million) of the new jobs created in these economies were taken by women, much of this in the service sector (ILO 2008). This pattern of job creation is mirrored in relation to youth employment – that is, more jobs are perceived as being for young women than for young men (ILO 2008).

The 2005 Labour Force Survey (Eurostat 2005) noted a clear difference in work patterns across the EU, with part-time working more common among the EU 15 than among the new member states and the latter also having the lowest employ-ment rates for women with three or more children. Different models of work partnership between men and women are apparent across the EU – for example, the man-only job is common in southern Europe; both working full-time is common in new member states and the full-time/part-time combination in the EU 15. Indeed, Eurostat thematic data updated in 2008 show that, women in work who want to alter the work–care balance, want to do so in surprising directions. Women working full-time want to work less and have more time for caring but women working part-time want the opposite! The UK Equality and Human Rights Commission (EHRC) provided evidence of the consequences of occupational segregation and the gender pay gap for fathers. Almost half of the men surveyed did not take paternity leave because they could not afford to. The loss of pay for mothers places financial pressures on families. Further, gender stereotyping in occupations makes it harder for men to request flexible working than women. Parenting has implications for material wellbeing and thus that of dependents. It also has long term impacts on career opportunities, and this is now the case for a growing number of men, as well as most women.

The ILO highlight the key issues facing our Geographical Zones – and these include the continuing impact of disease, especially HIV/AIDS in S-SA – on cre-ating a stable, fit, workforce. In the developed economies (USA, EU), among the issues identified is the continuing gender wage gap and the effects of an ageing society on both the age structure of the employment market but also on society's ability to pay for any future care for its people. Implications of these trends include:

- In poor Zones such as S-SA, those in employment must often work long hours and care with few resources, including the resource of time. Those out of employment have time but few materials or technologies to assist in care-giving.
- In wealthy, post-industrial economies, women are finding that engagement in waged work leaves less time for care but that gendered expectations that care is a woman's job persist.

Migration and mobility

A significant trend of the second half of the twentieth century is growth in migra-tion and mobility. Migration is generally defined as a change in permanent address involving movement across national or internal regional/state boundaries. Mobility refers to changes in permanent address within an internal regional/state territory. Based on UN statistical data, the International Organization for Migration (IOM) World Migration Trends Report 2005 put migrants at 2.9% (185–192 million) of the total world population in 2005, with the USA hosting the single largest number at 35 million people (20% of all migrants). In absolute terms, inward migration has impacted differently on each of our zones: figures spanning a 30-year period (1970–2000) show that only North America has continued to experience growth, with both Europe (includes all) and Africa (includes all) declining. Women accounted for almost a half (48.6%) of all migrants in 2005 (IMO). The nature of female migration varies between our zones. In North America (USA and Canada), female migrants have outnumbered legal male migrants since the 1970s and were 52% of all migrants in Europe in 2000. In S-SA in 2000, just under half (47%) of migrants were women and girls, and the proportion of female migrants has risen in parallel with the increased numbers of refugees among migrants (Zlotnik 2003). Whereas the main imperatives for women to migrate into Europe and North America were economic and social (following/reuniting with families), the main imperatives in S-SA were the impacts of natural or man-made disasters; for example, war, civil conflict, deforestation. Longino and Bradley (2003: 907), analysing US Census data, suggest that by 2013, when the baby-boom generation have begun retiring, '... even if there is a decline in the proportion of persons who make a retirement move, the numbers of older migrants will increase precipitously for two census decades.' And despite questioning the increasingly mobile (American) society, Wolf and Longino (2005: 9) found '... no evidence of declining rates of interstate mobility among those aged 65 and older, suggesting that the rates of retirement migration – typically entailing a long distance move – are unchanged'.

The economic consequences of migration for families and caring can be both positive and negative: it is a potential disruption to family relationships and direct economic support if the breadwinner leaves home to work elsewhere, but it might be an economic 'godsend' if monies flow back to the family, maybe even enabling some family members to undertake full-time care within the family rather than juggling family and work. A recent World Bank report on remittance trends (Migration and Development Brief 3, 2007, World Bank) pointed out that remittance flows to Europe and Central Asia went up by 175% between 2002–2007, and even S-SA recorded an 116% increase (although the publication's authors felt the real figure was likely to be considerable higher). These are the two highest growth rates in terms of the World Bank's Developing Countries Inflow zones for that period.

Social insurance system

The International Labour Office (ILO) estimates that '... only 1:5 people in the world have adequate social security coverage and more than half of the world's population lack any kind of social security coverage' (International Labour Office 2009: 2). There is no consensus as to the best way to provide such cover and our three zones are no exception. Indeed, because of the differing natures of the systems, the differing emphases within systems and the variable data collection/ presentation, we can only outline some key points from each zone, to give a flavour of the current situation.

In the EU (25), 'Northern European countries have followed the Beveridge type model of government funding via taxes and others the Bismark tradition ... based on insurance contributions.' (Eurostat 2008a). Although the two traditions – government funding and insurance contributions – seem to be converging as each adopts practices from the other, receipts show that the social insurance model still dominates, with 59% of all social security receipts, compared with 37% being government funding, the rest being private and administrative costs. The EU 25 spent 27% of GDP on social protection but that varied from a high of 32% in Sweden to a low of 12% in Latvia (Ibid). Ironically, strong economic growth does not necessarily protect or enhance its share of Gross Domestic Product (GDP)[5] and, as evidenced by the Baltic states, Poland, Slovakia and Slovenia, the share can actually fall in seemingly 'good times' as new monies are diverted to other sectors of the economy. Within the EU 15 and EU 25, old-age benefits (46%) were the main component of total social benefits, followed by sickness and health (29%), family and child (8%), disability (8), unemployment (6%) and housing/ social exclusion (3%) (Ibid).

The social protection system in the USA is largely insurance-based, underpinned by a mix of federal and state frameworks. Social security accounted for 4% of GDP in 2008 and the government health insurance programme Medicaid, 5% of GDP. The US system is probably most easily understood through its health insurance system. In 2007, the US Census Bureau reported that just over two-thirds (67%) of those covered used private insurance, with 28% being covered by government schemes, the largest of which is Medicaid. Of the private schemes, the largest provider were employers (59%). Fifteen percent of people had no health insurance cover – that is, 45 million Americans. Just under a third (32%) of this uninsured health group are Hispanic, with 19% Black American and 10% white non-Hispanics. The 2000 US Census found that age was an important factor, with those in the 18–24 years group twice as likely as any other age group to be uninsured. Furthermore, nearly half (48%) of poor full-time workers were uninsured.

Social protection schemes in Sub-Saharan Africa (S-SA) take various forms, combining earnings related with means testing (in some countries) and compulsory savings plans. Although countries cite universal coverage for old-age benefits, thus far only three countries have non-contributory social pension schemes (Botswana, Namibia and South Africa) (see www.allafrica.com/Namibia). As Messkoub (2008) in his study of social security and population ageing in S-SA points out, the fact that such benefits are mainly earnings related, covering formal work sector employees, favours urban-based workers over rural workers both in terms of access to social protection schemes as well as ability to contribute. Botswana provides a flavour of the type of social protection system operating in S-SA. There is a universal pension and orphan care benefits paid by the government; sickness and maternity benefits are non-statutory with employers mandated to provide maternity benefits and certain medical services (that is, organise and pay for); there are no statutory unemployment benefits but employers are mandated to provide conditional severance benefits; last, family allowances are focused on those defined as destitute and comprise cash benefits and food rations. The country profiles provided by the International Social Security Association (see www.issa.int) shows exactly who provides what and the key differences lie unsurprisingly between the stable economies and those in conflict areas. Our three zones (EU, USA, S-SA) may seem different, but there is a common thread and that is the onus on the individual to contribute to their potential and actual social protection needs.

School education and policy

Universal primary education is one of the UN's key Millennium Goals and the recent review (United Nations 2008) of those goals shows that, in 2006, the net enrolment ratio for the developed countries was 96% compared with 88% in developing countries. Within this, it should be noted that Sub-Saharan Africa (S-SA), although still the lowest return, improved its position from 58% in 2000 to 70% in 2006. However, surveys in the region still highlight the fact that those from the poorest homes are least likely to attend school and there were no substantive differences between urban and rural settings in that regard. Gender parity has been an ongoing concern in the region and the review again shows real progress, with girls now at 80% of boy's enrolment levels. Yet the review also draws attention to the low retention rates among girls, particularly in Western and Central Africa where, they speculate, girls are being harder hit in terms of drought, famine, armed conflict and child labour. In terms of secondary education, net enrolment levels were 92% in developed countries, but just 54% in developing countries. S-SA fairs badly in this respect, with only 25% of those of secondary school age actually in secondary school and a sizeable 41% not in education of any type.

School systems in the USA and Europe have been moving towards a more integrated 'social' model. To a large extent, the USA led the way in the 1980s with their concept of A Full School Service (Dryfoos J 1994) in which schools would provide school-based health and social services designed to support individual needs. The key rationale behind the development was to address the perceived culture of failure within American schools through treatment, prevention and support not just to the pupil but also to their families. States developed their own versions of the general concept: for example, Florida put the emphasis on community services so that help was available on such matters as applying for public benefits and adult education. California developed 'Healthy Start' legislation, which covered all health and family support and youth development services. Indeed, some models even offered off-site referral to health, career, employment training, welfare and housing services.

In Europe and especially the UK, these ideas were reincarnated and adjusted under the banner of new community schools (New Community Schools Project; Scottish Office, 1998; www.scotland.gov.uk/library/documents-w3). Again, the aim was to integrate provision around families and pupils and, in so doing, encourage pupils and parents to adopt more positive attitudes to learning. The rationale was to bring out the best in the children and their parents through a concept of family learning and positive parent/child interaction. The community aspect came through providing out-of-school childcare services; student and family welfare services; and to act as a focal point for lifelong learning within the community. Indeed, the health component was intended to link to the World Health Organization concept of health, promoting schools (WHO 2004). Both the original US approach and UK adaptation were implicit recognition that education cannot exist in a box and the wider care context of the child had to be addressed through family and relevant services if the child was to achieve their potential.

Although these developments were going on at a national level, to mark the start of the new millennium the UN, in concert with world leaders and other supranational agencies, set an agenda of Millenium Development Goals (MDGs) designed to improve people's lives across the world but particularly people in poorer countries (UN 2000). A range of targets were set and, among them, that every child should have access to primary education by 2015 and that gender imbalances in access to schooling should be addressed. This latter target links to the target of ensuring gender equality by opening up opportunities for girls and women and reducing relative neglect and inherent bias against them in the home, work and community. The targets also recognised the crucial role that poverty, bad nutrition, sanitation and poor water quality made in under-minding educational performance. Added to the supra policy mix was United Nations Children Fund's development of the Child Friendly School (CFS), a cross-cultural model emerging from the human-rights-based approach to programming and based on the principles of child-centredness, inclusiveness and democratic participation. The model promotes the idea of a gender-sensitive, healthy and protected learning environment for all learners (UNICEF 2006). However, for those children living in S-SA, access to and the ability to participate and complete any form of education is being heavily challenged by the effects of the HIV/AIDS pandemic. Schools are being looked at in a new light, as centres of care (Boler 2008). Building on the child-friendly school model in response to the changing demands placed on schools, UNICEF has recently funded a major study in five S-SA countries examining school-based delivery of essential services. Central to that research was the design of an index of key indicators to provide planning guidance to schools in the new realities of becoming centres for care and support to pupils (Learning Plus Initiative: Schools as Centres for Care and Support, UNICEF Jan 2009). The key categories of services included in the Index are: Education; Psychosocial Support; Physical Health; Water and Sanitation; Nutrition and Safety; and Security. In particular, the psychosocial aspect of the Index recognises the gaps occurring when family cannot, will not or do not know how to address the grief, depression and anxiety that many children experience in facing up to the effects that HIV/AIDS has on their families and themselves.

Thus, in each of our zones, 'care' within an educational context has moved centre-stage regardless of the underlying motivations, and common aspects are emerging – for example, the need to involve the community, the need to integrate services, and the need to support the child and family as individuals but also as a unit.

Comparative time use

Table 1.2 gives an insight into the division of time among people in employment across our three Geographical Zones. How people say they spend time, and how this is categoriszed, adds depth to our analysis of care relationships. Data presented in Table 1.2 is derived from time-use surveys conducted within each regional zone. In the case of S-SA, the only time-use survey available at the time of writing was that of South Africa; therefore, South African Black African population results were utilised as proxies for S-SA. The time frames for each survey were: South Africa (2001); the EU (2004); and the USA (2006). The numbers relate to minutes per day. Because of the comparative difficulties with the data (for example, differing age groups, variations in employment categories and in time frames for the survey), the overview is broadly illustrative, not definitive.

In all three zones, personal care consumes the highest amount of time over a day but that is simply because a broad range of activities, including sleeping, have been subsumed in this category. The USA's employed population (men and women) spend the most time per day in paid work activities, followed by those in S-SA, and lastly people in the EU. Interestingly, the gap between men and women in terms of employment time seems to be narrowest in the USA. Women in the EU appear to use less of their daily time in employment than women in either of the two other zones. This could be due to the high levels of part-time work among women in the EU. S-SA employment time distinguishes between formal and informal and when both are accounted for in daily time use, S-SA men seem to be spending the same proportion as US men – that is, about a quarter of daily time. Only around 1% of daily time is spent in study regardless of zone or gender, although EU women seem to spend the least time in study (0.5%).

Unsurprisingly, women spend the highest absolute and proportionate amount of daily time in domestic activities. Men across each zone spend more time on leisure than women. Given the dominance of women in all forms of care work, combined with the many images of women in caring roles, the gap in leisure time is perhaps narrower than might be expected. It should be noted, however, that there are compositional differences – for example, women in the EU and USA spend less time on sports and computer-related leisure activities and more speaking with people on the telephone than men!

Care in action

Below we present four People Scenarios. These are vignettes based on imaginary families and relationships – however, in creating these, we have drawn on existing academic studies and media reports. Each draws on a topic of particular relevance to the Geographical Zone that forms the backdrop. In the EU, old and new, the topic is combining caring and working. In the USA, it is eldercare, migration and migrant labour. In South Africa, S-SA, it is the impact of HIV/AIDS on generations and intergenerational care.

Table 1.2 Broad-Based Comparative Time Use of Men and Women: EU, USA, S-SA. Minutes per Day.*

	EU Men 25–44 years	EU Women 25–44 years	US Men 15 years+	US Women 15 years+	S-SA Men 10+ years	S-SA Women 10+ years
Personal Care	639	654	553	575	681	682
Employment	308 (23%)	179 (13%)	516 (34%)	444 (30%)	312 (24%)	239 (19%)
Other Employment	–	–	–	–	41	39
Study	11	7	27	32	13	14
Domestic Work	116 (9%)	271 (20%)	80 (5%)	134 (9%)	73 (5%)	173 (14%)
Volunteer Work	10	8	8	8	8	5
Leisure	264 (19%)	230 (17%)	328 (22%)	283 (19%)	199 (15%)	141 (11%)
Comparative Time Total	*1348 (22.5 hours)*	*1349 (22.5 hours)*	*1512 (25.2 hours)*	*1476 (24.6 hours)*	*1327 (22.1 hours)*	*1254 (20.9 hours)*
Care of Persons						
All Household members	–	–	98 (20)	142 (43)	5	44
Non-Household Members	–	–	98 (11)	97 (14)	–	–
% Daily childcare	Highest Belgium, 12%; Lowest Latvia, 4%	Highest Norway, 15%; Lowest Latvia, 9%				

Sources: The Lives of Men and Women (Eurostat 2008b); South African Time Use Survey (Statistics South Africa 2001); American Time Use Survey (ATUS) (US Bureau of Labour Statistics 2007)

* The categories cited are the ones that are broadly comparable and therefore do not add up to all minutes spent on activities during a day. Furthermore, the definition of personal care is based on care for the disabled, sick or elderly, and domestic labour does not include informal care work. Thus, informal care is only partly documented – across two categories – and this reinforces our argument on limited data sources and why that continues.

EU: EU figures are minutes per day and cover 14 countries – a mix of north, south, east and west within the EU 25. Within leisure, men spend more time on sports, computing and television; women more on socialising with family. EU % Daily Household Activities Childcare is drawn from a sample aged 20–74 years.

USA: Figures are given for two splits as per ATUS. In brackets, the 'civilian' population; out of brackets, 'persons engaged in the activity'. In terms of analysis, this has had to be juggled – e.g. for 'study', we use only the civilian population, otherwise the large body of students included in 'engaged' would distort the time factor and the same is true for volunteering. Leisure is also measured for the civilian population.

S-SA: Figures relate to the African ethnic groups who participated in the survey. The S-SA figures are given as the employed group. The S-SA survey splits work into three categories, namely (1) work in establishments, (2) primary production, (3) work in non-establishments. The first category has been taken as the equivalent of the EU employment category and a separate category created for the rest.

Working and caring in the EU – Marcella and Henk Korteweg and Peter and Maria Prazak

The EU tries to help families to reconcile working and caring. In large part, this agenda is driven by economic issues – in particular, the drive to re-configure the EU as a set of economies based on knowledge industries, such as banking, finance, information and communication technologies, and education. The EU seeks to position itself as a major knowledge-based economy but is, however, composed of member states with varied historical, political and welfare systems. Economic development has varied between and within countries. The expansion of the EU has meant it is no longer a 'club' formed of post-industrial societies. The growth in members has brought with it enhanced recognition of the variability in patterns and practices of combining informal and formal care with paid work and the welfare problems and inequalities associated with this variability.

In EU 15, the old EU, governments and families have grappled with combing caring and working for several decades, often with limited support from the state. Marcella Korteweg and her family live in Hilversum, which is 30 minutes by train from Amsterdam. Henk and Marcella have lived together for 12 years and have two children; daughters of 10 and 1 years of age. Henk works full-time, overseeing the day-to-day management of a number of cafés and restaurants across Amsterdam, starting his shifts late morning and working into the evening. Marcella works part-time as a receptionist during the day. Without both incomes, they feel that they could not survive as a family and they have moved out of the city to be closer to family members and to where housing is affordable. Family members help with childcare when Marcella works but she is the main carer. During school holidays, Henk and Marcella organise leave so someone can be at home. Their lives mirror those of many families as they work on a daily basis to construct and maintain a patchwork of childcare activities in order to combine caring and working.

In contrast to Henk and Marcella in The Netherlands, the Prazak family have lived through a period of rapid political and economic change. Peter and Maria moved to Prague 3 years ago from just outside Brno, to improve Peter's chances of work. They have one teenage boy aged 16 years and two young twin boys aged 6 years, both of whom suffer from severe asthma. Peter works in a local glass factory but it looks as if it might close and the family are already struggling to make ends meet. Maria has a full-time job cleaning and the family have access to a small allotment that has become a life-line for food, supplying vegetables and fruit. Before the move, they were able to use Peter's mother to help with the twins and Maria misses the practical and emotional support as she and her neighbours all work and local childcare places are currently full. On top of this, recent changes to the Czech healthcare system means the family have to pay fees to access the ongoing medical care that the twins need, which has underscored the need for both parents to work. So from a number of angles, the family are under pressure in terms of caring for themselves as individuals and a family.

In contemporary post-industrial societies, women and men are expected to be active in paid work regardless of their parenting or care status. The growth in women's participation in employment has been coupled with increased rationing of welfare services and policies. Much of that growth has been linked to, and largely driven by, changes in the role of women. These changes, however, are more evident in public spheres than private aspects of life. Across the globe, we find that the increase in women's work outside the home has not been met with a concomitant decrease in responsibilities inside the home.

Migration and care relationships in Orange County, California, USA – John Terhunen and Nancy Hernandez

After a busy working and home life, peppered with hobbies and physical activities, John has reached his 80s. He's a bit surprised to have got to this age as it seemed to him that not that many of his older work colleagues lived beyond 70 years of age. But here he is. Last year, John was widowed, and that, combined with a decline in his mobility, has left him feeling vulnerable. John decided to move to the west coast of the USA and seek a warmer climate in anticipation that this would offer some relief from arthritis. Living in a gated senior citizens housing complex, John feels fairly safe. A nearby community centre runs a range of activities and offers opportunities to meet other residents. However, John's relatives live thousands of miles away in New York State, and lead busy lives, which curtails their ability to visit and contribute to his care.

To help John stay in his own home, he has joined a care network run by the owners of the housing complex. He pays a monthly sum for a carer to help him with housework and personal care. For example, he likes to have someone in the house when he bathes in case he has a fall or gets stuck in the bath. In the last 6 months, his carer, Nancy, has become important to his life. She is from Mexico and has limited English, but a big heart. She is kind and generous, often bringing him cakes that she has baked. Nancy cannot understand why John does not live with one of his children (his isolation seems alien to her) and she knows how much he needs her and looks forward to her daily visits. They enjoy a laugh together, and in slightly different ways it's a great comfort to both of them to know that Nancy arrives at the same time each day. As they have begun to enjoy each other's company, Nancy has said more about her circumstances, and John knows she has family outside the USA and that they depend on the money she can afford to send home. They are both 'migrants', whose lives have become interwoven around mutual needs and family circumstances.

The experiences of John and Nancy reflect global trends in morbidity, everyday lives, migration and experiences of care. In post-industrial societies, a range of residential shifts may occur as adult children and parents live their lives and address care issues related to the parents growing older or becoming widowed. Older men who become widowers are more apt to suffer severe support loss at widowhood because, in more traditional families (especially rural families), they have not been central to the tasks associated with keeping up family ties with migrant children (Russell 2007). As a result, widowers like John are more likely to seek a response that is less linked to close family members. Although an older person's migration to an environment with the potential to meet their specific needs (for example, to communities geared to support older people with mobility, health and social support issues) can relieve pressures on family members to provide care, the distance involved can raise anxieties and concerns among family and friends. Relatives and friends may undertake much travel, in addition to phone calls, emails and letters, to keep in touch, and feel increased concern as a result of managing care across distance.

Inter-generational care in Sub-Saharan Africa – Mary Ngaiza

Mary looked forward to becoming a grandmother. She was overjoyed by the birth of her first grandchild, Joy, 15 years ago. Now with three grandchildren, she is keen to support them to become happy and fulfilled adults. In the few moments she has to muse on life, however, Mary is bemused at how quickly her anticipation of later life has changed. For the last 5 years, she has been the main and full-time carer for her teenage grandchildren. Her daughter died from HIV/AIDS, the children's father died from the disease 2 years before her after several years working hundreds of miles away from home and coming back only rarely. On the few occasions that she can sit down to reflect on life, she gets worried. What of the future for children in communities where adults have to migrate for work? And HIV/AIDS is still rarely discussed but is leading to so much illness and death among adults who are often parents. What will happen as her health fails? The youngest grandchild is 8 years old and not in good health. How many years has Mary left to live? She wonders about the church-run orphanage nearby. When Joy was born, it was unthinkable that any grandchild of Mary's might be placed in an orphanage but now this might take place. Mary is concerned that Joy's future is not limited through becoming a full-time carer for her siblings before she is 20 years old. How can Joy be helped to avoid getting HIV? Times change, she mutters; who could have imagined any of this when her daughter was growing up? Dreams shattered; anticipations that were not realised. Best not to think too much and just get on with protecting the grandchildren.

With almost half of the population of Sub-Saharan Africa aged 15 years or less, the impact of infectious diseases has led to increased levels of intergenerational care among kin. Grandparents, aunts, uncles, older siblings and cousins are caring for younger relatives. The churches and international NGOs assist but there is some stigma about accessing welfare services, especially if these are linked to caring for people with HIV/AIDS. Not quite the pattern of growing up and growing older that many expected.

Summary

In this chapter, we drew data from international sources to present key dimensions of the variable global context of care; trends in population, health, labour markets and how people spend time. The device of Geographical Zones – EU, USA and S-SA – allowed us to illuminate change, continuities and contexts. Obvious examples of change are the impact of disease, HIV/AIDS, life expectancy, growth in labour force participation and urbanisation. These changes have varied impacts in each Geographical Zone and these differences result from different histories, welfare systems, cultural mores and experiences of war, unrest and natural disasters. Continuities are evident in the gendered nature of informal care and formal care work and the ways in which care is fundamental to human flourishing. The very different material and political contexts of care are signalled by differences in the power of the state to support informal care through the provision of formal care services and through different types of financial support for carers. The People Scenarios will allow us to explore these continuities and differences throughout the book. Disease and ageing are major concerns for Mary in S-SA, as she struggles to care for her grandchildren in an uncertain and insecure situation with limited state support. John and Nancy have forged a friendship through payment for care and that friendship offers emotional support for them both in a context in which older people are encouraged to remain 'independent' and to provide for their own care through use of money earned through paid work. In the new EU, which includes The Czech Republic, the outlook for the Prazak is bleak. The family is trapped between the experiences of the old state and the realities of the new. Although, in The Netherlands, the cost of housing and the juggling of childcare adds to the stresses and strains of family life for the Kortewegs in a context in which state encouragement for gender equality and for women to enter the labour market also relies on unpaid family resources to provide care. In subsequent chapters, we will develop the People Scenarios to aid the exploration of how time, space and place inter-weave with care interdependencies to form caringscapes.

This chapter has provided details of the material and social variability of the social and economic contexts for care around the globe and has hinted at cultural variability in caring expectations and practices. In the next chapter, we move on to explore the concept of care and the social processes involved in informal care. Together, Chapters 1 and 2 are intended to form a context within which we will go on to explore how informal care is bound up with our journey through the lifecourse.

Notes

1   In 2008, the EU comprised 27 countries. Given restrictions with the availability of data, consider EU 15 and EU 25. EU 15, also known as 'old' EU, comprises: Belgium,

France, Italy, Luxembourg, The Netherlands, West Germany (who were, in 1952, founding members of an economic collaboration that provided the basis for the European Union). In 1973, Denmark, Ireland and the United Kingdom joined; in 1981, Greece; in 1986, Portugal and Spain; in 1995, Austria, Finland and Sweden. EU 25, also known as 'new' EU, includes the 15 plus 10 countries that joined in 2004 and are predominately Eastern European: The Czech Republic, Estonia, Hungary, Latvia, Lithuania, Poland, Slovakia, Slovenia, Cyprus and Malta. In 2007, Bulgaria and Romania joined and the EU now has 27 members. Data, however, on the two most recent members continues to be patchy and hence they are excluded from our analysis.

2 Sub-Saharan Africa (S-SA) is a geographical term used to describe the area of the African continent that lies south of the Sahara or those African countries that are fully or partially located south of the Sahara. Only six African countries are not geographically a part of S-SA: Algeria, Egypt, Libya, Morocco, Tunisia, Western Sahara (claimed by Morocco). Together with the Sudan, they form the UN subregion of Northern Africa. Mauretania and Niger only include a band of the Sahel along their southern borders. All other African countries have at least significant portions of their territory within Sub-Saharan Africa.

3 Serial monogamy is a common trend in most societies. In post-industrial countries, this is facilitated by legal measures, especially legislation on divorce. In previous centuries, death of a partner, commonly through childbirth, made this possible. Sadly, maternal mortality continues to be a major factor in partnership changes in poorer countries.

4 Gross National Income (GNI) comprises the total value produced within a country (that is termed the Gross Domestic Product (GDP)), together with its income received from other countries (notably interest and dividends), less similar payments made to other countries.

5 Gross Domestic Product (GDP) is is a basic measure of a country's economic performance. It includes the market value of all final goods and services made within the borders of a country in a year. It does not include unpaid domestic and care work.

2 Care and Interdependency

Introduction

Care relationships are central to our everyday lives. Emotional and physical forms of concern, anxiety and labour are evident in care relationships. Rather than being dependent or independent, people are, at different points of their lives, both responsible for and reliant on the caring of others. Moreover, it can be argued that this interdependency is a necessary part of what is described by philosophers as 'human flourishing' or, that is, 'true happiness' (Paul and Miller 1999). But, there is a paradox: the everyday informal caring that is *essential* to social life is often taken-for-granted and undervalued.

Giving and receiving care is the embodied manifestation of our interdependency. Many kinds of care have been framed as 'natural' and 'normal' through a conflation of biological determinism with social roles and rules. However, we will argue that the way in which we care and who we feel we should care for are not 'natural' attributes but learned social behaviours that we acquire, practice, and develop in particular times and places. Hence, it becomes important to understand how and where we learn to care and what difference this may make to the caring that we exchange with others.

In this chapter, we explore 'informal care' as a social process in time and space. We start by exploring the concepts of care and caring and the notion of an ethic of care; we then look at some of the ways in which the social practices of care are shaped. Throughout this book, we will be emphasizing the importance of analysing what can be described as ideologies or social discourses that delineate who should give and who should receive care and in what social circumstances. Here, we start by examining the discourse of 'dependence' and 'independence' which, alongside a particular understanding of 'the family', has become so important to western conceptions of care. We continue by exploring the role of emotions and ideas of reciprocity in care and then examine the process of negotiation through which care practices are shaped.

'Care' and 'caring': meanings and morals

In this section, we first discuss what we understand by the terms 'care' and 'caring', drawing attention to the complexity and variety of the activities that might be considered to constitute 'care'. To give care is normally thought of as a positive and moral act. We thus also consider the notion of developing ethical guidelines, drawing on the everyday moralities of care-giving.

What do we mean by 'care and 'caring'?

Tronto (1993) has suggested that there are four phases in the process of care-giving:

- 'caring about' – noting a need and deciding it should be met
- 'taking care of' – assuming responsibility for the need and deciding how to respond to it
- 'care-giving' – an activity state that refers to the 'direct meeting of needs for care'
- 'care-receiving' – which involves assessing that the 'object of care' responds to the care it receives.

This last phase, she argues, is important because it recognizes that care can be ineffective or wrongly provided. She points out that paying attention to the effect of care – care-receiving – alerts us to the dilemmas of having to prioritize different needs and choose between alternative ways of meeting them.

Tronto's identification of the four phases of caring is intended to draw out essential features of caring to be found in any situation in which caring occurs. Its characterisation of the process of care is helpful both in identifying the necessary steps in care-giving and because it raises a number of important questions about each phase in the process. Thus, it raises the question of how needs come to be noted and recognised as legitimate; why one person or group rather than another might take responsibility for meeting that need. It draws attention to the fact that the same need might be met in diverse ways, or not met at all in the case of neglect. Furthermore, there are different ways of assessing the adequacy of care. So this leads us to the topic of how particular ways of meeting needs are chosen and assessed. The specific empirical answers to these questions will vary in different situations and the identification of the factors involved requires extensive comparative research. These issues will come up in various guises in the discussions in this and subsequent chapters.

However, in much empirical work, we find that meanings of care are often taken for granted, rely on cultural assumptions about the term, or allow defining factors to emerge from the particular perspective being taken (for example: Folbre and Bittman 2004, Forbat 2005). Thomas' review of the caring literature in the early 1990s drew attention to the problematic nature of the concepts of 'care' used. She critiqued researchers who presented their own interpretation of the concept as encompassing all caring activity, when, she suggested, the concepts of care employed were only partial representations of the totality of caring. She suggested that different definitions of care and caring exclude and include different sets of social relations in caring relationships (Thomas 1993). She examined the work of

Graham (1983, 1991), Parker (1981) and Ungerson (1990) to consider how the social identity of the carer, the care recipient and the inter-personal relationship between the two are considered in their different definitions. Reflecting on these studies, she concluded that care exists at the 'level of everyday familial and political discourse' and the term 'care' is commonly used to describe the 'totality of society's people-centred work' (Thomas 1993: 666).

'Caring' is a more fluid term than 'care'. It explicitly suggests the act of doing rather than a specific action or service provided, given or received, whether formal or informal. By emphasizing 'doing', it also focuses attention on the relationships involved in care – that there is a recipient of care and that the recipient is as important as the carer (Bondi 2008). Indeed, Thomas went on to identify seven dimensions of care, the first three of which emphasise this relationship. The remaining four emphasise the significance of the social and economic contexts within which care and caring are constituted. These dimensions can be combined in different ways to define different 'types' of care – for example, formal elderly care in America provided by a private firm; informal care exchanged among family members in Africa or 'free' childcare provided through a state-run nursery in Europe. These dimensions are:

- the carer
- the recipient
- the interrelationship between carer and recipient
- the nature of care
- the social domain
- the economic character
- the institutional setting

In each type of care, the answers to the questions raised by Tronto about how and why needs are acknowledged, how they are met and the quality of care assessed, may be different. Thus, conclusions drawn from empirical research about a particular 'type' of care cannot simply be transferred onto another 'type'. In this book, we are concerned with informal care. We address a challenge posed by Thomas (1993: 652) to include all the domains in which care takes place (such as the family, workplace, hospital), as well as the many types of relationships (including intimate partners, relatives, friends, work colleagues) to explore the multi-faceted nature of care.

Part of the difficulty of defining care can be seen in the dual meanings associated with the English word 'care' – 'caring for' and 'caring about'. The former has been described as an activity state, while 'caring about' someone is a feeling state (Thomas 1993: 652). In other languages and cultures, the notion of care is broader and includes care and caring in various settings (Ungerson 1983). In Finnish and German, for example, a number of words and terms exist to describe caring relationships and these allow for broader interpretations of the tasks and social relations of care and caring than in English. Ungerson (1983) identified 'caring about' with affection, affinity and emotion, whilst seeing 'caring for' as associated with servicing needs, specific tasks, obligations, and Parker's term 'tending' (1981). Arber and Ginn (1999) suggest that although both women and men 'care about', it is women who tend to carry the responsibility for 'caring for', although they acknowledge that men are more involved with 'caring for' than has formerly been noted. However, there are still gender differences in the kinds of caring for that is undertaken by men compared to women; for example, in both Europe and S-SA, men are less likely to undertake personal and intimate care (Arber and Ginn 1999, Arber and Gilbert 1989, Taylor *et al.* 1996, WHO 2002, Drew *et al.* 1998).

Another definitional issue of particular importance to us, as we are focusing on informal care, is the distinction between this and formal care. Formal care is usually defined as paid care, which is formally organised and regulated through some employing organisation, which can be either state-run or private. It is some-times presented as instrumental – designed to meet a clearly defined need. Formal care can be seen as a commodity to be bought and sold, measured and allocated, monitored and controlled. Informal care, by contrast, is not paid and is not provided according to a set of formal rules of care-giving. It is held to flow from commit-ments of kinship, community or belief system that embody both 'caring about' as well as 'caring for'. Rather than being carefully measured and allocated, it is flexible, responding to the variable and particular needs of care receiver and care giver. However, in practice, the division is less clear cut. Fink, in her edited col-lection (2004) aimed at exploring what care means (particularly in relation to social policy), suggests that care '… straddles and unsettles the boundaries between paid and unpaid employment, work and home, rationality and emotion, masculine and feminine' (1497). First, we may note that informal caring relations may develop in the process of providing 'formal' care (Thomas 1993, Qureshi 1990). Second, it can be argued that often 'effective' formal care not only engenders but requires 'caring about' emotions. Third, some informal care is provided in an instrumental and calculative spirit.

Thomas' concern was to ask if care can be re-conceptualized in a way that adequately addresses its diverse nature. She concluded that the construction of a single unified theory of care would be inappropriate for a concept that she considers to be an 'empirical category, not a theoretical one' (Thomas 1993: 668). We find her analysis persuasive; therefore, in this book we are not attempting to produce a grand theory of informal care and caring, but rather to provide a survey of the range of issues that a wide-ranging study of informal care provokes and also to provide a framework for investigating how caring activities and beliefs are bound up with human social behaviour over time and in place and space.

The ethic of care

Since the 1980s, an important and growing body of writing has focused on the 'ethic of care'. This refers to the idea that exploration of the principles involved in everyday caring can form the basis for the development of ethical principles that should underpin social behaviour and the organisation of society (Noddings 1986, 2002, Tronto 1993, Groenhout 2004, Held 2007). Such writing draws attention to the necessity of attentiveness to the needs of others and relatedness in care and caring and the particularity of caring relationships. For example, Held argues that care is a 'relation in which carer and cared-for share an interest in their mutual well-being' (2007: 35) and Tronto (1993: 134) suggests that: 'Caring is by its very nature a challenge to the notion that individuals are entirely autonomous and self supporting'. These ideas can be used to interrogate ideas of citizenship and pinpoint the shortcomings and strengths of actual practices and policies of care (Sevenhuijsen 2000). Their implications for our obligations to 'others' living 'at a distance' have also been recognized as important (Smith 1998, 1999 and Cottingham 2000) and have been valuable in the examination of the motives for specific examples of 'caring at a distance', such as charitable donation or consumption of Fairtrade products (Silk 2000, Barnett *et al.* 2005).

Writing in this 'ethics of care' tradition, Groenhout (2004) suggests that a successful theory of care *has* to incorporate an ethical dimension, a 'voice' in Gilligan's terms (1982) that reflects the moral component of the human condition. This perspective sees responsibilities and relationships as fundamental to 'human flourishing'. It thus challenges a mainstream point of view (an ethic of justice) that prioritizes impartiality and utility over emotion when considering right and wrong and, in so doing, risks dismissing the everyday experiences of care, particularly those of women. Because this challenge had come largely from feminist theorists, it has been seen as focusing particularly on the tasks and roles usually carried out by women (child and other forms of personal care). The focus on the experiences of women has been criticised as failing to provide 'an account of human life …
[that] … consciously works towards inclusivity … not an account of women's lives alone' (Groenhout 2004 p. 17). We agree that care is neither neutral nor value-free nor is it the province of women alone, although it is also the case that, globally, women appear to do more caring for than men. Tronto has challenged the feminist suggestion that an ethic of care is 'a factor of gender difference that points to women's superiority' (1987: 662) in her demands for a full theory of care. She has drawn attention to four elements of an ethic of care that she identified as necessary to be a morally good person, which are linked to the four phases of care discussed above:

- *attentiveness* – that is, noticing that care might be needed generally and specifically
- *responsibility* – that is, taking on caring practices (in contrast to obligations or rules)
- *competence* – that is, being capable of a caring practice or ensuring that a caring practice is undertaken properly
- *responsiveness* – that is, acknowledging 'the possibilities for abuse that arise with vulnerability' deriving from the need for care (Tronto 1993: 135) and being attentive to the way in which others articulate their need for care.

For the practice of 'good care' to work, the integration of these four elements is, according to Tronto, essential, as well as the recognition and 'assessment of needs in a social and political, as well as personal, context' (Tronto 1993: 137).

One challenge to an ethic of care is the observation that many actual caring relations involve dominance and exploitation. Practices of care can be seen frequently to involve interactions between people who are unequal (however brief these interactions may be) and so imply some degree of dependence and limited choice. This is particularly true of care for people who are frail, very ill or very young (Feder Kittay and Feder 2002). Morally good care for those who are highly dependent requires actions, but also anticipation, planning and making choices on behalf of others. It requires sensitivity to the feelings and views of the people we may be caring for and about: children need to explore as well as be kept safe; as we grow old, we want to make our own choices for as long as possible, as do the ill and infirm within the limits of their condition. The place of the care-giver can also be vulnerable and subject to exploitation. Feder Kittay and Feder (2002) make the point that informal care, relegated as it tends to be to its 'natural' location of 'the family', ensures that the costs of caring are borne by individuals (family members, wives, mothers), even though the benefits of care are felt and enjoyed by all of society in the sense that informal care ensure that adults remain and children become productive and content members of society. Fink uses the term 'a continuum of care' from Twigg (2000: 2), to suggest that this 'can range from love, nurture and personal attention through to abuse and neglect' (Fink 2004: 147). We find the latter notion particularly useful. Discussion of care can be bedeviled by the tension between our ideals of 'care' and 'caring' and the messy reality of human behaviours. Real relationships involving care can embody a complex mixture of love and abuse, and an emphasis on the social value of care must not ignore the problems of its absence or inadequacy or the exploitation of care-givers.

Care and caring: ideas and practices

In this section, we explore the ideas and practices that underpin caring in everyday life. We start by exploring the importance of what some might describe as ideologies and others as social discourse – sets of ideas that have become pervasive popular understandings of the world and that help to structure our behaviours and moral interpretations of behaviour. In relation to care, the dichotomy between 'independence and dependence' is of particular importance, and we start by discussing this. We then explore the significance of emotions to care and continue by examining the role of two important, but often tacit, features of relationships – reciprocation and negotiation.

Independence and dependence

In post-industrial society, it is clear that living in a state of independence has come to mean and continues to be seen as the ideal for the individual (Fraser and Gordon 2002). Although most of us may be attracted to the idea of not having to rely on others, in fact, as Feder Kittay and Feder (2002: 4) assert: '... independence results from invisible or unacknowledged dependencies on others, or on economic or political institutions and on social understandings of what constitutes dependence and independence'.

Fraser and Gordon (2002) have described a 'genealogy of dependence' to explain the development of the western ideology that underpins current understandings of dependence. 'Dependency', they explain, originally just meant being lower in status or unfree (as in serf or slave), but with the move to industrial capitalism it has come to mean being in a morally reprehensible state. This change in the nature of dependency, from an indicator of social status to that of an individual character trait, parallels the emergence of a Protestant work ethic alongside industrial capitalism that encouraged the view that independence could be achieved through (paid) work. As wage labour became the norm, unpaid activities became non-work and invisible. Paid employment has come to mean independence and independence tends to be equated with self-sufficiency. Young makes the point that:

> '[E]ven with a progressive understanding of "self-sufficiency" that refuses to accept that low-wage unskilled jobs can make poor people self-sufficient, the ideology of self-sufficiency still makes independence normative for autonomous people, and thereby judges those whom for whatever reason the society finds overly dependent as less worthy.'
>
> (Young 2002: 47)

In other words, the very use of a term such as 'self-sufficiency' implies that this can be attained, when it is clear that even the most privileged in status, power and financial resources will rely on the direct and indirect care of others at various points in their lives. Fraser and Gordon suggest that at the same time as being dependent (on others, on the State) attracted a stigmatized moral identity in an employment-driven world, a feminisation of dependence emerged that suggested that this was a state appropriate for women but not for men, alongside a racialisation that suggested dependence was appropriate to non-whites (Fraser and Gordon 2002).

Hockey and James (1993) suggest that the feminisation of dependence and the social marginality of children and older people who do not do paid work in the West can be traced back to the conflict between, on the one hand, the Western belief that independence is a desirable and natural state and, on the other, the reality of illness, ageing and death for adults. They suggest that this conflict is resolved, in part, through the use of metaphors that infantilise older people and construct children as necessarily dependent and helpless. Such metaphors, or discourses, are embedded in a wide range of social institutions and practices – in particular, a familialist ideology, the treatment of children as not fully 'persons', and the social construction of certain bodily characteristics (such as incontinence and confused memory) as childlike rather than as characteristic of certain adults. They contrast this treatment of older people in the West with a range of alternative understandings in other cultures. For example, they refer to the Sherba people of Sierra Leone and the Venda-speaking people of southern Africa, where signs of ageing are interpreted positively as indications of a growing closeness with the world of the ancestors or spirits. In such circumstances: 'While a daughter may have to give the kind of physical care to her helpless mother which she as a help-less infant received, that care endorses, rather than diminishes, the status of the elderly women' (Hockey and James 1993: 96–97). These examples show that our understanding of the necessity of physical or emotional care for particular groups of people – here, 'the elderly' – are products of particular cultural and economic circumstances rather than simply 'natural'. Moreover, the same care task – looking after an elderly mother – may involve very different understandings and feelings for both parties in different times and places.

Hockey and James (1993) argue that the form of gendered care that is central to Western family life, in which care is given to 'dependent' children and adults, predominately by women, is constructed as 'normal' because family care-giving is understood to spring from a 'natural' sense of obligation and emotional com-mitment. Hence, they claim that 'the centrality of the family is drawn upon to make manageable the notion of human need, thereby allowing dependency to be incorporated within a capitalist system grounded in the principle of individual-ism' (Hockey and James 1993: 126). The western familial ideology has assigned the role of adult dependent and carer to women. In the recent past, women were expected to care for but also to be dependent on the male wage earner and to care for children and the elderly. Women's dependency was socially approved but simultaneously positioned them as lacking power in society. However, women have challenged this position and sought 'independence' and social recogni-tion through entry to the labour market and political activity. This challenge has produced unresolved conflicts and confusions over family care relationships and responsibilities. These conflicts arise not just because work is not shared 'fairly' but also because these tasks are understood and practiced as constituting gendered identities (VanEvery 1997). Thus today, the notion of 'the housewife' has (ironically, from a feminist perspective) moved from an accepted and accept-able 'natural' role for women to that of parasitic dependence on support from a male breadwinner, or in his absence, the State. As many feminists have noted, this view ignores the unpaid caring work undertaken in the home (largely) by women, which subsidises the family and enables (male) paid employment. It has also resulted in an increased entry of women into paid employment, without an equivalent reduction in their responsibilities for domestic 'work' (Sullivan 2001, Hochschild 1989).

In many Western countries, the development of welfare state regimes has seen the State take on the responsibility of support for those who are vulnerable, when the 'natural' place for such support – that is, the family – has failed or is seen as failing. Being 'welfare dependent' is a stigmatised state, but also, at times of eco-nomic or physical vulnerability, state support is seen as a 'right' following from a person's past or future contribution to society through paid work (Deacon 2007). The intensity of debates over the proper roles of the State and family in caring for children, the elderly or the unemployed, and the complexity of people's feelings about accepting formal State care or becoming 'a burden' to family carers, are wit-ness to the power and contradictions of discourses of dependence and independence and ideas about family care. A simplistic duality that denigrates dependence and applauds independence, whilst ignoring the relationship between these two, has become widely accepted. Such ideas, although originating in Western capitalist societies, have been spread by Western policy-makers and funders through policy prescriptions for economic and social development in a variety of situations and countries (Sen 2001, Deacon 2007). This flawed division allows both people and the State to rely upon, without due acknowledgement, the universal necessity for mutual interdependence.

Caring about: an emotional process

The fundamental nature of emotion for all social action and communication has been examined by a number of sociologists (for example: Turner and Stets 2005, Bendelow and Williams 1997, Williams 2001, Crossley 1998, Hochschild 1983). We argue, as has Crossley (1998), that emotion is not just a series of private internal feelings that follow from and influence major and minor day-to-day experiences, but is central to the rational and public social world. Emotion informs the morality of choices and decision-making (Williams 2000).

Emotions are central to care-giving, as is implied in 'caring about'. We may be spurred to perform caring tasks by our emotions – because we care for someone, because we 'feel' we should do so or because we fear the social and emotional consequences of not doing so. Moreover, instrumental acts of performing a care task can set up an emotional relationship between carer and cared-for (Qureshi 1990, Twigg 2000, Brown 2003). The ethic of justice suggests that emotional commitments may lead to inequitable decisions over who to care for and how. In contrast, proponents of the ethic of care argue that emotion is inseparable from our decisions but also that good care requires empathy and emotion, although we need also to examine carefully the efficacy of the care we give (Bondi 2008). However, although good care may require emotions, it is also the case that care exchanges can involve the manipulation of emotion, and withholding or giving love and affection can be used as a means to exert control by the carer over the cared-for (Lee-Treweek 1996, Twigg 2000). Although this issue of using the emotional potentiality that is inherent in care exchanges is more usually discussed in relation to formal, paid care, it can also be characteristic of informal care.

Much may take place during an emotional expression or as a consequence of it that may not be understood, but will contribute to future actions and choices. Williams (2000) suggests that emotion guides reason, helping us to prioritise the different choices or options that we have at hand. He also suggests that 'primary' emotions (being part of our 'evolutionary biological makeup' (Williams 2000: 566) are constantly and continually developed and elaborated over time and place, history and culture. So, just as care and caring may evolve over time and in different settings, and through specific actions and behaviours, emotions are likely to evolve in similar ways and become more complex through this interaction. Emotions thus are not individual responses but are socially conditioned (Hepworth 1998). As ever, cause and effect is unlikely to be just one way and, although emotion may oil the wheels of care and caring, the bodily in-the-world socially mediated experience of caring will influence the feelings that we have about all aspects of our caring activity.

The expression of emotion is subject to social expectations about the appropriate methods of expression at different times and places. Indeed, social expectations about how we *should* signal our feelings are likely to influence those feeling themselves. Ideas of public and private affect social expectations about how different emotions can be expressed. In popular discourse in the West, the 'private' domain of the family has come to be viewed as the social space within which to express emotions (both negative and positive), and to expect those emotions to be attended to. In the 'public' domain of paid work and politics, many kinds of emotional expression – such as outbursts of anger, grief and hatred – are felt to be normally socially inappropriate. But there are also social expectations about how far people in different social categories and of different social status should express emotions and this will also be judged according to age, class, context, cultural traditions and many other social 'categories' that we impose on ourselves and others (Oleson and Bone 1998). Carers may feel obliged to present a socially acceptable 'mask' to the world that is very different to their inward feelings (Hepworth, 1998). Thus, Milligan notes that, in informal care work, 'the social performance of 'respectable emotions' requires informal carers to engage in a self-conscious distancing from their subjective feelings' (Milligan 2005: 2109).

Negotiation without emotion will not necessarily improve an outcome or make a process more rational. Family negotiation (discussed below), as a taken-for-granted process, assumes the emotional involvement of family relationships. The history of any individual family will, of course, be influenced by the wider cultural understandings of a particular time and place (Brannen 2006), but when choices are made the feelings of the participants will be influenced and developed through everyday actions. Love, affection, pride, loyalty, contentment and satisfaction can influence caring activities in the home, between friends and in the workplace, although they may be expressed and prioritised differently in each setting. Equally, disappointment, anger, envy and resentment can restrict or re-direct positive negotiations about actions, goals and decisions, influencing positively or negatively the shape and form of a group or a team over time and through generations.

Caring for: the meaning of reciprocity

The *exchange* of care between individuals is central to building relationships of mutual support. However, the 'payment' for an act of care by another act of care does not have to be immediate or formally acknowledged as a 'debt' to be effective in setting up such a relationship. The work of Finch (1989) and Finch and Mason (1993, 1999), concerned with family obligations in Britain in the 1980s, drew attention to how family members construed the exchange of assistance and support and the influence of duty, obligation and responsibility upon the process that translates *ought* into *action*. They noted that that there are no precise norms or rules of obligation – rather, there is a process of interaction in relation to care and support that they defined as 'developing commitments'. They concluded that everyday interactions involving monitoring, caring and supporting, rather than being the *consequence* of a relationship, could be seen to *constitute* relationships, especially if repeated routinely over time:

> [R]esponsibilities ... are the product of human agency and not an external property of social structure over which individuals have no control. But there is a sense in which they become structural features, in that they both constrain and facilitate future actions.'
>
> (Finch and Mason 1993: 173)

Thus, in many families, work groups and neighbourhoods, the exchange of care between individuals becomes part and parcel of ongoing relationships in which norms of reciprocity become features that 'constrain and facilitate future actions'.

The existence of webs of relationships sustained by norms of reciprocity is central to the concept of social capital (Coleman, 1988; Bourdieu and Wacquant 1992; Putnam 2000; Portes 1998). The large literature on social capital has shown how people can access valuable resources by virtue of their membership in a network of social contacts. Their ability to access these resources is underpinned, in part, by the knowledge that if they give to someone at one moment in time, in the future they will be able to call on that person, or someone connected to them, to give to them in turn. The social capital literature looks at the exchange of a variety of resources, including information, money and jobs, but also the physical and emotional support that constitute care. We are not concerned here with the debates over the role of social capital in development in either rich or poor countries (Woolcock 2001) or with arguments about its role in 'civic engagement' (Sen 2001). Rather, we simply wish to note that the rich array of empirical studies carried out on social capital have shown that networks of relationships in which norms of reciprocity are built up over time and enforced through various social sanctions are important to care relationships in a variety of countries. For example, social capital has been invoked in studies of transnational family care-giving (Zontini 2004), neighbourhood relationships (Forrest and Kearns 2001) and the social support networks of poor African-American and Latin-American mothers (Domínguez and Watkins 2003).

The process of exchange of care that is bound up in the term 'reciprocation' occurs over time. Social norms about the period of time that can pass before reciprocation is required are important. Some acts of caring, which are part of such reciprocation, such as the everyday exchanges of care between partners, parents and child or worker and co-worker, have a daily or weekly periodicity and often involve synchronisation of co-presence – for example, cooking an evening meal for a partner who does the washing up in 'return', or exchanging emotional support with a work colleague over a weekly lunch. In such cases, the 'equality' of the exchange may or may not be significant to the participants – but if reciprocation is too unequal it will undermine the relationships. Other caring-for tasks may not be reciprocated for many years and may not be expected to result in easily defined reciprocal acts of care – for example, although parents do expect some 'return' in terms of love, care and consideration from their children for the many acts of 'caring for' involved in bringing up a child, most are prepared to wait some time for some of these returns. However, the exchanges that take place in the home, community and workplace over different durations and periodicities create and re-create relationships of informal reciprocation that enable (or disable) social life throughout the lifecourse.

Caring about and caring for: negotiation as a way of life

The term 'negotiate' has been defined as: 'to treat (with another) in order to make a bargain, agreement, compromise', and also 'to arrange, to bring about, to procure by negotiation' (Oxford Dictionaries 2008). The general use of the term is usually seen as a formally conducted, overt transaction, but when used to describe the everyday interaction between people, a more subtle interplay can be identified. When we talk about accommodation of the needs and preferences of different family members, it is rare for this to be undertaken in a formal, contractual manner. In the informal setting of family or friends, the tacit process by which some form of consensus is reached often involves an ongoing and interpretative testing of territorial and activity boundaries and flexibility of roles. Family practices, to which caring makes such a significant contribution, are often achieved through a complex process of presumption, dependence, rapport and, only sometimes, direct communication (Finch and Mason 1993). Gendered assumptions that rely on notions of the natural often underpin such negotiations. The implicit character of negotiation in this form contributes to the invisibility of 'caring about' activities, particularly as undertaken by women.

In the paid work setting, there are formal roles and rules both as part of a general work ethos, and specifically attached to a particular work setting. Beyond these requirements, people can establish informal understandings of how they might care for and support each other in the work environment. Such understandings will often rely on both reciprocation and negotiation. For example, the ways in which a worker might organise their work hours to accommodate paid work requirements and non-work care expectations may incorporate formal and informal forms of negotiation, which can both clarify and obscure the links and boundaries between these settings. The informal arrangements that people make allowing them to bring children into work on occasions, or taking work home to meet a deadline, or swapping shifts to attend to personal appointments are more likely to be informally negotiated arrangements between colleagues and workmates. They rely on mutual trust, friendship and a sense of reciprocity often developed over time and/or in settings in which such give-and-take is seen as normal (McKie *et al* 2008, 2009).

Time is important to both reciprocity and negotiation – time is needed to develop the understandings upon which they both depend and also to carry out the caring tasks that are their subject. However, place and space are also integral to their operation. Negotiation requires communication, whether that be through body language, tone of voice or written communication. Much of the tacit and informal negotiation that underpins informal care requires co-presence and so is characteristic of groups who spend time together in a work, leisure or family setting. However, more explicit negotiation – for example "I'll do the shopping if you can pick the baby up from nursery" or "Could you cover my shift and I'll cover yours next week" – can be conducted more remotely by phone, text or email. By learning of the negotiations of others and their outcomes, we also build up a picture of what sorts of exchanges are accepted and expected – of what is 'normal' in a particular locale or setting.

Everyday understandings of a normal life, whether at work or in the home, are established through negotiations rooted in ongoing and developing understandings of what *should* be. Among any family, community or work team at any point in time, there can be a range of 'shoulds' that evolve into 'cans' for that particular group. This is not to say that the 'normal lives' that are negotiated are always satisfactory to all groups, or individuals. Negotiation is the means by which people *organise* their lives, but also acts as a process by which they *normalise* their lives. The social norms of what friendships, work teams or the family *should be* can act as a backdrop to how people negotiate both the everyday or the new and the unexpected, using past experiences in conjunction with present patterns and future plans. Moreover, although we might want to assume that social norms will imply positive, progressive, caring behaviour in any social setting, entrenched uncaring social norms in specific groups, communities or nations can mean a dialogue that confirms rather than challenges the negative in social behaviour.

Moving from Part I to Part II

In Part I of the book, we have considered the importance of the differing contexts for care around the globe (Chapter 1) and introduced and considered a number of concepts relating to informal care (Chapter 2). Having provided foundations to our exploration of informal care in specified parts of the world – the Geographical Zones – we now flesh out notions of time and space. The People Scenarios offer a vehicle for a renewed examination of existing literature and theories. In Part II of the book, we develop our ideas on how time and space are bound up with informal caring practices in the family, among friends, between 'strangers' and in the workplace. The People Scenarios bring into focus how past, present and anticipated notions of care are evident in everyday activities and longer term plans. They also help to illuminate the similarities and differences of the temporal and spatial dimensions of informal caring across the world and how these can change suddenly. Here, we detail how our frameworks of caring and carescapes have evolved. We start Part II by exploring, in Chapter 3, the topic of living with care as we grow up and grow older. As we have explained in the Introduction, we have deliberately placed 'learning to care' after 'living with care' to emphasise that learning about care is not something we only do at the start of life but takes place continuously, and is as much to do with space as time.

Part II

3 Living with Care

Introduction

This chapter focuses on how the consideration of time contributes to our understanding of informal care across the lifecourse. We start by discussing the importance of different conceptualisations of time to caring and then explore how considerations of time are bound up with social processes and social control. Care over the lifecourse is then explored in terms of the role of memories and anticipations of care in structuring our journey and the importance of gendered expectations and practices. The chapter moves on to consider the ways in which people cope with expected and unexpected change and, last, examines the shifting nature of care between the generations.

Care, time and social processes

The multidimensionality of time and care

Caring takes place through time and occupies time. Anticipations of the future, ideas of the socially expected timing of events and of the ways in which we should and do 'spend time' all will affect practices and beliefs about care and caring. There is a large literature on time use, which tracks the amount of quantitative time people allocate to different tasks (for example, Gershuny 2000). Chapter 1 gave examples of time use in our different Geographic Zones. These data can provide snapshots of the time spent on different caring activities but tell us little about their repetition or relationship to other activities. In her study of the temporal organisation of daily life, Southerton (2006) quotes Fine's five dimensions of time:

> 'Periodicity refers to the rhythm of the activity; tempo, to its rate or speed; timing to the synchronisation or mutual adaptation of activities; duration, to the length of an activity; and sequence to the ordering of events.'
>
> (Fine, 1996: 135; quoted in Southerton 2006: 436)

These concepts can be used to explore the patterning of activities in time, which is linked to problems of synchronising and co-ordinating activities with one another. Some caring activities may be of short duration and may not involve much synchronisation or be sensitive to sequencing (for example, ordering something on the internet for a older person who does not have a computer), whereas others may be strongly linked to the activities and time constraints of other people as well as requiring sequencing (for example, taking someone to the doctor and then to pick up a prescription). Some caring activities must be regularly repeated to be useful (for example, feeding or disciplining a child), whereas others may only need to be carried out once.

Studies that focus on synchronisation, duration or the allocation of time to different tasks still tend to measure time in quantitative 'clock' time. However, there are other ways of thinking about time that pay more attention to the subjective. Limiting time to the quantitative ignores the complexity of social time and how it is tied up with space, gender, caring and power, and hence how meanings and understanding of time will differ between cultures (Southern 2006, Brannen 2005, McKie *et al.* 2002, Daly 2001, Adam 1995). For example, and as previously mentioned in the Introduction, Adam's (1995, 1998) 'timescape' perspective starts with *quantitative* time (as in clock time), then adds the *context* (bringing together time and space) and the *multidimensionality* of time (that is, the different, but simultaneously experienced, timescales on which time functions).

The implications of switching to these more complex understandings of time can best be understood through an example of undertaking a recognisable routine caring task: getting from home to school to work. For this task, quantitative time would just involve consideration of how much clock time it would take to do the trip from home to school to work. However, the context within which this takes place might include the time needed to bring together the children and their accoutrements (such as homework, gym equipment, lunchbox), as well as form of transport (car, bus, walking), the physical locations of the two destinations, the flows of traffic between them and the timing of the work and school day – all of which are influenced by the local and national state, rules and traditions, and the local economy.

Consideration of the multi-dimensionality of time reminds us that the journey will be embedded within a number of different timescales and social understandings of time – for example, there are the timescales of the day and its scheduling, of the school year, of the parent's career, of the child's development – all of these different timescales can affect the parent's and the child's experiences of the journey and how they interpret the significance of the journey for themselves or each other. These different temporalities will affect how the time of the journey is experienced and perceived by each one and how it is organised in relation to other activities; how it is prioritised, undertaken and remembered. Already, we can see how a simple task includes complex contextual and temporal considerations.

Continuing the 'school run' example to provide a picture of the care implications of this simple set of actions, we now need to add the many social dimensions associated with getting children to school, such as: the gendered nature of parenting that still expects mothers to be the person primarily responsible for their children; the class-led assumptions about location and resources that limit school choice; work-led priorities that emphasise full-time and continuous employment as the criteria for salary and promotion considerations. These considerations will also be embedded in a particular historical period in a particular country in which there will be a given welfare regime and set of social and economic expectations, which themselves all change over time (Brannen 2006). From this example, we can see how time is both a driver for and an outcome of social life.

Time, care and 'control'

Adam (2006) has made the point that, since time has been made measurable (and that measurability has come to be seen as the 'natural' way of assessing life), this has strongly contributed to a capitalist system that places value *only* on time that can be measured. She suggests that, in trying to control time, time has come to control us – bringing with it a notion of instantaneity that undermines (and makes invisible) any group or set of systems that cannot be brought within that remit.

> 'With information and communications technologies (ICT) time compression has reached its zenith: succession and duration have been replaced by seeming instantaneity and simultaneity. Duration has been compressed to zero, elevating human capacity to that of extraterrestrial beings, that is, to be everywhere at once and nowhere in particular ... Children and the elderly, the unemployed, carers the world over and subsistence farmers of the majority world inhabit the shadowlands of un-and under-valued time. Women dwell there in unequal numbers. Their time does not register on the radar of commodified time. ... it is rendered invisible.'
>
> (Adam 2006: 124)

This instantaneity and simultaneity is perhaps most evident in the world of neo-liberal capitalist paid work, where 'flexible working' has made the location (where), the timetable (when) and the duration (how long) of working so fluid and adaptable that the boundaries between home and work have become increasingly blurred. Work time seeps easily into 'home time' – not least because home (social) time is not measured (costed) in the way work time is (or at all). This flexible way of working demands a self-regulation that gives an illusion of control over time, but means we can find it difficult to assess a 'reasonable amount of time' for work (or, in fact, any activity). It creates a constant state of 'busyness' that allows little opportunity to be other than in an extended present – so little attention can be paid to the future or even plans for the future (Brannen 2005).

Indeed, much has been said about the tension between an ideal of 'family time' (Folbre and Bittman 2004) and its lived experience, with a positive moral value accorded to family time that leaves members feeling they are constantly falling short of their and society's 'family' ideology. Family time has been described as a prescriptive term implying a set of traditional values not easily realised in work/life challenges (Bernardes 1987); any one family can be seen as, effectively, two different families that live in a state of tension, "the one they live with and another they live by" (Gillis 1996: xv). Daly (2001) suggests that this is manifested in ideas of sacrifice and putting the children first (ironically, according to Daley, more likely to be a concern of parents than children). It is revealed through feelings of guilt and disappointment, that is, aspirations that they see as beyond their grasp, and so requiring '... a need to hold on to the "reassuring myth of family past" that serves their present needs and future aspirations' (Daly 2001: 293).

Time and the development of caring relationships

Caring practices between individuals, whether in the home or at work, often start in small ways over a coffee with a friend or in passing with a neighbour. They occur within defined social roles and rules, particularly in social settings that are recognised as appropriate, and the relationship that is developed through each encounter constitutes a potential for mutual caring processes. For example, caring for the neighbour's cat each time he goes away, cumulatively may develop a reciprocal cat-caring set of responsibilities, but may also lead to further caring exchanges that involve looking out for each other in other ways and the possibility of becoming friends. Such caring interdependencies not only have significance at the micro level of the individual, but also at the macro level of society (Thomas 1995). Such interdependencies affect our understanding of time and lead to the imbrication of temporal norms and social organisation. Muzzetto (2006), examining the views of Alfred Schutz on time and meaning, suggests that, for Schutz, "the basic element of the social world is the experience of 'sharing' the form of experience – that is, of time. Thus, the construction of a common time is the construction of the 'social'".

Tabonni's analysis of Elias's understanding of social time suggests that time is meaningful as a concept through interactions that create 'long chains of interdependence' that link everyone to everyone else (Tabonni 2001: 11). Care, as a social norm, provides a lived experience of internalised temporal rules. Tabboni (2001: 6) asks:

> 'Since conceptions of time change, what concept of time can take account of the experience, both individual and collective, which the idea of time evokes?'

and

> 'How is it that everyone, in making a choice, constructs their own personal time while still remaining subject to the restraints of social and natural time?'

Her answer is that 'The social construction of time ... goes back to a specific human ability to work on the experience of change, to react, to organize and confer meaning on the experience' (Tabboni 2001: 7). Through this process, she suggests, '[R]ight from the first experience the idea of 'time' would seem to suggest an experience of change which is ordered, capable of meaning, and within which choices can be made'. These, she goes on to suggest, imply temporal norms that 'play the

... social role of guaranteeing the organisation of work, the systematic satisfaction of reciprocal expectations in people's behaviour towards each other, at the same time as they express evaluations and moral positions in face of the fundamental experience of change ... .' (Tabboni 2001: 9). As part of, in Elias' terms (1982), a civilising process, interdependent lives in complex societies encourage the development of a 'social sensitivity' to these temporal norms – a temporal *habitus* in which 'respect for temporal norms in these societies gradually becomes a 'feeling for time" (Tabboni 2001: 11).

A significant theme for this book is the functional nature of *inter*dependency for human flourishing. If the social groupings within which caring is routinely practiced become fragmented (through distance, or competing responsibilities, or work pressures), they become less functional, and there seems to be less and less time and space for care. For example, if practices that are seen as a 'normal' part of family life that also promote caring opportunities (such as the family meal, or Granny babysitting) disappear without the development of new 'family' practices that also encourage care, we may find a transformation of family as a 'relationship' to family as an 'idea'. For example, the loss of the 'family meal' is a loss of opportunity to learn and practice caring. If it is not replaced by other, equivalent opportunities, it can result in a reduction in family interdependencies. Like many social practices, caring is learned through practical application and social interaction; it is an ongoing process rather than a one-time lesson. Without ongoing reinforcement over time through everyday activities, care and caring can wither and decay.

Caring over the lifecourse

A focus on specific periods or points in the lifecourse (such as childhood or the transition into full-time paid work) has the tendency to imply that these are static and stable, certainly in relation to care and caring. In our examination of the movement and flow of interdependency across the lifecourse, we aim to show the ways in which it is, in fact, fluid and changes over time, and, more importantly, that interactions at different points of the lifecourse have implications for decisions and relationships (and therefore dependencies) at other points of the lifecourse.

As babies, we are dependent on others to care totally for us; as children, we explore the boundaries of care; as teenagers, we start to define and redefine who we are and that impinges on and redefines the care we now receive and are willing to receive, as well as what we are willing to give in return. As adults, we try to take charge of what care means in our lives and this is shaped not just by past experiences but by the way we construct relationships with others now and plan to live in the future. In later life, we try to stay in control of how we give and receive care, especially the latter, as it may challenge both our identity and what is acceptable to us as a life. The notion of the lifecourse as a journey whose end should be resisted as long as possible ignores the potential reciprocities between those who are ostensibly dependent and independent, as we have pointed out in Chapter 2. Moreover, people move in and out of caring situations during this journey and their care status can be ambiguous. For example, a teenager may receive care but may also have to give care where a parent is ill or has limited physical capacity. As a young single adult living away from home, they may become less involved in family care and more involved with care of and from friends. Moving on in their life, they may acquire a partner and children and change their care role as a result. When the children leave home. the nature of their care-giving and receiving may change. Later, they may have to relinquish some of their care-giving role and increasingly become the subject of care. Most people never fully step out of a care role in their lives but the care role varies in intensity and form.

Memories and anticipations

When we are called upon, in different ways, to provide care for others, we fall back on our caring histories and biographies to help us know *whether* to care, and, if so, *how* and *where* (Finch and Mason 1993). We also draw upon our past experience as well as the experiences of those around us to plan future caring; for example, we may plan to remain childless, expect that friends will be a major source of emotional and practical support or assume that we will provide care for ageing parents. Each of these expectations is likely to lead to particular courses of action. An important feature of such practices and 'plans' – however vague the latter may be – is that they embody moral judgements about how we 'ought' to behave. Many of these moral judgements revolve around the idea of 'family' and the social obligations and duties that different members of a 'family' owe to one another – such as mothers, fathers, daughters and sons, siblings and grand-parents, as well as more distant relatives. In Chapter 5, we will explore in more depth the significance of care from friends and acquaintances, but 'kin-care' (Graham 1991, Thomas 1993) is a particularly important arena for care practices and expectations and so we focus on this here. Memories and anticipations and the family caring practices that people have been part of in the past help to create these moralities. In other words, the family is an institution in which, over time, particular understandings of informal family care are developed, modified and passed on across the generations through the interplay of memories and anticipations.

The '*idea*' of family, as well as the actual lived reality of family, is important to the development of such caring practices across the lifecourse. Moreover, every-day practices both reflect and create anew, ideas about family. Thus, the institution of the family provides, for the people involved, a dual role in their lives. Whilst undertaking the tasks and activities that allow family to perform *functionally*, each member's contributions towards daily routines also provide a day-to-day construction and reconstruction of the *meanings* that the family generally have for them. These meanings are constituted through the interaction of everyday routines with social representations of family life from a variety of sources. Morgan has suggested that there are 'family practices': 'which deal in some way with ideas of parenthood, kinship and marriage and the expectations and obligations ... associated with those practices' (Morgan 1996: 11). The term 'kin', frequently associated with definitions of the family, introduces notions of duty and obligation through a sense of reciprocity that, nevertheless, must be negotiated (Finch and Mason 1993).

However, what constitutes particular 'family practices' varies between cultures and over time. The term 'the family' as a social institution is recognised across most cultures (not just those in the West) as the institution within which most people, at some point in their lives, live and conduct the private and personal aspects of their lives (Cheal 1991). However, the form of this institution and the meaning of family and family practices are highly variable across cultures (Carsten 2000). Furthermore, in much policy and some academic literature, there is a conflation of 'family' and 'household'. Thus, people may live in a variety of types of 'family' households – for example, polygamous family households, households in which genetically unrelated people feel they are a 'family' and 'nuclear' family households. They may also interact frequently with a wider set of family members (kin or fictive kin) who are not co-resident. In recent years in the West, popular understanding of the co-resident family household has shifted from a heterosexual, once-married couple with children to encompass a broad range of (semi)permanent liaisons that have the common aim of creating a sense of completeness and continuity based on mutual love, affection, kinship and responsibility. This term has come to include: lone parents, foster or adoptive parents, same-sex couples, cohabiting couples and remarried couples with step-children, all of whom will, today, describe themselves as 'a family' (Bernardes 1987, Morgan 1996, VanEvery 1995, 1996, Cheal 1999, Williams 2004). Among these 'families' and also the growing number of single people, there are also often strong caring relationships with other, non-co-resident kin. Ideas of families, of what family obligations, behaviours and relationship entail are very powerful in creating social, political and moral expectations. These are embodied in a host of everyday habits of speech and behaviour, media representations and political rhetoric in different societies.

The types of care that the family is socially expected to provide vary with the welfare regime in which it is embedded. In situations in which the state provides very little, people must turn for care to family, friends or a social group with which they are identified. This may be a religious group, an ethnic group, a production-related group or a territorial group. Although such social groups are important, around the world we find that 'family', variously defined, continues to play an important role in such care. Thus, for example, in many poor countries in which state pensions and welfare benefits are rare and/or have limited coverage and/or low value, it is the person's children or other relatives who become socially obliged through 'tradition', to provide care and organise care for older people or orphaned children. However, such sets of beliefs and practices are not fixed – they may change in response to 'events' such as changes in state provision, war or disease that affect the practicability or desirability of the arrangements.

Limited welfare and support systems add to the issues that families have to grapple with. In post-apartheid South Africa, for example, the state pension is now paid to 80% of age-eligible Black South Africans. It is estimated that more than 80% of the elderly have no access to income apart from the state pension. With the monthly pension twice the median monthly individual earnings of Black South Africans and women eligible at 60 years of age, many families have come to depend on this source of income. The households of older women increase when they start to draw a pension, with relatives from different generations being dependent on this source of income. Older Black women are increasingly assuming the role of primary economic and care resource and intergenerational transfer of resources is evident (Duflo, 2003). In contrast, evidence suggests that older Black men, who receive the pension at 65 years of age, are less likely to transfer resources across the generations. For example, in Tanzania, the government, with the support of global agencies and NGOs, is developing strategies to tackle poverty, especially in rural areas, focusing specifically on primary health care and schools. In addition, the government is promoting skills and financial education in agriculture to enhance the potential for better returns and cash income to support families (Tanzanian Government 2001). Such strategies have the potential to impact on intergenerational economic and care relationships.

Changes in political direction can have significant impacts on family welfare. For example, in the Czech Republic the decline in day nursery provision for children that started in the early 1990s continued through the change in regime (1999) and membership of the EU (2004). There were 1040 state-funded day nurseries in 1990; they had declined to 52 by 2007 (Radio Prague, 21 March 2007). The private sector and NGOs have become the main providers. This, coupled with the fact that few businesses offer childcare places, means that mothers with very young children (0–3 years) who wish to work find it difficult to do so.

Brannen (2006) provides an excellent example of the ways in which some family practices have changed in response to changes in the welfare regime. In a study of the cultures of intergenerational transmission of resources and care of 12 multi-generational families in Britain, she shows how the advent of the welfare state changed some families' ideas of what kinds of obligations were appropriate between family members. 'A culture of 'getting on' and 'independence from family' was evident among members of the Second World War grandparent generation, both men and women, who … were able to draw on the benefits offered by the expanding growing welfare state to help advance themselves' (Brannen 2006: 150). But she also shows that some families resisted such a shift, retaining highly solidarised patterns of behaviour with a gendered exchange of resources between men and care between women across the generations. For example, across S-SA, cultural attitudes and policies about orphaned children differs between countries, regions and local communities. In different regions, depending on the cultural foundations, orphaned children are expected to be taken in and cared for by either matrilineal or patrilineal relatives – albeit often in return for those children doing work for their relatives and being placed in subordinate social roles (van Blerk and Ansell 2007). As we have said, these arrangements are coming under increasing strain as a result of the impact of HIV/AIDS in a situation of poverty. The Czech Republic, by contrast, has among the highest number of children in orphanages in the EU. Combined, the influence of religious ideology, provision of church-based orphanages, limited access to contraception, an increasing sexualisation of adolescence and growing inequalities have led to a dependence on orphanages to provide care (Fultz *et al.* 2003). These examples show how people adapt family practices of care in response to major changes in the resources available or in the demands made on them.

In countries with a well-developed welfare state regime, families may still play a very important role in informal care provision and in *accessing* state aid for family members. Moral beliefs about the rival merits of formal state, private or voluntary care, and informal 'family' care are significant to families' behaviour and may vary considerably between families from different class and ethnic backgrounds (Brannen 2006, Duncan and Edwards 1999). The desirability of 'family' care – usually provided by women – is particularly morally contentious in relation to care of the elderly and care of young children. For example, in Brannen's research, mentioned above, she found some families who believed strongly in State provision and independence from family when it came to care of the elderly. They did not provide care for their own elderly parents and did not expect it from their children. As one respondent put it: 'We grew up expecting the state to do things, and I'm still very much in favour of that ... I don't think I would want my children to feel that they had to look after me' (Brannen 2006: 144). This contrasted with others who felt equally strongly that the family should care for elderly parents and behaved accordingly.

Across the globe, women's increased involvement in paid work has resulted in many women now having the dual burden of both working and retaining the main responsibility for care in the home and family. In a study of women's attitudes to combining paid work and mothering, Duncan and Edwards (1999) have argued that women's attitudes and actions are not structured in terms of a 'rational' evaluation of financial costs and benefits in relation to their 'human capital' – as is often assumed by policy-makers – or as the result of 'preferences' as argued by Hakim (2000, 2002), but rather that different groups of women have different 'gendered moral rationalities'. Duncan and Edwards' research in England suggests that these gendered moral rationalities differ between different groups of women defined in terms of class, ethnicity and residential location (itself a reflection of economic constraints and desired lifestyle). For example, they identify three different 'gendered moral rationalities': mothers who believe they should physically care for their children and that paid work decisions must be subordinated to this requirement (primarily mother view); those who feel that full-time employment is part of good mothering (mother-worker integral view); and those who feel that their identity as a paid worker is separate from their role as a mother (primarily worker view). Mothers in working-class social positions living in old industrial towns tended to the primarily worker view; those in peripheral working-class social positions, living in similar areas, adhered to the first, primarily mother, position. Mothers in professional managerial class positions living in a high-status suburb also adopted the 'primarily mother' view – but those that Duncan terms 'gentrifying partners' living in Hebden Bridge, an old industrial town that has become gentrified with the influx of artists, leftish professionals and 'yuppies', adopted either the 'primarily worker' view or the 'mother-worker integral' view. The latter was also characteristic of mothers of African-Caribbean background living in inner areas of London. Those of higher class were more likely to favour the 'primarily worker' view (Duncan *et al.* 2003).

Duncan (2005) argues that these gendered moral rationalities are socially constructed through the experience of individual biographies lived in the context of particular 'regionally specific gender cultures' and which are also, importantly, 'classed cultures' (Duncan 2005: 73). McDowell *et al.* (2005, 2006) also discuss how women make decisions about mothering and paid work in London and Manchester, arguing that they are influenced by 'local moral geographies' in which 'women's experiences and meanings of motherhood are mediated through the networks and cultures in which they are embedded as well as influenced by the types of childcare available locally' (McDowell *et al.* 2005: 231). Similarly to Duncan (2005), they argue that 'class, lifestyle and locality interact to produce complex resolutions in which class position and financial assets are perhaps of overwhelming importance' (McDowell *et al.* (2005: 231).

People develop ideas about caring, infused with moral expectations, derived from their past experiences and expectations of possible and probable futures within a particular time–space context. The context – the economic and social relations of a particular historical period and place – affects the opportunities and constraints within which people make decisions and reflects classed, gendered and racialised inequalities of power. However, the complicated interactions that bring about change in ideas and behaviour are not always smooth or synchronous. It is a picture of imperfect articulations, and contested and contradictory adjustments, although there may be an illusion of continuity in the way that ideas change. Through these adjustments, the image of 'family as natural' endures through its links to 'gendered caring as natural'. These assumptions contribute towards what Giddens terms our 'ontological security' – that is, a 'person's fundamental sense of safety in the world', which 'includes a basic trust of other people' (Giddens 1991: 38). Thus, these ideas are part of taken-for-granted ideas about human nature. Put another way, they are part of what we consider to be 'normal' human behaviour. We now turn to examine the role of such ideas of 'the normal' in helping people cope with change.

Coping with change

There are a number of transition points and events in the lifecourse at which informal caring comes to the fore in individual people's lives either as a care-giver or recipient. Such transitions and events may relate to oneself or relatives or friends and cover transitions and events such as family change (for example, birth, death, divorce or marriage), moves through education (such as taking exams or starting at a new school or university) or employment events (for example, a new job or redundancy). Whether expected or unexpected, such transitions and events require adjustment in people's everyday lives and often in their interpretation of their own identity and self-worth. These adjustments may involve major reorganisations of social expectations and informal caring practices or more personal individual adjustments of caring relationships. These points are illustrated below by, first, reference to the adjustments people make to their caring relationships in response to the chronic illness of a member of their family and second to people's adjustment to an expected but feared transition – the move into frail old age.

'Nowadays with infectious diseases far less threatening in *mass* terms, chronic illnesses have assumed a greater importance, and sickness has become a way of life, not a way of dying' (Stacey 1988: 143). For patients and for the rest of their social group, chronic illness may be an ongoing lived, sometimes a lifelong, experience (Anderson and Bury 1988, Williams 1984). When faced with such a future, we are frequently encouraged to both follow medical and lifestyle advice and, at the same time, to lead a 'normal' life. This tension between 'leading a normal life' and following medical advice comes out of an assumption that 'being normal' implies not being ill, which, in turn, contradicts the need to follow medical advice. Thus, any 'normality' to be had will be found in understandings and expectations that have to be developed, negotiated and refined (most frequently in the family setting) over the course of the illness, which may be for a lifetime. These issues are illustrated in the people scenario in Box 3.1. Here, we illustrate how a diagnosis of illness, in this case Type II Diabetes, has everyday implications that are both practical – in terms of shopping for food – and emotional, as Marcella takes time to think through food and diet for her husband and family.

Box 3.1 In Sickness and in Health: Hilversum, The Netherlands.

In Hilversum, Marcella is doing her food shopping. She thinks about how her shopping has changed since Henk was diagnosed with Type II Diabetes 2 years ago. Gone are the biscuits and cakes they both used to enjoy! For a while after the diagnosis, shopping had been a slow and anxious business as Marcella spent time reading labels in search of hidden sugar. Henk had been unwilling to accept that he had a chronic illness and for the first few weeks when he went shopping he didn't bother to check the labels. They had always shared the food shopping but it was Marcella who wrote the list of things to buy. So Marcella had taken to writing more explicit instructions about what brands to buy and both of them had got used to the fact that their diet would have to change. But they had had to go on buying some biscuits and snacks so that their daughter wouldn't feel odd when her friends came round and so they could continue to offer a biscuit with the coffee they liked to share sometimes with their neighbours. Marcella ate the same diet as Henk although she did not have diabetes – that had seemed a better way to handle the new situation than giving him special dishes – it would have made him feel different from everyone else. If family or friends came round to eat, she gave everyone the same – apart from those biscuits with the coffee!

Marcella had been frightened when she read about the problems that people with diabetes could face in later life and she was determined to ensure that Henk stuck to his diet – he was lucky because he had the sort of diabetes you could control with diet alone but he wasn't very willing to think of himself as someone with a problem – still less as someone with a disease. With his job and the changing shift patterns, it was difficult to eat regularly and correctly. She had started making him food to take with him rather than leaving him to buy a snack as he had quite often done in the past. She had tried to impress on him that this would be good for their finances – after all, money was tight and snacks were expensive. She thought he would find that a more acceptable reason than the notion that he was ill – although they both knew what was really behind her new pattern of provisioning. But she knew he found it difficult – after all, he was often offered food or a coffee in the restaurants and cafés he was managing and he didn't like to let people know about the diabetes. However, there had been quite a lot of publicity about the disease recently and she thought he was becoming less sensitive about people knowing now that it seemed a more 'normal' problem to have. She'd been quite surprised the other day when he had mentioned it to one of her friends as if it wasn't a big deal and she hoped this meant he was coming to terms with the idea that this was now part of their lives for ever.

The issues outlined in Box 3.1 are further illuminated in a study undertaken by one of the authors of this book (Gregory 2005) into how families manage when one member is diagnosed with a diet-related medical condition. This study revealed the extent to which new forms of informal caring can be accommodated into everyday life, with little recognition of how demanding this can be for the person with the condition and, in some cases, especially for their main 'carer' (although the term 'carer' was never used by participants). Although the participants in this study varied in terms of their satisfaction with the nature and form of their family relationships, all seemed to recognise as legitimate the view that it was within the family that caring and support should take place. Activities around food and meals were construed as functions of family life in which all family members should be involved, wherever possible. The demands of the special diet involved extra work and it was clear that family members, particularly the female, were committed to provide that support routinely.

The 'caring for' and 'caring about' work in these family relationships was most commonly undertaken by wives and mothers and routinely absorbed into their existing family responsibilities. Any contribution from male partners was more likely to be time limited and contingent upon specific events. However, the support from spouse to spouse, in families generally but particularly in the face of chronic illness, was not determined purely on gender grounds. The study revealed family practices that had developed and evolved over time but were subject to social norms *and* the contingency of the moment. For example, one man who had (reluctantly) retired due to ill-health took over the shopping and then the cooking in the family, primarily for practical reasons – he had more time and his wife wanted to develop her career, but, over time, he had become more and more interested in doing the cooking as, not just his interest, but his role in his family. Many people reach for the 'normal' as a guide to which path to take through the terrain we call caring. Bernardes suggests that: '… whilst we all like to think of ourselves as somehow 'special', we also like to think of ourselves as essentially 'normal'' (Bernardes 1987: 54). But what is 'normal' may be subtly redesigned in the face of illness. Illness and its consequences can then be absorbed and a new 'normal' emerges. Roles are consolidated and adjusted in the light of experience.

We have already drawn attention to the impact that the advent of HIV/AIDS has had on family caring relationships in Southern Africa. Expected patterns of intergenerational and familial care are disrupted as relatives who would have taken on the care of an orphan in the past find that the death of productive adults and consequent poverty makes this impossible. Evidence from Evans and Becker's (2009) work in Tanzania and the UK suggests that, in some cases, lack of alternatives mean that gendered norms are being de-stabilised and boys are taking on caring tasks that were previously felt to be appropriate only for girls. Here, an appeal to the 'normal' may be difficult to sustain, yet people make sense of the changes by appeal to the necessity of maintaining care standards: 'According to our culture it is not good [for a boy to bathe his mother], but I had to do it [...] I couldn't leave her there like that when everything was soiled' (Good Luck, aged 18 years, Tanzania, quoted in Evans and Becker 2009: 260). Here again, we have the interactions of social norms and the contingency of the moment to produce an adjustment of roles. In a similar vein, Duvdevany *et al.* (2008) show how fathers with spinal cord injury in Israel were able to parent effectively despite negative social attitudes towards their parenting, by ensuring that their children felt that they had a 'normal' father but understood and accepted their father's physical condition: 'And somehow ... I make them feel that "you have an ordinary father" ... But they also know the limits of what they can ask [of me]' (Duvdevany *et al.* 2008: 1027).

Although the onset of chronic illness is not normally predicted, the frailty that accompanies ageing is less surprising. Of course, many people die before such a stage is reached but it remains a real future possibility that people may or may not consider as they travel through the lifecourse. One potential consequence of increasing frailty is the need to move from reliance on informal care to formal care. The need for formal care tends to be seen as something to be delayed and avoided by the person needing the care and, often but not always, by those currently taking responsibility for informal care – family members, friends or neighbours. This reluctance to move to more formal care support is born out of the belief that 'normality' and personal identity can best be preserved through maintaining the individual's 'independence' and that if care is needed it should be family care. The notion of family care is, as in the case of mothers' care for children, suffused with moral beliefs about obligations and the value of family care. This, combined with concerns about lack of respect for the vulnerable and neglect or even abuse in formal care institutions or from formal carers, leads to reluctance to use formal care.

Yet there is a tension between these reservations and the difficulties that emerge when family and friends attempt to care for those becoming increasingly frail or requiring more and more specialist support. On the one hand, the time involved in providing informal care alongside other time commitments such as paid work and other caring tasks may be too great to be sustained and prompt a move to formal care. There may be a lack of the requisite medical or other skills required for appropriate care. There may be a clash of cultural conventions – for example, when a man finds himself having to bathe his elderly mother; or when an elderly mother must provide physical care for a sick middle-aged son. Such gendered or age-based cultural expectations can create barriers to care. For example, in a study of households affected by HIV/AIDS in rural KwaZulu Natal, Montgomery *et al.* (2005) argue that, in South Africa, negative stereotypes of men as irresponsible and unwilling carers both limits recognition of the care they do and, in fact, is in opposition to gender norms, but also 'creates an environment hostile to widespread change in gender dynamics' (Montgomery *et al.* 2005: 16).

Box 3.2 An Ageing Parent: the Czech Republic

Peter and Maria in the Czech Republic are worrying yet again over what to do with Peter's grandmother Agneta. She is now nearly 90 years old and lives in a small village some 60 miles away from them. Peter's mother, her only child, died of cancer 15 years ago and all her remaining family live in or near Prague. Until 3 years ago, she had managed very well – she had lived and attended church in the village all her life and, after the death of her husband 25 years ago, had been surrounded by many friends from the church and from her youth. She had always been very independent and physically active. Peter is very fond of her as he used to spend time with her when he was a child.

Three years ago she had a fall – she had been concussed, badly bruised and shocked – and that had been the start of the problems. She had been unwilling to accept she needed any care but it was evident when visiting her that she could no longer manage to cook for herself safely, her hands trembled and lifting the pans was difficult. Preparing food for cooking was clearly an effort. And she wasn't keeping the house or her own clothes clean; she couldn't see as well as she once did. Her feet hurt with corns and in-growing toenails and because she couldn't bend to reach them to treat them she was hobbling around the house. When they visited, she did let Maria look after her feet – provided Peter left the room.

It had taken many months and the persuasion of several friends and members of the family until she would acknowledge that she needed not only daily help with the house but also some care for herself. It was only because they had found that Ivana, the daughter of one of her school friends, whom she had known all her life and who lived in the village, was willing to come in to help, that they had finally persuaded her. Ivana has received a carer's allowance from the state to help with Agneta's care and they had hoped the problem was solved – but things had not gone entirely smoothly. Agneta had become frailer but still would not let Ivana help her wash and dress, although eventually she did let her cut her toenails! Ivana said that Agneta was taking longer and longer to get washed and dressed in the mornings and she was fearful she would have another fall – she also said that she did not think Agneta's washing was very effective. There were arguments because Agneta was critical of Ivana's cooking and claimed that Ivana bought food without consulting her. Ivana said that Agneta forgot what they had agreed.

Despite these difficulties, it seemed that they had a viable solution but a few weeks ago Ivana had rung up to say that her husband has become ill and that she could no longer go on caring for Agneta. She asked Peter if there were any possibility Agneta could come to live with them. But Maria feels this is impossible – they cannot manage their jobs, look after the children and care for Agneta even with the extra money that the carer's allowance might bring in. Peter is less sure that they could not manage – but he won't be doing the lion's share of the work! But it is difficult; when they went to visit last week, Agneta was adamant that she can manage by herself although it is plain to everyone who knows her that she cannot. No-one in the family is happy about the thought of her going into long-term residential care – especially in view of the bad publicity such care homes have had recently, such as stories of understaffing, negligent nursing and bad food. But they can see no alternative. So far, no one has plucked up the courage to make this suggestion to Agneta – but they will have to do so soon.

The people scenario in Box 3.2 describes a situation familiar to many families across the world. An older relative is keen to retain independence, her children worry and seek solutions that ensure safety and security whilst maintaining familial relationships. Often, modes of care are stitched together like a patchwork quilt, but in the knowledge that pieces of the quilt will not hang together for long.

We have social understandings that caring (for and about) should be exchanged at different rates and forms at different points of the lifecourse, and in all cultures, and this is particularly the case between parent and child and adult child and parent. Over time, over the lifecourse, we develop expectations around care (good and bad) that reflect cultural norms *and* personal experiences. These create ideas of 'normality' that may be a valuable resource in difficult times. Within social settings, it is through ordinary everyday tasks and activities that we act out our normal lives. 'Being normal' is not so much what you *are*, but what you *do* and *how* you do it. It seems to guide and mould what we choose to do, or even find ourselves doing without much thought or planning. Informal caring activities, which both represent and constitute 'caring for' and 'caring about', are not just, in Frank's terms, the 'repair work' (1991) for disrupted lives, but are also the building blocks for the identities that form our lives.

By re-imagining 'normality', we may find ways of adjusting to change. However, ideas of how people of different genders, classes, ethnicities and ages should care, if strongly embedded in social institutions and behaviours, can also act as a barrier to change and appropriate adaptation. These points are also exemplified in intergenerational caring.

Intergenerational caring

Intergenerational care is a major form of care in families. Memories and expectations of intergenerational care are central to the development and transmission of family 'cultures' of care and of family resources for care over time (Brannen 2005). Hence, disruptions to such care pose severe problems to individuals and societies. Intergenerational care can take a variety of forms from (for example) the iconic image of mother and child to grandparent and grandchild, to uncle and nephew. It also covers adult children or young children caring for parents and grandparents.

Such relationships occur between family members both within and beyond the home. Although here we focus on intergenerational relationships within the family, such relationships are not confined to kin. They can occur in any setting that affords contact between younger and older people – for example, neighbourhoods, community facilities, and even health care settings where the younger patients in a ward may informally help the older patients as an adjunct to the formal care being provided. Such relationships typically involve the exchange of both physical care and emotional care and are often vital to the survival and wellbeing of participants. They are arguably important to societal well-being through promoting intergenerational understanding and exchange of resources.

The care given by a parent to a child is understood as part of a move through the lifecourse in which the physical and emotional tasks of 'caring for' in the present will be reciprocated in the future. As we have mentioned above, in poor countries with a limited welfare state, this reciprocation will be expected to start sooner rather than later with household or livelihood tasks. As parents age, there will be a social expectation that a child will care for them, although the precise nature of the obligation, whether it is the role of the eldest or youngest or of a son or daughter and whether there are different obligations to mothers and fathers is variable. But it seems that, in all cultures, some measure of reciprocation is expected from children to parents as they grow up. But it is also the case that the caring obligations of parents do not normally vanish as their children grow, although they may change. Perhaps as they become grandparents, they will be socially expected to care financially, physically or emotionally for the grandchildren or, as parents, they may find themselves called on for emotional support by their children throughout their lives.

However, the existence of reciprocation does not mean that there is some neat equation of the 'costs' of parental caring with matched care from children in later life. Indeed, some parents do little in the way of caring and may actively injure their children emotionally or physically. Children may not be able or willing to care for their parents. The 'costs' of parental care may be more than any child could 'repay'. Indeed, many women have, over the years, felt that the caring role of mother 'cost' them too much in terms of personal autonomy, social respect and career choices. At the same time, the delight and enjoyment of motherhood is often presented as 'its own reward'. As Melissa Benn has fervently pointed out: 'My children cause me the most exquisite suffering ... It is the suffering of ambivalence: the murderous alternation between resentment and raw-edged nerves and blissful gratification and tenderness' (Benn 1998: 21). Emotion is bound up with the pleasures and pains of both motherhood and fatherhood and hence becoming a parent is not simply an instrumental choice – although instrumental considerations will usually be involved (Ribbens 1994).

Nevertheless, becoming a parent does affect the lifecourse in materially important ways – it involves the expenditure of time on parenting that could otherwise be spent on other, economically or socially beneficial activities, while children's contribution to the household economy once they leave babyhood may be substantial. For example, in rural areas of low-income countries, being childless is likely to severely limit peasant farmers' economic prospects, as children are a valuable source of household labour (Kielland and Tovo, 2006). Recent data from the United Nations Children's Fund (2008) found that 1 in 3 children aged 5–14 years in sub-Saharan Africa is working, compared to only 1 in 20 in the Central and Eastern European/Commonwealth of Independent States. Children living in the poorest households and in rural areas are most likely to be involved in child labour, including agriculture, mining and manufacturing. Boys are more likely to be engaged in child labour than girls, whereas household chores are overwhelmingly undertaken by girls.

In post-industrial societies, the number of women occupying multiple social roles continues to grow. The stresses induced by the time–space crunch of combining paid work and care have resulted in many mothers working part-time, or taking some time out of the labour market, or missing promotions opportunities and taking less well-paid work than their qualifications would suggest. These choices contribute to the gender pay gap and the poverty of older women (Women's Unit of the Cabinet Office 2000, Connolly and Gregson 2008). The result of increasing life expectancy and later childbirth has also meant a growth in the so-called 'sandwich' generation who give care to ageing parents and for dependent children at the same time.

In a study of women in their 50s living in a major city in Scotland, Airey *et al.* (2007) analysed data on the experiences of women caring for both younger and older relatives and friends, in addition to their paid work and daily domestic chores. They concluded that the nature of employment, in terms of its spatial and temporal characteristics, has implications for women's management of their work and care obligations. Women lived close to both their workplaces and young and elderly dependents. Proximity was crucial to the everyday management and sequencing of their work and care activities. For some of the women in the study, the shop floor served as a locale for 'caring encounters'. This overlapping of the times and spaces of caring and working represents a blurring of the boundaries between women's gendered 'public' and 'private' roles, albeit in a manner that was apparently sanctioned by employers, as it did not pose a threat to workplace organisation and the smooth-running of business. As with caring for children, care for older parents requires that other activities are forgone and can lead to considerable hardship, exhaustion and social isolation.

Although people in the West are more likely to be able to turn to structural (State, voluntary or private) support systems when caring for older people, the 'orchestration' of this care has been shown to have considerable personal and employment costs to both sexes (Rosenthal *et al.* 2007), but especially to women. Adult children's responsibility to care for ageing parents may vary from culture to culture, but this seems to be by degree rather than as an absolute (de Valk and Schans 2008). However, it is important to remember that older people may well provide care and support as well as receive it (Gierveld and Dykstra 2008). However, the importance of their contribution will vary. For example, the 'babysitting' that a grandmother can offer her working daughter may be very useful for the management of time in a busy dual-career family, but tends to be time-limited both within the day and across the lifecourse. The full-time care given by a grandmother to orphaned grand-children turns familial care support into essential parenting, changing the lifecourse of adult and child radically and irreversibly.

Below, in the people scenario in Box 3.3, we note the similarities in care-giving by two grandmothers – expressions of concern and anxiety for their grandchildren – but marked differences in the practical tasks required and resources available.

Box 3.3 Two Grandmothers: Tanzania, Sub-Saharan Africa; Hilversum, The Netherlands

In Africa and The Netherlands, two grandmothers are busy caring for their grandchildren.

In Sub-Saharan Africa, Mary is organising the day for Joy, Abel and Grace. All are attending school but there are many chores to be done at home and a long walk to school so everyone must start early. Joy and Abel go and fetch water before breakfast – they are lucky because it is not very far to go. Meanwhile, Grace, who is 8 years old, helps Mary get the stove going and prepare some food for them to eat. Grace is not well so Mary does most of the work. At 7.30 am, the children leave for school – they will be late but it can't be helped. Mary needs them to do some household chores as she is less physically strong than she used to be. After the children have left, Mary sets off to work on her smallholding – a walk of half a kilometre. Mary has been determined that the children will attend school – but affording this has been difficult, the school here is free but there are uniforms to buy – and sometimes the children have been sent home because they had no shoes or exercise books.

Joy had missed a lot of school when her mother was ill – she had really looked after the young ones by herself when her mother first became ill and, even when they had moved to stay with Mary, she had played a major role in her mother's care – and so she is only now completing her primary schooling. When her daughter had become ill, the family had ended up moving to live with Mary – her daughter had wanted to die and be buried at home. That had been a difficult time – she had had to take them, although the children ought to have gone to someone in their father's family; that was what would have happened in the past. But her daughter had begged her to keep the children after her death – she had worried that her husband's brother would not care properly for the children. This was not how it ought to be – but the old ways were changing. When they moved to the country, Joy and Abel had found it very difficult to adjust – Grace had been too young to notice much, but the other two missed their old home.

Mary worries that Grace's poor health will mean she too will miss much schooling. A worker from a local NGO who provided home-based care to her daughter when she was dying and who still visits the children, has suggested that Grace should be tested but Mary is reluctant – if Grace was given medicines, Mary could not afford to feed her the good diet Grace would require. Joy will soon leave school and will need to find work – Joy wants to return to the city and, without her help, Mary is not sure that she can continue to manage to look after the other children. But she is sure she is doing the right thing in keeping going for as long as she can. She wants to avoid asking for outside help for as long as possible.

In Hilversum, Henk's mother Janneke has just arrived at Henk and Marcella's house to look after the baby, Lotte. Janneke travels for an hour to come from 11 am to 2.30 pm on 3 days a week to help out until Marcella can get back from work. Sometimes, she stays longer if Marcella has errands to do in town or has to stay on at work for a meeting. On the other 2 days, Lotte goes to Marcella's sister who has a small baby of her own but works the other 3 days. Occasionally, Janneke's husband comes too, but he is a keen fisherman and is not sorry to have the time to himself. Janneke enjoys the work – her little granddaughter is mostly delightful but, as she has got more active, crawling round the house, Janneke finds it quite tiring to keep up with her, change nappies and feed her. Of course, the house is well equipped with fridge, dishwasher and washing machine, which makes the chores easier.

She is glad to help and, although she finds her daughter-in-law's housekeeping standards lower than her own, she thinks she is a good mother – and that is what matters! Of course, it is sometimes irksome to have to forgo meetings with her friends or trips out with her husband, but these days, she thinks, it is hard for mothers to stay at home as she did, it is so costly to pay for a house, car and all the things that children seem to need. She is happy to do this until Lotte is able to go to state school, when she is 4 years old. Some of her friends think she should not be helping – they say her son is grown up, and he and his wife must manage for themselves and send Lotte to a private nursery, but Janneke knows this would be too expensive for Henk and Marcella. |Besides, she thinks that family is important and that because she has the time available since she gave up her own part-time job, she ought to help. Anyway, she enjoys being useful and likes the feeling of being part of her son's and grandchildren's lives. But her husband is 10 years older than she is and she thinks that once Lotte has gone to nursery she will prioritise spending time with him.

As we have mentioned above, at times of individual stress or societal disruption, the 'normal' pattern of intergenerational care may be reversed. Children may care for parents or grandparents; grandparents may care for their grandchildren. The advent of migrant work and HIV/AIDS has challenged the cultural norms of care-giving and added considerably to existing pressures on families. In S-SA, two main types of society exist – patrilinear and matrilinear – with care responsibilities following those lineages. '*Care migration*' is an established pattern in most African societies, particularly in relation to children. The use of extended families (local and non-locally based), gave an inbuilt degree of flexibility in matters of childcare and employment. It was not unusual in some societies for very young children to be sent away to live for a number of years with relatives and return later to the family home to resume their life with the primary family. The advent of HIV/AIDS can negate the 'return factor' in two ways: through AIDS-related poverty, negating any possibility of coping with an extra mouth, and through dissolution of the primary household as rising death rates remove the main bread-winners, accompanied by the stripping of assets to pay for funerals. '*Generational care migration*' is occurring in terms of care responsibilities. By this, we refer to changes in availability and depth of care across the generations. Younger and older family members are having to reassess their expectations of what they can expect by way of care and how much more care for others they may have to now take on. In decades previously, aunts and uncles might have been available to care for nieces or nephews orphaned or whose parents migrated for work, but this is the generation that HIV/AIDS has most affected.

Van Blerk and Ansell (2007) argue that '*intergenerational fractures*' are occurring as the adult working generation succumbs to the disease. They posit that 'intergenerational contracts and clusters' were disrupted by these fractures, the major problem being the lack of a working generation to provide resources to the younger and older family members who depend on them. New types of contract and care arrangements and new time frames for delivery were emerging.

- The time frame within which contracts take place has been significantly reduced, with immediate reciprocity favoured over longer term moral obligation to old and young.
- Contracts were becoming more explicit, e.g. to get education paid, a child must do so much housework.
- There was evidence of inequality in the provision of resources either from the previous life to the new one and/or from one person to another, e.g. child to grandmother.

In Southern Africa, the advent of HIV/AIDS has meant that the burden of caring has fallen on older or younger people at a time in their lives when they might expect to be cared for themselves. Grandparents take on the job of caring for orphaned children, while children and young people may find themselves caring for a dying parent or taking the place of a parent in the lives of their siblings (Evans and Becker 2009, van Blerk and Ansell 2007). In these situations, the physical and emotional capacity of an old or young carer and the clash with expected norms of care may become an issue.

For example, a young carer in the UK interviewed by Evans and Becker (2009) talked about the changed relationship with her mother since she had begun caring for her: 'We used to be quite close and sort of drifted apart recently [...] it's become like less close, like it's not like mother and daughter, it's more like helper and daughter more, helper and mum yes [...] I'm quite used to it, but it's when I stay at friends and I see how they act with their parents that it's sort of different' (Evans and Becker 2009: 170). A national survey of young carers in America found indicators of psychological stress and behavioural problems among young carers (National Alliance for Caregiving 2005). Some felt isolated and sad, and this seemed to be more prevalent among boys than girls. We speculate that this may reflect the fact that such caring is more socially expected for girls than boys. In a different study in Canada of children living with parents with mental illness, the authors found that children focused both on keeping a day-to-day rhythm of relationship with their parents and maintaining a relationship while preserving their own psychological safety. The authors comment that 'Adolescents appear to be struggling with their parents' illnesses and their greater awareness of "ideal" family lives and the stigma associated with mental illness' (Mordoch and Hall 2008: 1142). Again, expected ideas of care and the practical and emotional difficulties of care for parents by young people are emphasised. Despite these pressures, many young carers show considerable resilience and want to provide care to their sick parent, grandparent or sibling, but often lack sufficient informal and formal support to do so without major physical and emotional effort. Furthermore, it is not a one-way relationship. Evans and Becker (2009) found that parents continued to provide valuable and valued emotional support to their children and advice on coping with the world.

In the USA, it is estimated that 2.4 million children are being brought up solely by their grandparents; the majority in informal, private arrangements (Letiecq *et al.* 2008). For most of these children, these grandparents are providing a vital service. A small-scale study of 6 custodial grandparents and 5 grandchildren in New Mexico from Anglo, Hispanic and African American backgrounds emphasised that, for the grandchildren, grandparents often offered stability in lives that had been disrupted by the chaotic lives, illness or violent death of their parents. Grandparents were, for these children, a 'safety net': '"They want me ... and they choose to keep me instead of giving me to someone else just like my mom. And they love me a lot" (9-year-old granddaughter)' (Goodman and Rao 2007: 1126). In common with many full-time grandparent carers in the USA, these grandparents were on low incomes, often living in cramped accommodation and in poor health. They needed support but, as Letiecq *et al.* (2008) explain, many informal grandparent carers face an uncertain legal position, lack information and fear that the welfare system might remove their grandchildren from their care. This often means that they do not access the support that does exist. They find themselves in an ambiguous situation – providing what is socially considered to be informal care, although if provided by a foster family it would be considered to be a paid formal care role.

Grandparents find that informal caring for grandchildren brings rewards as well as loss of opportunities. Jendrek (1993) carried out a study of 114 grandparents in Ohio in the USA (96% of whom were white and 97% of whom were female) who were either caring full-time for grandchildren or who provided day care for their grandchildren. In the case of the former, most grandparents had taken on this care because of emotional or drug/alcohol problems faced by the child's mother, whereas the others were providing care while the mother or, less often, the father, worked full-time. A belief in the value of home-based family care was important to these latter decisions. Jendrek found that many grandparents talked about the loss of 'freedom' and the cost of care but also of the fun of caring. For example, one custodial grandparent said: 'Before I had all the freedom, I didn't need a baby sitter; I didn't need to check to see if I could go out of the house or when I had to be back [...] If I pay the babysitter then I don't have the money to go out'. But another whose daughter and grandchildren had lived with her for 5 years said: 'The change in my enjoyment of daily activities has been for the better. ... They're fun kids' (Jendrek 1993: 616). As with the young carers, these grandparents found that they were sometimes seen as behaving in ways that were socially inappropriate to their age and this sometimes curtailed their relationships with their peers while opening up other relationships – for example, with younger parents.

In Africa, grandparents who care for their grandchildren as a result of HIV/AIDS do so with limited financial and physical resources. The majority are women – for example, in a study of older carers over 50 years of age in Zimbabwe, 71% were women, many of whom were caring for their children with AIDS or orphaned grandchildren, some of whom were also ill. Many also face stigma and rejection of the HIV/AIDS sufferer, which is carried over onto the carer who is blamed for failing to 'socialise our children well, which is why they got sick and are dying from AIDS." (WHO 2002: 24). The loss of those in the family who have died of AIDS also often means the loss of remittances or farm labour and creates severe financial difficulties. Many older carers consequently become ill under the worry and stress of caring. Support from the Church and NGOs and the government is helpful but inadequate (WHO 2002).

These studies show the importance of intergenerational care in the face of problems with 'normal' patterns of care and the significance of emotional involvement to the exchange of such care. Both grandparent and young carers have found it difficult to gain the social recognition that brings support. These studies also suggest how such exchanges of care may be woven into new understandings and practices of future caring.

Summary and Conclusion

In this chapter, we have argued that it is relationships practiced through time that constitute the cultures that underpin kin care. Our theme of landscape allows us to think of care and caring as part of the journey that we take, metaphorically, through the lifecourse, accumulating ways of behaving and ideas and beliefs about how we could and should be concerned about others that we come across along the way. It is a journey that involves links between people of both the same and of different generations who have started their journeys at the same or different times but who interact with one another along the way as their routes touch, intertwine and sometimes separate. These interactions involve the need to synchronise and sequence activities with others and to control or respond to their duration and periodicity. Each person's current behaviour and ideas are influenced by memories of the places, events and people that they have seen en route and their ideas of the way forward. On the way, people pass through expected transitions but must also react to unexpected events. Thus, for most, it is a journey that involves managing change and the unexpected while maintaining continuity.

We have already touched upon the ways in which a particular 'culture' of care may be developed in a given place during a particular historical period but have left the questions of place on one side. In the next chapter, we further develop these ideas about 'cultures' of care in relation to 'learning' to care and focus on the significance of space and place to such learning.

4 Learning to Care

Introduction

The focus of this chapter is on the key spaces and places within which we learn and re-learn caring practices over the lifecourse. The most obvious place in which informal care is learnt is the home – the place in which most children are brought up and, for some, the place in which older parent and adult child may learn new ways of relating to one another. However, there are clearly many other spaces of relevance to the learning in which we engage in the course of our everyday practices – school, community spaces, a variety of leisure venues and, for many adults, the workplace. In this chapter, we focus on the home, school and 'neighbourhood'. Spaces of leisure and volunteering will be dealt with in Chapter 5 *Networks and Chains of Care*, and the workplace in Chapter 6, *Working and Caring*. We begin with a short consideration of the meaning of space and place in relation to learning to care. We then consider the home as a learning environment at three key points in the lifecourse: growing up, being ill and growing old. In the next sections, we consider learning to care within the school and then the neighbourhood. In the last section, we summarise the key points of the chapter.

Spaces of caring

A 'space' once was thought of simply as a fixed area within which an activity might be performed – a 'stage' upon which social activities are acted out. However, this notion of space as socially inert and unchanging has been transformed by the work of geographers over the past 30 years. In their new 'relational' approach, spaces are understood as being constantly made and re-made through human interpretations and economic and social material practices (Massey 2002, Thrift 2006).

Care and caring are carried out in material spaces and places. Such spaces may influence the experience of care or even the possibility of care. The size, layout and privacy of a space, as well as its furnishing, equipment, heating and so on, also influence the ease with which care can go forward. Looking after an elderly person in a cramped, cold, dirty room with minimal furnishing and equipment is physically harder than looking after the same person in a warm, comfortable and well-equipped environment. However, it is not just the immediate material space that is important to care – it is also the changing social *meanings* associated with that space or *place* that are important. Is this a place in which both carer and cared-for feel 'at home'? Is it a place whose furnishings and design convey to those involved a sense of security or insecurity; do they feel socially 'unwelcome'; are caring encounters in such a place socially appropriate or inappropriate?

Furthermore, the characteristics of a place do not result simply from what goes on within it but are influenced by its relationships with other places and spaces. Thus, a place can be understood 'as being a moment in a wider relational space – a particular point in the wider intersections of social relations' (Massey and Thrift 2003: 281). In relation to caring, this starts to focus our attention on the social relations, operating through space and time, which affect a particular caring encounter at a particular time and place and these will be complex, rich and variable. The importance of the links between everyday 'local' practices of care and neo-liberal globalization are vividly shown in Dyck's (2005) insightful exploration of women's 'hidden work' of care in place-making. This illustrates that spaces are not created simply by interactions within a space, but by the uneven processes of production and social reproduction and hence reflect all forms of inequality of social and economic power. In relation to informal care, this means that we have to consider how the material and cultural characteristics of places that are relevant to care are influenced by processes of production, social reproduction and the political relationships that relate to these.

Recognising that places are implicated in a web of economic and social relations extending over space brings to the fore the issue of spatial scale. The informal care that is carried out in the home may be shaped by processes operating at the scale of: the neighbourhood (e.g. local cultures of parenting); the local urban area (e.g. local labour market relations; transport, school and nursery provision); the nation state (e.g. the creation of policies governing school and nursery provision and employment rights for parents); and the globe (e.g. the international division of labour, the international exchange of policy and cultural ideas). The scales of most relevance may change – as political or economic relations are 're-scaled' upwards or downwards so that the dominant influences on informal care will shift. Thus, a further aspect of space and care is recognition of the different spatial scales over and between which processes affecting caring may occur.

Learning to care at home

The idea of 'home'

In this context, we take the 'home' as a socially designated built-form or area within which it is expected that 'family' activities take place. But we recognise that, in relation to the care of older people, 'home' also encompasses formal care locations such as residential and nursing homes. Ideas of home and family bring together location and relationship to define a space and time within which family practices are seen as not only appropriate but natural (Bowlby *et al.* 1997). The complexity and intensity of the meanings of home are linked to its role as the space within which 'family' caring relationships are expected to be focused and shaped.

The social meanings accorded to the home are complex and intense and bound up with ideas of the safety provided by intimate and secure social relationships; control over who may enter the space; and roots or belonging (Somerville 1992, Bowlby *et al.* 1997, Mallett 2004, Blunt 2005). The decoration of the home, the memories of events that have unfolded there, the photos, ornaments and other memorabilia that they hold also reflect and represent people's social identities (Gurney 1997, Gram-Hanssen and Bech-Danielsen 2004, Reimer and Leslie 2004). Our repeated bodily 'performances' in the spaces of the home create an embodied memory of place and social interactions that shape the meanings that the physical place of home has for us. Homes are spaces whose multidimensional meanings shift and change over time with changes in their inhabitants' lives and interests. For many people, short- and long-distance migration mean that kin relationships are sustained between multiple linked locations and (changing) notions of home may refer to several places linked through the lifecourse and over space (Zontini 2004, Jamieson 2005, Parrenas 2001, 2006). Thus, family caring operates across distance as well as linking generations.

Another powerful set of social ideas that link family practices with home is the concept of the division between public and private. Ideas of home, family and the domestic, as associated with the private – the sphere of the personal and of intimacy and of women – are important in structuring our expectations of behaviour in the home and outside it. Feminists have challenged this dichotomy empirically and theoretically as an ideology that justifies women's confinement to family, home, caring and nurturing (Armstrong and Squires 2002). More particularly, feminist geographers have produced a rich body of work to show the empirical inadequacy of this dichotomy in relation to the home. They have shown how the private space of the home is enmeshed in the relations of the public sphere of production and civil society, and that the 'mapping' of the private/public dichotomy onto the private spaces of home and the public spaces of the street are culturally specific and temporally and locationally variable (Mackenzie 1989, Saegert, 1980, Hill Collins 2000, McDowell 1998, Bondi and Domosh 1998). In consequence, later in this chapter, we will discuss the wider residential environment or 'neighbourhood' within which individual 'homes' are found. Chapter 5 discusses a wider networks of informal care provided by friends and leisure interactions.

Despite the criticisms of the idea of the home as a private space of intimacy and care in opposition to the 'public' sphere, the informal care for other members of the household carried out by women remains empirically important. In the West, women's entry into the labour market has led to women taking on the 'double burden' of waged work and domestic caring work (Hochschild and Machung 1989). As a result, there has been a slowly growing shift to men taking on more caring work in the home, although few men take a share equal to that of their female partner or relatives (Sullivan 2006, Ciscel *et al.* 2000). In many countries of the Global South, it is said that women bear a 'triple burden' of productive work, social reproductive work and community managing (Moser 1989, Momsen 2004, Evans and Becker 2009), with women being responsible for the health and up-bringing of children, the health and well-being of adult members of the household, and for food preparation and cooking, as well as subsistence production of foodstuffs.

Growing up in the home

It is in the home that we expect (but do not always find) the love and affection that are supposed to be part of 'family' life. In particular, the home is understood as the space within which parents, but more particularly the mother, should care for small children (Ribbens 1994). Popular debates in many Western countries about whether small babies and children should be cared for in nurseries while parents are at paid work often elide 'maternal care' and 'care in the home' to create an emotionally powerful picture of ideal 'family' care in a home space. However, this picture is culturally specific in its understandings of 'family' and of 'home'. In many African and Asian households, the nuclear conjugal family is not the norm – in South Africa, for example, homes include 'children of all ages, siblings, other relatives' (Amoateng *et al.* 2007: 56). This form seems to be persisting and even increasing following the end of apartheid with the relaxation of controls on where non-white people can live. In such extended family households, childcare is more easily shared between the mother and other relatives – although it is usually shared with other women and children rather than with men.

There is nothing quite like 'learning by doing' for understanding and remembering caring within the home. 'Doing' childcare, as many would agree, often involves a steep learning curve, especially in the early years. The resources in and the nature of childcare space will have an impact not only on the caring at any one time, but also on future understandings and expectations of care (giving and receiving); that is, the person receiving caring (at any age but especially the very young) watches and learns about the gendered nature of caring, carrying on these ideas into new settings and contexts. A corollary to this is that 'doing caring' is hardly ever a one-way activity. People of all ages rarely receive or give care passively, or without having feelings and opinions about the level and quality of that care, or without absorbing ideas about what care means, to individuals, in social settings. The youngest of babies can convey its (dis)satisfaction when fed, or bathed or cuddled (or not) very clearly, without the need for words. And the act of being fed or bathed or cuddled goes beyond the moment into the embodied memory and is drawn upon in a range of future experiences, particularly of doing care or being cared for over time and in particular spaces. Thus, in their home, children learn what it feels like to be cared for by parents, relatives or nannies (or about the absence of care when neglected or abused); parents learn what it feels like to do caring – practically (through feeding and soothing or tending and anticipating) and emotionally (through loving and feelings of pride or worrying and feelings of anxiety). These knowledges are achieved within home spaces and with resources that have been deployed to serve behaviour that is 'appropriate' to the setting. Of course, the behaviour that is seen as 'appropriate' is influenced not only by the development of caring practices within a home over time but also by media, political and other social representations of homes and families – that is, by ideas of how we should care within the home and family. The resultant practices become part of the behavioural repertoire of those involved, influencing their future ways of 'doing home' (Bowlby *et al.* 1997).

Care for young dependent children usually requires a level of proximity of the carer to the cared-for, not just to provide essentials such as nourishment and to ensure their safety, but to convey the social expectations of behaviour and identity formation (more on proximity and care in Chapter 5). Homes offer a defined space within which such proximate care can easily be achieved. Adult household members teach children what will be expected of them, partly through direct instruction about what may or may not be acceptable (from toilet training, through punishment and praise for specific acts and actions, to the imposition of tacit and explicit rules and guidelines), and partly through co-present examples and performance of actions within the space of the home. For example, a recent (2008) anti-smoking advertisement in the UK media attempts to show how children will observe and copy the actions of parents long before they realise what the activity really involves (a 5–year-old playing at holding a pencil as if it was a cigarette with Mummy in the background smoking by the garden door). The power of this advertisement rests on viewers' recognition of the importance of such co-presence within the home as part of learning.

Care is learnt through co-present examples and interactions, but also through the allocation of caring tasks to children. The tasks that children are expected to carry out within and outside the home are part of their socialisation into family caring and, as such, are culturally gendered and change with the child's age (Valentine and Holloway 2000; James *et al.* 1998). They reflect different social and cultural conceptions of childhood and the capabilities of children (Valentine and Holloway 2000, James *et al.* 1998). For example, in many poorer countries, children are expected to contribute to the family economy through paid or subsistence 'work' from what many would consider too early an age (Kielland and Tovo 2006). In largely subsistence household economies, the division between caring and 'work' is not always very clear, as most tasks are focused on maintaining the family livelihood. As Scanzoni comments, this ensures that children learn both how they should care at the same time as they learn livelihood skills – the two are not experienced as separate (Scanzoni 2001).

There are important cultural variations in whether and how boys and girls are allowed to go alone outside the home. For example, in Tanzania, girls are expected to help their mothers within the home and are given little time or opportunity for outdoor leisure, whereas boys are expected to help with such tasks as grazing cattle outside the home, which also gives them greater independence in outdoor spaces (Evans and Becker 2009). Katz's research in Sudan in 1981 showed that both girls and boys were allowed to roam freely from home and to participate in outdoor tasks – running errands that took them far from the *hosh* or houseyard (a semi-enclosed outdoor space around which the houses of extended family are arranged and within which much family caring takes place) (Katz 1993). However, at the age of puberty, this freedom was curtailed for girls, although they continued to collect wood and water. The way in which they moved through spaces beyond the *hosh* changed as they were required to dress modestly before going out. Katz comments that, in the Sudan, as elsewhere, where the practice of purdah (the confinement of most of adult women's activities to the home) limits adult women's ability to undertake outdoor tasks; these tasks are performed by children whose labour thus facilitates purdah and reinforces a gendered division of domestic care tasks (Katz 1993). Girls are more constrained than boys in exploring the environment outside the home in many societies, but gendered expectations can also give girls greater freedoms in some situations – for example, in the UK, Valentine (1997) shows how parents' evaluations of the 'maturity' of young teenagers often worked in favour of girls, with boys being seen as less competent and 'sensible'. As these examples suggest, as children grow they also learn to care within a variable pattern of physical, social and cultural ideas of who, when and where responsibility and independence can be exercised. These cultural codes affect the learning of and future practices of informal care.

Care is often about control and, conversely, control can be presented as care. Much caring control within the home concerns how children or adults, men or women, should behave within particular spaces. The setting of the home is not internally homogeneous and researchers from a variety of disciplines have noted the importance of the symbolic and material layout of the home in both reflecting and affecting social differences of gender, age and status (Carsten and Hugh-Jones 1995, Mallett 2004, Blunt 2005). In particular, children's behaviour within the home is often expected to be different in different parts of the home – with particular rooms in which adult rules are dominant (Wood and Beck 1990). Except in particular spaces (for example, their own rooms, if they have them), children are usually less powerful than adults in relation to what may be done where within the home. Their behaviour is often under adult surveillance, and children and adults may adopt a variety of socio-spatial strategies to avoid or maintain such surveillance – for example, children may use hidden spaces in the house for their games; adults may require that children only use the internet in common 'household space' so that it is subject to adult surveillance (Stevenson 2008, Valentine and Holloway 2000). This surveillance may be understood by both parties as adult care as well as adult control.

Children do not experience care in the home solely from their own parents and siblings nor within their own home. Friends and relatives move in and out of the home, sometimes with differing care norms to the child's parents: the indulgent grandparent appears in all cultures as does the austere! Children experience different norms of care if they visit the houses of friends and relatives. Care experiences in the space of the home are thus connected to other homes, spaces and caring experiences through children's and adults' variable time–space routines. In particular, in some families, paid childcare workers are brought into the home. These may be formally employed people, or paid partly in kind – for example 'au pairs' (Cox and Narula 2003) or, as in some part of Africa, poorer relatives who are given board and lodging in return for housework, including childcare.

The growth of waged work among women in the West has led to increased demands for childcare based outside the home (in the shape of nurseries) or inside the home (in the shape of nannies and childminders). The latter solutions are often presented as more desirable for the child – as more 'natural' in the sense that they are more 'family like'. For those rich enough to pay for others to care for their children at home, it is usually other women who are employed. Indeed, one of the ironies of childcare in many countries is that women from poor countries migrate to care for the children of the wealthy in their homes, leaving their own children behind to be cared for by female relatives, local female domestic workers or, less often, by their fathers. These arrangements are part of the globalisation of care (the 'global care chains'), with women from developing countries substituting for women in developed countries who now feel they must go out into the paid work-force or have no inclination to be 24-hour mothers. Their employers often assume these migrant women have 'natural' caring skills both because of their femininity and 'culture' (Ehrenreich and Hochschild 2002, Pratt 1998, Parrenas 2001, 2006). Such relationships, often facilitated through rules that give a particular immigration status to domestic work, create new 'spaces of care' within the family context, formed through interactions operating across a variety of spatial scales.

The nature of caring relations in the home will be influenced by the time–space demands of other activities. Thus, the locations of other services and activities such as schools, nurseries, shops and health care, as well as waged work locations, influence the time–space budgets of all household members and affect the caring interactions of family members (Hagerstrand 1970, McDowell *et al.* 2005, 2006). In particular, the rhythms and locations of waged work affect the time available for home-based care. The moral understandings of who should undertake family care work that we discussed in Chapter 3 underpin the ways in which different parents accommodate their activities to the time–space demands of waged work. In general, it is fathers who commute furthest to work and work the longest hours, while mothers look for work closer to home so that they can manage to combine caring and working (Hanson and Pratt 1995, Jarvis 2005), thus reflecting and reinforcing the gendering of care within the home. In Chapter 6, we discuss the policy contexts that facilitate or hinder the combination of family care work with waged work.

The spaces of the home provide different ways for children in different cultures to absorb and develop their own caring understandings as they grow and change their roles within the family and wider society. Different spaces, scales and times of care are embedded in the processes of learning to care in the home.

Being ill in the home

As we have discussed in Chapter 3, the maintenance of what can be understood and presented as a 'normal' way of life within the home, helps people to adjust to the very real changes they may have to make to their everyday lives as a result of chronic illness in the family. Such adaptation can involve learning new ways of caring and shifts in relationships among family members as participants learn new physical and psychological patterns of caring and being cared for. Bury (1982) describes 'disrupted biographies' in which the illness becomes interwoven into the lives and identities of the sufferers (and, we suggest, that of their significant others).

He suggests that self-identity and self-worth will be changed as a consequence of the diagnosis of a chronic illness, but the level and direction of change will be influenced by the context within which it takes place. Recovery, even if it falls short of the normality the person has previously enjoyed, can be promoted within a space of care, or held back by a place devoid of caring.

Meal preparation is a common form of home-based caring that has strongly gendered connotations in most cultures. Women are usually responsible for this and the kitchen is understood in many cultures as a woman's domain (Hand and Shove 2004, Llewellyn 2004). In her study on family practices and diet-related medical illness, Gregory (2000, 2005) found a number of participants who had ambivalent feelings about learning to adapt to changes in meal preparation arrangements. We already discussed one of these in Chapter 3 and continue this example here:

> Mrs Rice expressed her frustration over her desire to follow particular eating patterns, ... [but].. reluctance to express this forcefully to her husband ... [so a] ... need to maintain recognized patterns of responsibility and control within the relationship vied for priority with her own dietary needs ... She also betrayed a wistfulness.. [about].. not being allowed to do the cooking now that she was retired, "*It is a kind of little element of caring that you rather miss, because I enjoyed doing that for my brother, but he* [her husband] *doesn't like – he likes the roles reversed in that respect. It is quite convenient so I just give up.*"

While his wife carried out her job as a teacher, the husband had taken control of all aspects of food preparation (shopping, provisioning and cooking) but now she was retired, she aspired (unsuccessfully) to taking back these tasks to improve both their diets generally, but also because she saw it as a 'normal' caring role. Thus here, we can add to our previous discussion of normality to note that particular activities in place (here, meal preparation in the home) become associated with 'normal', gendered caring roles in the home.

Although diet-related chronic illness of this kind may require little intervention within the home from formal carers, for many such sufferers as well as some older people, formal carers have to be brought into the home to enable the person to remain there. Their entry into the home space may also bring equipment – such as hoists, commodes, breathing apparatus – thus disrupting a 'normal' home and life. For many people, the home then becomes more 'public', less secure, less in their control and no longer 'their' space, with their unique presentation. Furthermore, the formal carers are 'strangers' who enter spaces of the home that are normally the preserve of family members – such as the bedroom – to perform intimate tasks such as bathing, which transgress normal expectations of privacy (Dyck 2005, Angus *et al.* 2005, Twigg 1999, 2000). These incursions may also affect those family members who have been caring, whether or not they live in the home of the cared-for person, as their own competency and commitment may seem to be challenged and discarded.

Caring for an ill person in the home who needs to be in bed or requires both physical and emotional care is a time when new ways of caring may be learned or existing allocations of care responsibilities reinforced. As we have already mentioned in Chapter 3, this may be an occasion for intergenerational care, with children caring for a parent or a parent caring for a child, as well as for caring between partners. Just as the incursion of formal carers into the home may disrupt the expected social uses of home space, so also the demands of the sick person may disrupt activities in the home. For example, some areas of the home may become 'no go' areas for children because of the need for quiet to allow the sick person to sleep, or children may only be allowed to see their relative for a limited time. If the sick person is a parent, their bedroom may become the locus for emotional care as the parent learns to exercise parental care through listening, advising, instructing, or reading to and 'playing quietly' with children. Children who are ill may need to stay in their bed or, perhaps, lie on the sofa in the sitting room watching television. These adaptations of behaviour again will disrupt 'normal' time–space routines within the home and may lead to the learning of new ways of caring or being cared for. As we suggested in Chapter 3, such care may evoke in children feelings of safety, security and love produced by parental care practices that may be drawn upon later in their own parenting. The ill person may need physical assistance to move about the home – to get to the bathroom or go downstairs. For those who are 'normally' physically fit, such physical dependence will create a new kind of caring relationship with the person helping them. This again is a form of care where age-based and gendered taboos affect the acceptability of physical care between different people (Twigg 2000).

Box 4.1 Remembering Care: Tanzania, Africa

Joy has been talking to her brother Abel about their dad. He was only 4 years old when their dad had died so he could hardly remember what he looked like – she didn't remember him that well either but she does remember that she had to do a lot of errands for her mother when he had come home sick and dying. Abel likes her to tell him stories about their dad – he wants him to have been a hero – or at least strong and impressive. It is difficult; she can only remember a thin, tired man lying on a bed in the corner. She remembers the room and the smell and it makes her unhappy. She remembers her dad demanding that she and her mum get him water; she also remembers helping her mother bathe him and how difficult it had been and how cross her dad had been with them both when they dropped the water. She hadn't told Abel about that, instead she had tried to keep Abel happy by repeating some of her mum's stories about the things her dad had done when he was well and strong.

Talking about the past makes her sad and happy at the same time. Although she doesn't remember so much about her father, she remembers better what it had been like when her mum started to get ill. Her mum had struggled on for some time pretending that everything was normal but then she had had to admit something was wrong. At first, she said it was only the effect of her husband's death and the exhaustion and worry of his illness. But soon she had had to admit it was more serious. There had been good days and then the days when her mother was too tired to get out of bed. It had been difficult – there was so much to do with the two small children to care for as well – Grace had only been a baby. Joy had had to do a lot of the food preparation and cooking and the house was small – only the two rooms, and there was always too much to do to keep it clean. At first, she had been angry inside, angry with her mother and angry at her father too for leaving them – later, when her mum had started to talk to her about her illness and how she felt and about how Joy would need to look after Abel and Grace, she had learned to be more patient and not to get cross when the two smaller children were awkward. Once she had begun to talk with her mum about her illness, they had got on so well; Joy felt she had learned a lot from her mum about how to live and how to look after the others. It makes her happy to remember those conversations and their closeness.

Later, when they had moved to live with her granny, it had been a relief because there was someone else to talk to and to take some responsibility. But then she did not always agree with her grandmother about how to treat the other children and how to look after her mother. She had wanted to do a lot of the caring herself and her granny had wanted her to go to school. Her mum had told her to go to school too but it was so difficult to concentrate and she was often tired. At school, some of the girls had talked about her mother being sick and that upset her – she wanted her family to be like other people's families with no ill parent to worry about. And she and Abel and Grace had been sent home quite a few times because her granny and her mum hadn't been able to afford the proper uniform as well as buying the extra food they needed – her granny's smallholding provided a lot but not enough for them all. Then she had decided to take time after school to do small chores for the neighbours to earn a bit of money to buy vegetables for the evening meal. Her mum and granny had been pleased, although worried about her school work. She and Abel still do chores for the neighbours and she knows it is useful.

Reflecting on the past and memories of her father's final days evoked memories of care practices and emotions. Joy witnessed the many care tasks related to her father's illness and feared that level of responsibility at her relatively early age. When her mother became ill, however, she learned a lot more about care both for her mother and her siblings. Joy also experienced the dilemma of having to choose between school and her future and caring for her terminally ill mother. Her grandmother wanted her to go to school to aid future security but how could Joy do this when her mother was so ill and there was so much to do at home?

Growing old in the home

Older people are potential recipients of and contributors to the learned care environment within a home. It may be their own home in which they live permanently, they may visit a friend or relative's home to care or be cared for (at time of their illness or to help out) or they may simply visit (regularly or infrequently). They inhabit different caring spaces and adopt varying caring persona depending on their needs and the needs of others. Interestingly, older people tend not to be conceptualised as learning new ways of being, learning new ways of caring and new ways of being cared for – they often are seen as passive recipients of care or, if not passive, as problematic and unruly. However, Powell (2006) points to a 'critical gerontology' that avoids the assumption that older people are passive, and cannot be active in organising informal care and the learning that surrounds it. Even as we reach old age, we have the capacity (especially if we have the time and space) to learn new perspectives on care and caring. Godfrey *et al.* (2004) studied the experiences of ageing among people aged between 58 and 97 years in two urban areas in the north of England. Many of the participants saw this as a period of actively managing change and developing new patterns of behaviour. As one participant pointed out:

> You can't know until you've been there what it's like to be old. They say 'well, you've had your innings' … . but it's the other way round. We've got over the rough unpleasant stuff – jobs, family, whatever – and now it's our chance. But they don't see that. You can't until you're old yourself see how precious every day is … now is the time to enjoy yourself.
>
> (Godfrey *et al.* 2004: 96)

The study found 'interdependency' and 'reciprocation' to be central to their participants' discussions of the 'opportunities and challenges of growing old'. In the summary of their study Godfrey *et al.* comment: 'Mutual exchange was a feature of valued relationships with family, friends and neighbours. The study revealed a rich pattern of reciprocity, with active older people playing a significant role as givers of help. As people became more restricted, high value continued to be placed on 'giving' and not just 'receiving'. For some, memories of the help they had given others in the past enabled them to come to terms with accepting support for themselves' (Godfrey *et al.* 2004).

Older people, through their actions, can affect the spaces and places of learning to care within a family and home and can choose how far they wish to be involved with any 'caring' tasks (baby-sitting, pet-sitting or financial support). They can chose the spaces and places in which they will exercise such care (within the family home, within their own home, within public places); they can choose the extent to which they will pass on their care learning. In making these choices, they both enhance and constrain the spaces and places in which learning to care occurs for the recipients but also those in which their own care learning or adaptation occurs.

Learning experienced by older people is also influenced by external developments that impinge on the home setting. Technology, such as computers, the internet, mobile phones and video cameras are changing the nature of family care from physical face-to-face care to care delivered via disembodied voices or pictures. These technologies enable different types of caring within and outside the home to emerge. On the one hand, these technologies are closing the care gap – those who live long distances away or in other countries can maintain some two-way caring input via such communication; not only checking on granny but granny checking on grandchildren. However, on the other hand, such technologies may also create a care gap – those who live close by can create physical distance from caring and lessen direct care by transferring to more impersonal remote monitoring. Such technology may also create a system of constant and intrusive care whereby both carer and cared for are almost instantly accessible: if the mobile is switched on there is no hiding place from care enquiries and demands. But people are now beginning to learn how to structure care around these technologies to monitor, deliver and control care (Milligan 2008b). Indeed, these new developments can be used to build connections between home spaces and other spaces and people in ways that older people can control and develop rather than limiting their interaction and creating home as a confined space controlled by others.

For many old people, there comes a time when they can no longer live in their 'own home' and must move into a residential 'care home'. As in the case of child-care, this is a move in which cultural ideas of 'home' and 'family' as the 'normal' and 'natural' locus for care raise intense emotions. Writing about the impact on the carer of the move of a cared-for person into a care home, Milligan (2008a: 12) writes: '[T]he care transition is experienced by most informal carers as a period of grief, guilt and great unhappiness, not dissimilar to the experience of bereavement'. It is not only that carers may feel guilty because they can no longer care for the person within the family and home, but also they feel the loss of the companionship and physical presence of the person. In the case of partners, in particular, this sense of loss is often re-emphasised by continuing reminders of the person's former presence in the house – clothes and possessions which, it is felt, cannot be removed because the person is still alive. Moreover, there is often a long history of the exchange of care between both people within the home, which now must be disrupted. In contrast, the residential 'home' initially lacks the meanings embodied in the rooms, furniture and decorations with which someone has lived for some time. Moving some furniture and decorations is a common means of making such residential care spaces into a more 'homelike' place.

The nature of the place and space inhabited by older people both shapes the care learning they can give and receive and the balance between these. For example, it could be argued that someone living in their own home has more freedom to carry out care as they wish than someone living in a residential care home. Places such as nursing homes and residential homes are seen as settings for older people to receive care (as passive recipients) rather than settings in which older people might give and receive care as active participants in care relationships. Yet, beneath the surface, much giving of care between residents does occur and residents suffuse these spaces with new ways of caring, as they learn to adapt their previous caring patterns to their new realities. For example, the gentleman who makes sure he is sitting next to the blind lady to help sugar her tea and then lifts her cup for her because her hands are sore today. The chair-bound lady who watches who has and has not appeared this morning in the day room and makes a point of asking staff about any missing person.

Many older people are able to continue to live in 'their own home' by moving into sheltered accommodation where some care and support is provided. Such moves will entail the loss of familiar surroundings, although furniture and decoration can provide a link with former homes if desired. The people scenario in Box 4.2 illustrates such a situation and the potential importance of the relationships between a formal carer and a cared-for older person. There is a mutual dependency, the exact content of which remains tacit. John's room reflects his initial desire to start a new life without links to the old. And Nancy is typical of many migrant workers in the care sector in sending home remittances to her family – in this case, to care for her son. The people scenario also illustrates cultural differences concerning the care for older people.

Box 4.2 A Carer and Friend: Orange County, California, USA

Nancy is sitting on the bus on her way to John's apartment. She is exhausted, she has been doing long hours to earn extra money and now she is going down with a cold. Nevertheless, she is cheerful – 2 days ago, John had asked her to go and buy some presents for his grandchildren. His daughter will be visiting from New York and the presents are for her to take back to the children. Nancy is cheerful because John has paid her in cash for doing the extra shopping – he's not supposed to do that – but she thinks he likes her, knows she is short of money and wants to help her, although he would never say so. She is pleased because this means she will have got together the money she promised to send home to her family this month on time. Now there is enough for her son's school fees for another term.

Nancy is fond of John; he reminds her of her grandfather who used to live at home when she was small. Like John, he was sometimes crabby and disinclined to talk much but could also be amusing and kind. She had learned how to look after old people by helping her mother look after him. Now she finds herself becoming fond of John – she does not understand all that he says to her, but they seem to communicate and she enjoys making him laugh and he enjoys teasing her. She thinks he does not get out enough – it is true that he spends quite a lot of time with a group of the other residents; she has seen them playing cards and she knows they watch sports on TV and often eat together, but she feels he needs to live with a family now that he is getting so limited physically. She wonders why he does not go and live with his daughter. And she also wonders why he does not try to make the apartment a bit less impersonal – there aren't many photos or pictures or ornaments; the living room is a bit like a hotel room.

John is waiting for Nancy to arrive. He looks forward to her visits more and more. She is always cheerful and often brings him small gifts of food – usually something she has cooked. She seems to like him and he likes her – they have a laugh together and he enjoys having a woman fussing about in his apartment – it makes it seem more like a home. Of course, he does not stay in the apartment all day. He likes to think he has made some good friends here. There are quite a few other people like him in the complex who have moved here from New York and they often get together. When he first arrived, he had found two people who shared his passion for golf and was kept busy playing and socialising around the local golf club. People in New York had thought it is odd that he moved away from his family, but he felt that the family part of his life had finished – he loves his daughter but finds her domestic, family preoccupations boring. He had always enjoyed spending time by himself, so living alone did not worry him. He had thought that moving to California after his wife died would be a new and interesting chapter in his life. And so it had been for the first 3 years.

But he has been disappointed by the recent rapid deterioration in his own health – he has had problems with his knees and has developed a heart condition – he has had to stop playing golf and to give up driving. Now he finds it tiring to simply walk around the housing complex. It is only when one of his friends who is in better health suggests a drive that he sees much of the outside world. His relationship with Nancy has become more important. He depends on her more and more for help around the house, but he has also become very attached to her. He had never known anyone from Latin America before, had never thought much about the problems of immigrants or of living in a poor country. He thinks that the difficulties of speaking to one another, given her small command of English, are teaching him new ways of relating to someone and new ways of understanding other people. She is now, he thinks, more of a friend than an employee.

In Milligan's study in New Zealand, she found that informal carers of relatives in care homes continued to take responsibility for many physical caring tasks, as well as being involved in social and emotional care. Importantly, in relation to our concern with learning to care, they learned new caring-related skills by monitoring the formal care provided (Milligan 2008a, Belgrave and Brown 1997). Thus, in some circumstances, the change of home setting can open up the opportunity or necessity to extend learning. Ironically, the comprehensive legislation that surrounds care homes can constrain input from family for fear of litigation if there is an accident and so limit the opportunity to develop new ways of caring that are beneficial to both carer and cared for.

In this section, we have argued that the home is an important space in which people, both young and old, learn and re-learn ways of caring. It is important because the idea of home and practices of 'doing home' are bound up with socially approved ways of caring. It is important because particular homes embody memories and meanings that are central to people's identities and which may be disrupted or enhanced by caring exchanges. It is important because the materiality of different 'homes' offers their occupants the opportunity to control or evade the control of behaviour in the different 'territories' of the home that are often part of 'caring'. We now turn to another space in which care and control are important – the school.

Learning to care at school

Spaces of schooling

The school is a particular type of 'place' in that it is a spatially, temporally and legally distinct venue that is demarcated by physical boundaries. A school has its own internal geography and spatial practices through which a complex set of social relationships are played out (Nespor 1997).The school brings together in time–space many young people of a similar age to interact with each other and their teachers. The organisation of the learning activity creates structured inter-actions between people that create a wide variety of formal and informal social relationships between pupils and pupils and teachers. Thus, whereas homes are spaces in which formal carers are often seen as 'out of place', school are spaces in which formal care and informal care are juxtaposed and are expected to inter-act. Schools are also an excellent example of spaces that can only be understood within the wider context of the residential geographies, state policies and economic forces that impinge upon education. Schools thus can be seen as places that are implicated in wider processes operating at a variety of scales, processes which therefore may both influence and be influenced by caring within school (Hanson Thiem 2008).

Within schools, the territories and physical layout of classroom and playgrounds offer opportunities for the imposition of formal adult control over who is allowed in different spaces and what they can do there in a manner that is analogous to informal adult control and care in the home. At the same time, they offer oppor-tunities for the evasion of adult control and the development of informal rules of behaviour within these spaces that are devised and operated by children. In particular, the space of the playground is one in which informal relationships between children – often structured by adults – may include care as well as cru-elty, violence and neglect. The playground is a space in which class, gender, and ethnic conflicts and inequalities created in wider society are literally 'played out' (Armstrong 1999).

Regulating care at school

Schools are designed to inculcate particular knowledges and ways of being – they are intended to control children's learning and behaviour. They are also expected to look after the welfare of their pupils. Thus, unlike the home and family, the formal and informal care interactions in school are, in part, governed by explicit rules and regulations created by local or national governments or agencies. Many of these rules relate to the obligation of schools to 'care' for their pupils. For example, many health and safety regulations can be seen as rules created by governments to oblige such institutions to look after the health and welfare of their pupils (Wilson, 2004, World Health Organization 2007). Many schools publicly subscribe to a moral-ity of 'care' and claim that they encourage young people to care for one another informally and their staff to 'care' for their pupils. Indeed, part of a teacher's job description is to provide help and advice to facilitate pupils' educational learning. Teachers are usually also expected to be aware of and helpful regarding any family or personal problems that may be affecting pupils.

Many schools in the EU and the USA have specific 'Guidance' teachers, whose formal job it is to address 'care' issues affecting pupils and to liaise with outside care agencies as necessary. We also noted the initiative to promote schools in Southern Africa as centres through which pupils can access care and support in coping with the impact of HIV/AIDS (Boler 2008, UNICEF 2009). These formal caring roles and initiatives are witness to the importance of school as a node in the daily activity patterns of children and hence as a potential place for linking children and their families to formal state or voluntary care agencies. However, the effectiveness of such policies may be limited by the lack of understanding among some teachers and parents and children's desire to keep their problems 'private' – that is, within the family. For example, in Evans and Becker's (2009) study of young carers, they found that many parents and young carers did not wish their situation at home to be known at school for fear of stigmatisation. When teachers were made aware, some were supportive and others not. Many young people felt that the support available at school was focused on problems with school work and was not relevant to their situations.

Furthermore, although such policies can be a valuable means of reaching out to vulnerable children, they may also in some circumstances be a way of the state or other agencies imposing their ideas of appropriate ways to behave on recipients. As such, they re-emphasise the tension between care and control that we have already signalled in the case of the home. This tension also is present in everyday interactions between pupils and teachers. There is a fine line between what pupils deem to be acceptable 'care' and what they deem to be interference in the conduct of their school life. Teachers' attempts to inculcate norms of civility and care can easily be perceived as being, or indeed be, attempts to control the behaviour of children for the convenience of adults. For example, Thomson, in a study of school playgrounds, concluded that 'the space of the playground was shaped, compartmentalised and manipulated according to the adults' whims and concerns surrounding children at play' (Thomson 2005: 69). An important way in which adults try to ensure their control is through maintaining spatial arrangements or room, playgrounds and spaces of circulation that allow continued surveillance of pupils' behaviour. This is nicely illustrated in Smith and Barker's (2000) study of after-school clubs in which the issues of control were further masked by the play-workers desire to present themselves as 'friends'. Pupils, in their turn, try to find ways of contesting and evading such surveillance in a similar manner to children evading parental surveillance in the home. The allegiances formed between children in these endeavours are one means by which they become friends.

Informal care and schooling

The school is a place for children to forge and enhance peer-group relationships. They are important venues in which young people can make their own friends, away from the influence of the family. Such friendships are a significant source of learning about ways of behaving and thinking other than those learned at home. These friendships can become very important to young people's self-esteem and sense of identity, and can offer opportunities to practice and learn the reciprocation and negotiation that are part of caring about and caring for others (Bukowski *et al.* 1996). However, these friendships may not be used to give emotional or practical care relating to family relationships. Young people facing problems in their relationships at home often see time with friends as a way of 'forgetting' their home-based problems – a separate 'space' (Evans and Becker 2009). Indeed, peer relationships are recognised as an important resource for young people in forging identities apart from the family. Thus, the school may be a space in which new understandings of care and relationships are learned that become alternatives to those learned in the home.

What goes on in school or college is, of course, linked to the local community and local economy and affected by the actions of local and national political agencies. Schools and colleges reflect and interact with the local community or region in which they operate (Nespor 1997). Thus, they bring into the playground, classroom and student residence, expectations about age, gender, ethnicity and ability that influence friendship groupings and hence potential informal care relationships. They create or reproduce inclusions and exclusions of gender, race and disability in ways that structure possibilities and actualities of care relationships between girls and boys of different ethnicities and abilities (Scott 2002, Karsten 2003, Thomas 2005, Holt 2007). For example, Thomas (2005), in a study of the everyday performances of young girls in a US High School in Charleston, shows how such everyday behaviours as where different pupils sit in the cafeteria reveals that they are 'practitioners of race' and also of gender, but that these practices arise as girls 'come to accept, repeat, and embody racialization' (Thomas 2005:1246). Thomas raises but leaves open the extent to which these practices can be understood as developing from regional history. However, we might expect that such performances and the naturalised understandings that they express and re-create will be linked to such regional histories, economic relationships and state actions.

Learning to care in 'neighbourhood' spaces

The final space that we consider in this chapter is that of the 'neighbourhood'. In Chapter 5, we will consider in more depth the importance of friendship and the ways in which friendship practices 'make space' – including spaces of neighbourhood. Here, however, we are concerned with the way in which the physical dimensions of a neighbourhood can create and affect caring behaviours within its spaces.

Neighbourhoods and activity spaces

Definitions of 'neighbourhood' usually focus on three key characteristics: it is a spatially demarcated area within a larger town or city; it is a social community; and, in theory, there is considerable face-to-face interaction among its residents. We may contrast the experiential space of 'the neighbourhood' – the area that people themselves define as such with the neighbourhood as defined by policy-makers. The latter may or may not coincide with the former. In a seminal study, Lee (1968) showed that different people understood the idea of neighbourhood differently – some as a small, highly localized area of a few houses, others as an area encompassing their everyday 'activity space', including shops and schools. Moreover, the idea of the neighbourhood as a 'community' is questionable in that 'communities' are not necessarily spatially defined or practiced. Like the idea of 'home', the idea of 'neighbourhood' is laden with meanings that present it as an 'ideal' space of caring and community. Some people may move to particular neighbourhoods in search of a 'caring community', as Little and Austin (1996) and Valentine (1997) have shown in relation to moving to the countryside. Whatever the conflict between ideal and reality, it remains the case that the wider areas around people's dwellings – their social characteristics, services and physical form and upkeep – are felt to be important to people's everyday lives. Indeed, housing prices are everyday reminders of the importance of such neighbourhood characteristics.

The neighbourhoods of policy-makers are given names, postcodes and other identifying markers that create the 'officially known' area. The neighbourhoods that have meaning to people reflect their own invisible markers, which are created through their own past and present uses of the area and the places within it that have a meaning for them personally. Those meanings can be derived from memories of family experiences, individual memories of interacting with the spaces within the neighbourhood, the experiences of friends, as well as ideas about the ideal neighbourhood. Nor is the notion of neighbourhood static: if we remain there for the whole of our life, it can grow and shrink in our minds and experience as we move over the lifecourse. If we move house, we may still maintain physical connections to each of the neighbourhoods that we leave: thus, over our lives and experiences, we may be simultaneously located in more than one neighbourhood. In what follows, we focus on the notion of neighbourhood as the product of individuals' overlapping everyday activity spaces, paying particular attention to its social meanings to individuals and groups. We focus on caring for young children and the elderly, as these are two groups whose activity spaces are often locally constrained and for whom the neighbourhood may be a particularly important space in relation to care.

Caring in the neighbourhood

Very young children are highly dependent on their parents and others as to their experience of their neighbourhood: they will usually be escorted when they are outside the 'home' and follow the routes those they are with choose to take. Their external independence is usually confined to controlled and easily surveilled spaces connected to the home, such as gardens, the immediate street, the local park. What they have learned and experienced about the neighbourhood in which they live is limited and largely defined by the actions and reactions of others. As children become older, they are allowed greater freedom, but the age at which this freedom is experienced is culturally dependent on different ideas of childhood and children's competence (Cosaro 1997, James and Prout 1990, Christensen and O'Brien 2002). In the West, going to school is usually the first prominent independent experience of the neighbourhood, whereas in poorer countries toddlers join with older siblings in play and doing household tasks that take them beyond the sphere of the home.

The 'caring control' of parents regulates access to the neighbourhood. In some neighbourhoods and cultures, much caring for young children may be 'shared' among other, non-kin, neighbourhood adults. This can reduce the strain of caring that is often felt by mothers. However, such sharing is usually predicated on the shared caring of women who have either 'chosen' not to go out to paid work or for whom this is not an option because of cultural restriction on women's independence (Bould 2003). The degree of parental sharing of care and restrictions on children's freedom to move beyond the home will be dependent on the nature of the neighbourhood. For example, in a study of African American fathers' strategies for keeping children safe in a violent neighbourhood, Letiecq and Koblinsky (2004) found that constant supervision and restricting the neighbourhood contact of pre-schoolers was a common strategy. Other strategies were teaching the children how to remain safe when outside their homes – strategies that created the neighbourhood as a space of fear. Thus, children may experience the neighbourhood as a space of safety, caring and familiarity, or of fear and lack of care (Harden 2000, Spilsbury 2005). In less violent neighbourhoods, parents will usually prescribe some distance beyond which the child should not go as a way of maintaining physical proximity between child and adult in case of the need for care. However, notions of 'proximity' have become more fluid, with the development of technologies that allow communication over greater distances. A mother may require that the child or young person takes a mobile phone so that the parent can keep in touch with them and be called in an emergency. The availability of such technology may enlarge the independent activity space of the child or young person or may increase parental surveillance. For example, parents are now being urged to buy children phones that give parents a constant update on their children's whereabouts.

However, caring and learning to care in neighbourhood spaces is not confined to parent–child or adult–child interactions. Care between older and younger children is also an important form of caring behaviour in which divisions of gender and age are expressed, learned and reinforced. For example, this may be part of the experience of the walk to school. And this generally applies in all our three Geographical Zones. The difference in many remote rural areas of S-SA is that the walk may be long but the learning of care or lack of care between children is similar – making sure you and your friends get there and back; who might you meet, who and where to avoid. The journey may be a journey by bus rather than a walk, and care here may relate to making sure friends have caught the bus and travelling with friends for mutual support. However, in many Western societies, perceived insecurities have led many (especially more affluent parents) to 'care' by driving their children to school, after-school activities or friends' houses, regardless of distances or access to public transport (O'Brien *et al.* 2000). This caring control limits children's ability to learn independence and limits their knowledge of the local environment and neighbourhood.

The spaces of the neighbourhood are also significant to the exchange of care for older people whose physical mobility is limited by physical impairments and frailty. For older people who have lived in a place for some time, the local neighbourhood can be imbued with meaning and a sense of belonging. In Godfrey

et al's (2004) study they found that the residential neighbourhoods were important to participants' sense of identity and belonging, in much the same way that
the home can be. The local areas held memories of people and events that were
linked to physical landmarks. This identification with place helped facilitate social
relationships with others living in the area. Everyday activities such as shopping
also led to routine social encounters with friends and acquaintances. However,
the quality of the material environment, the availability of transport and people's
sense of safety were important to their ability to move around the local area. Here
again, technologies of transport and communication can facilitate or hinder older
people's ability to maintain interactions within the local area.

Caring in the space of the neighbourhood can be limited or enhanced by the characteristics of the physical material environment, as well as the social environment.
We use examples relating to children to highlight the issue but the point applies
to all age groups. The route from home to school and back might require passing
through 'hostile' territory (the street of a known bully, the sub-neighbourhood of a
local gang). As a result, there might be an agreement among the children travelling
the same route, to meet up at an agreed point before the 'hostile' territory to present a stronger physical presence in negotiating that territory. In this example, the
spatial entanglements (Sharp *et al.* 2000) of the social with material spaces have
elicited and structured caring behaviours between the children. Another example
of such spatial entanglements is the experience of street children trying to live in
neighbourhood spaces. Lucchini (1996) points out that the 'street' is a place of
learning for a wide range of behaviours, but that these locations have existing cultural and institutional identities that, in turn, affect the behaviours practiced in the
space. Young (2003) picks up the theme, in her study of Kampala street children,
when she notes the way in which the children have had to create their own private
spaces out of the more untouched public places such as underground water system
tunnels. Looked at another way, it could be argued that here is a physical environment, that by its very nature offers the children a relatively safe, secluded place
to relax and care for themselves and each other away from the contested public
spaces occupied by Kampala's residents.

The physical spaces of neighbourhoods can be altered over time, even destroying
much of the original setting: for example, when run-down tenement-based neighbourhoods are revitalised with new semi- or detached houses. These new spaces
may well result in very different types of caring behaviours and learning environments. Keeping an eye on the old lady who lived downstairs in your tenement block
has now become making an effort to walk up the street to her new house, instead of
knocking the door on the way in or out of the tenement. Thus, the physical context
of the neighbourhood is not neutral in relation to people learning to care. Its form
not only shapes care but can elicit new types of long- and short-term learning and
care practice. What is learned and practiced by way of caring can be contingent
on the nature of the spaces to which we have access.

In the final people scenario in this Chapter we illustrate the interconnections between the spaces of the home, neighbourhood and school in the context of mobility.
An important conversation about school between mother and daughter takes place

in the car, en route to the familiar home of grandparents. The space of the family car can be seen as a mobile 'home' which is both public and private. While it is potentially open to public view, speech remains private and its enclosure and the lack of eye contact can promote intimate and caring talk (Ashton 2008). Knowing what is ahead when staying with Granny and Granddad reinforces a sense of well being attached to place for Aleta. But she will be less able to expand her new found independence outside the home and the care needed by her little sister may limit her activities outside her grandparent's home.

Box 4.3 Travelling to Grandparents: Hilversum, The Netherlands

Marcella, Lotte and Aleta – her 10-year-old daughter – are in the car together on their way to their grandparents' (Janneke's and Frank's) house. The children are going to stay there for the weekend while Marcella and Henk go to the wedding of a friend who has now moved to Hamburg. Marcella and Aleta always enjoy talking on car journeys together. Now Lotte is part of the family, it is a little different; Lotte sometimes interrupts by crying but, more often, she falls asleep and then the two of them talk. Marcella has found that Aleta often tells her things in the privacy and enforced togetherness of the car that she would not say in the day-to-day busyness of their lives at home. Today, Aleta is in the front seat as a treat. This is partly because Marcella thinks that Aleta is worried about something and hopes the car journey will give them the opportunity to talk. Aleta has been unusually subdued these past few days. And, sure enough, after 15 minutes of driving, Aleta starts to tell her about how one of her best friends at school, Dorine, who has been behaving in an unpleasant way, getting cross about nothing and saying hurtful things. Aleta had asked her to come over for the afternoon and had been refused with some unkind words – and then, 3 days ago, Dorine had started to argue with another friend and there had been a fight between all three of them in the playground. The teacher had broken it up and had said how disappointed she was in their behaviour. "*I feel bad because I really like Miss Jansen and now she won't like me. Why is Dorine behaving like that, Mum, we've always had such fun together? It makes me hate her*" Marcella has a shrewd idea of what the problem is – she knows that Dorine's mother walked out of the house and left her family 10 days ago but feels she cannot tell this to Aleta if Dorine has not said anything. "*Perhaps she is unhappy about something, Aleta. Sometimes friends are unkind because they are upset about something else. Don't be angry back – try to talk with her somewhere quiet and say you are sad she is being unkind but that you still like her. That would be what Miss Jansen would like you to do, I'm sure. It may not work but it is good to try and help our friends when they are unhappy and people are often nasty when they don't really want to be. Like that time you did badly in a test – you didn't want to tell us and you were grumpy with me and dad for a couple of days and we were cross until we found out what the problem was*". They continue to talk it over and, after a while, Aleta seems happier and determined to see if she can talk to Dorine.

When they arrive at Janneke and Frank's house, Aleta runs upstairs to see her room. She has stayed at their house quite a lot over the years. She loves the room, which Janneke has decorated with children in mind. There is a blue china rabbit on the shelf that Aleta is particularly fond of. When she was younger, she had asked to take it back home but Janneke had said that the rabbit lived in the room and looked after it when she was away and would be waiting for her to come back. Ever since, Aleta has thought of the rabbit as keeping the room and her safe when she is visiting and she loves sleeping in the room with the rabbit even now that she is too old to believe the story.

This is the first time that Lotte has been here when she has stayed without her mum or dad and she hopes granny and granddad won't spend all the time playing with and looking after Lotte. At home, now that she is 10 years old, she is allowed to go out with her friends to the park and the local shops and since there are quite a few of her friends who live nearby she doesn't have to be with her parents if she wants to go out of the house. The area around her grandparents is very different from home – it is countryside and although she enjoys the space and quiet she is scared to go out alone and, indeed, her grandparents wouldn't let her go anyway. Her granddad has promised to take her out fishing and to visit his friend who has a farm – she has been there before when she saw baby calves. She hopes he hasn't forgotten.

Summary

In this chapter, we have drawn attention to the importance of the spaces and places in which care 'takes place' across the lifecourse. We have drawn particular attention to the cultural and emotional significance of the home as a space within which care (or not caring) can be learned and re-learned. However, we have also suggested that care can be learned in other spaces – in particular, we have focused on the spaces of school and neighbourhood. In all three, we have noted the tension between care as nurture and support and care as control. Although control is necessary for the exercise of care – no-one would advocate letting a 2-year-old cross a main road unsupervised – care can easily become an excuse for the exercise and abuse of power. Furthermore, relations of inequality structure the exchange of care in each space.

Consideration of these spaces has moved us from thinking about care within the family and home to caring relationships outside the family – relationships with friends, acquaintances and neighbours. In the following chapter, we turn to examine how both time and space are bound up with these relationships of care beyond the family.

5 Networks and Chains of Care

Introduction

In this chapter, we consider the idea that caring can involve *networks* or *chains* of individuals, resources and sometimes organisations that are linked together in care relationships across space and through time. In a network, there are cross-cutting ties between some or all of its members. In a chain, there is a simpler forward or backward link between pairs of members. But, in both cases, a care event can involve many people. The simplest example would be a network of friends who care for one another. They may 'care' by exchanging physical care, helping when someone is ill, for example; but they may also provide emotional care for one another through meeting up at home or in a variety of social and paid work venues, as well as through phoning, texting and emails.

We can also consider chains of individuals, organisations and resources that are linked together in care-giving relationships. For example, care for HIV/AIDS orphans in Southern Africa may usually be provided by the extended family, but there are also people working for NGOs, some paid and some unpaid, who may provide care in the orphan's home, community spaces or orphanages. These NGO workers may be supported by donation given by 'caring people' in other parts of the world. In the USA, the formal care work done by many immigrant workers may be part of *their* need to provide informal care for their families by sending home remittances.

The quality of care in any setting will also be affected by the availability of a range of material resources – electricity, transport and communication technologies – provided by public and private agencies operating at a range of scales. As we have argued in Chapter 4, since caring *takes place* in different venues and contexts, the places and spaces matter: acts of caring may create 'places of care' or be affected by the places in which they occur; they also require relationships and exchanges of resources across space.

In the earlier part of this chapter, we consider the roles of networks of informal caring relationships over a person's lifecourse. Such networks can be thought of as a 'personal community' made up of the people that an individual feels are important to them (Wellman 1982, Spencer and Pahl 2006). The membership of this personal community will shift over time and may extend far across space or be locally concentrated. It can be made up of a varying mix of friends and family. In the second part of the chapter, we consider the unpaid care-giving that is provided to 'strangers' by volunteers in non-profit organisations.

When family are friends and friends are family

Context plays a significant role in shaping the form of care from friends and family. What we expect of friends and family and who is defined as a friend or family member differs between cultures and changes over time. For example, in countries with a shortage of goods and services, poorly functioning labour and commodity markets, and fractured state health and welfare provision (such as some members of the old Soviet bloc, and areas of S-SA), the contacts provided by a network of family, friends, and ethnic or religious social group may be vital to accessing paid work, goods and services. Such situations inevitably affect the nature of friendship and family relationships; the types of supportive relationships valued in 'comfortable First World milieus' will be very different from those in 'social systems that are less economically and politically secure' (Wellman and Wortley 1990: 583–584).

In the West today, the popular understanding of 'family' is the co-resident nuclear family and, usually non-resident, grandparents, cousins, aunts and uncles. This meaning is also extended to include step-parents and step-children and other step-relatives. This understanding of 'family' is limited to a particular time and place. For example, in the past in Britain, the term 'family' would include servants and unrelated household members. 'Families' in other parts of the world may be polygamous and define 'kin' in very different ways to those common in the West (Carsten 2000). Furthermore, expectations of what types of care kin or friends might provide are culturally variable. In some times and places, the societal ascription of familial or friendship roles may largely determine the type of care exchanged between people; in others, care given by kin and friends is the variable product of negotiation and practices that develop and change over time. In Western countries today, individual contexts and contingencies are more important in affecting the resultant patterns of care than role ascription (Finch and Mason 1993). Such differences between times and places are not fixed, rather the nature of personal communities and the caring roles of 'family' and 'friends' within them alter as part of slow (e.g. economic growth) or sudden (e.g. war and epidemics) social change.

The significance of such change is clear in debates over the changing role of the family in post-industrial societies today. Some argue that what they identify as a post-war trend towards isolated, nuclear-family households places major strains on parents, hinders the development of more equitable sharing of household labour between the genders, and limits children's ability to be legitimate and influential social actors. For these commentators, the solution is the development of 'giving and receiving' between people living in a consciously developed alternative type of neighbourhood (Scanzoni 2001). Recent political and social debates have focused on the linkages between households, neighbourhoods and philosophies of life. Examples include Hilary Rodman Clinton's thesis detailed in the book *It Takes a Village to Raise a Child* (Clinton 1996) and social justice debates promoted by Kevin Rudd (2006), when leader of the Australian Labour Party in opposition and, subsequently, as Prime Minister. Others argue that the conventional 'nuclear' family in such societies, focused around hetero-normative sexual relationships and procreation, is already becoming less important. They suggest that alternative 'family structures' for the exchange of emotional and practical support and care are being developed (Weeks *et al.* 1999, Roseneil and Budgeon 2004). They suggest that the conventional family is now bolstered or even replaced by the growing importance of 'families of choice' based on friendships (perhaps including lovers and ex-lovers). These suggestions are tied to arguments that the West is now witnessing moves towards increased individualisation, de-traditionalisation and the self-reflexive creation of individual identities and biographies (Giddens 1992, Castells 1997, Beck and Beck-Gernsheim 2002).

However, the idea and the ideal of family are so central to socially embedded understandings of obligation and reciprocity in the 'family discourse' that the de-centring of 'family', both from social science and society, seems unlikely. Rather, the ideal of 'friendship' seems to be infiltrating family relationships (Spencer and Pahl 2006). The term 'family' is also used to describe interactions between unrelated people in non-family settings to convey relations of affection, loyalty, reciprocity and reliability ('we're just like a family'). Nevertheless, there is a widespread social expectation (not always realised) that family members will be the default for long-term and onerous forms of care for the chronically sick or frail or for children.

Social expectations of friendship are assumed to involve freely chosen relationships between people, in which they may share enjoyable experiences, or exchange practical help and confidences. Friends, unlike kin, can choose to sever the relationship and (usually) 'regard and treat one another as social equals' (Allen 1998: 76) whether or not they are so 'objectively'. In relation to our concern with care, it is important to note that not all friends provide 'care', but many do. Some people are simply 'fun friends' – people with whom you share an enjoyable activity but with whom you would not expect to exchange practical or emotional support. However, other members of a person's 'personal community' do provide care, and do so in a range of ways.

For example, Spencer and Pahl (2006), in their recent research on friendship in Britain, identified a series of types of 'friend' who do or may provide different forms of care (recognising that these 'friends' might also be kin). They argue that although some relationships are 'given' rather than 'chosen' (this could be kin, neighbours or work colleagues), choice is becoming significant in the development of the 'given' relationship. They suggest there are *given-as-chosen relationships* (e.g. a family member or neighbour who becomes a close friend) and also *chosen-as-given relationships* (e.g. a friend who had become 'like one of the family') (Spencer and Pahl 2006). In terms of care, it seems that some friends may be expected to play 'family-like' roles in giving practical help and emotional support. Similarly, we increasingly expect 'friend-like' qualities in our relationships with our partners. Partners (married, living together or in civil partnerships) are seen as chosen by each other and this is assumed to involve liking as well as loving. So these partners are increasingly expected to act as companions and confidantes and to give both practical and emotional care. This kind of change in social relationships indicates a waning of a meaningful distinction between family and friendship for the future, with new expectations to be developed and negotiated.

In this chapter, we are considering the care provided within 'personal communities' – whatever the mix of family and friends that makes them up. We have already mentioned that such personal communities may include people living close by and far apart. This prompts the question: how does distance between people impact upon care giving? The next section discusses this issue.

Spacing care in a personal community: co-presence and caring at a distance

'S/he was always there for me' – this is a commonly used expression when people talk about the valued care they have received. But what does 'there' mean in this context? How far is it necessary or important for care to be provided by people who live 'nearby'? Can 'care' be provided by phone or via the internet? What affects *'thereness'*? Clearly, the answer to these questions will depend in part on the sort of care that is being exchanged and also on the quality of the care given. It will also depend on the frequency with which the care must be received and the time involved. The most important issue is whether co-presence is necessary. Many practical acts of care from washing a child or elderly person to taking someone shopping or fixing a faulty tap require co-presence or at least access to the living space of the person being cared for. Wellman and Wortley (1990) in a study in Canada in the late 1970s found that such practical care required people to be no more than a day's drive apart – which in Canada, at the time, meant 300 miles. However, although driving this far to give occasional practical help is feasible, it is not possible to pop in twice a day, every day, if it involves a 300-mile drive.

Care requiring co-presence is most often needed by those people who need physical assistance – children, older people and those with chronic illnesses. Living with or near carers may be necessary and the care required is often physically demanding and may also require considerable amounts of time. In Chapter 4, we have already remarked on the focus of much of children's activity and of care for children around the home and neighbourhood because of the need for co-presence or the ability to quickly achieve it. Physical, hands-on care may require the carer or cared-for to move residence and often involves long-term commitment and sacrifice – although it may also provide spiritual or personal rewards of satisfaction (Healy 2008). Moral beliefs built up over time in specific contexts, associated with gendered family or friendship obligations, are central to the relationship. For example, the difficulties of providing co-presence are central to the dilemmas of both adult children in Western countries who feel they 'should' care for elderly parents and the residential decisions of older people. Some older people decide to move near to or to share a house with their grown-up children, sometimes so they can help to care for grandchildren while parents work but also so that, as they age, their adult children will be able to care for them. Such moves are by no means always successful – leaving a set of local friends and increasing dependence on adult children, can be problematic for both parties (Phillips *et al.* 2002, Healy and Yarrow 1997). In contrast, as they age, other people may decide to rely on friendship and partners rather than children and move to sheltered housing and/ or to warmer climates near other potential friends and services (King *et al.* 1998). Expectations about intergenerational care may create stresses and guilt, as well as relief from obligations for the children of such parents, and these feelings are illustrated in the people scenario in Box 5.1. The adult child, Ellen, worries about her ageing father's health and senses disapproval from his carer Nancy. At the same time, she cannot see how the geographical distance and emotional gulf can be bridged.

Box 5.1 A Friendly Carer: Orange County, California, USA

In Orange County, John's daughter, Ellen, is visiting her father. Ellen lives in New York and it has been difficult to get the time to make this trip, as she works full-time as a legal secretary and has two teenage children. She has dreaded the visit, as seeing her father brings to the fore a host of complicated feelings – guilt, resentment, love and concern.

Before her mother died, her parents lived only 200 miles away from her and she and her husband were able to visit with the children at Thanksgiving and for two or three weekends during the year. She used to ring her mother every week and talk about everyday happenings but she has found it harder to talk with her father on the phone, especially recently as he seems to be less interested in hearing about what is going on in her family and repeats stories that he told her last week – usually stories and complaints about other residents in the housing complex or stories about Nancy, his carer. She has been encouraging him to buy a computer and use email but he has not done so.

When she sees him, she is worried by his increasing frailty and feels guilty that he is not living near or with her. Her parents had brought up their children to be independent and had always said that they did not want them to feel that they had any obligation to look after them in old age. But she compares herself to her friend Ann who has encouraged her parents to move into an apartment in the same neighbourhood as herself. She knows that when her father told her that he was moving to California, she did not try very hard to dissuade him – she said to herself that the winters in New York would not be good for him – but she also knows that she was quite relieved by his decision. She did not have a very easy relationship with him and she could not see how she would manage to care for him, her partner, Dave, and the two children while keeping on her job. The job is vital to their financial security – both her children hope to go to college and this will make big demands on the family finances.

She is with him when Nancy comes, bringing cakes and laughing with her father in a way that Ellen finds difficult. She feels that Nancy disapproves of her and that her humour and warmth are an implicit criticism, that Nancy is showing her how a daughter *ought* to behave. She thinks about the times when she did feel close to her father. When she was a little girl, he sometimes took her and her brother to the cinema – on those occasions, she had been proud of her father and had felt secure when he was in charge. Now he seems so different, dependent, tetchy and yet distant. But she is aware he is lonely much of the time, that he feels he is losing his independence and is becoming marginal to her because he can no longer visit her in New York. She resents being made to feel partly responsible for this.

This people scenario illustrates the potential importance of both family and formal carers as friends in the lives of older people. Ellen is having to battle with complex and contradictory feelings about her father and social expectations of how a daughter should care. Such care relationships may be more difficult for family members living in different continents as the result of migration. For example, older South Asians living in America or Europe may debate whether to move back 'home' and refresh networks of relationships with siblings and friends of their own age from the past or stay in their 'host' country and rely on children whose way of life may seem somewhat alien. However, improved and cheaper transport has made caring across long geographical distances feasible. For example, in transnational Caribbean and Italian families, as studied by Reynolds and Zontini (2006), there were examples of family members living in Britain who travelled to Italy or the Caribbean to provide 'hands on' care when a family member was ill. More commonly, 'flying grandmothers' (Goulbourne and Chamberlain 2001, cited in Reynolds and Zontini 2006) might come to care for children in Britain during the school holidays or look after children in the Caribbean or Italy during the long summer school holiday. However, long-term illness or frailty cannot be dealt with on such an episodic basis and requires close physical proximity.

In decisions about who to call on to provide care, gendered expectations and views about the trustworthiness of family or friends in relation to money seem to be of particular importance. Although we argued above that, in the West, family relationships are becoming more 'friend-like' and friends are sometimes taking on care that was previously provided by the family, there are still expectations that onerous or long-term care should be provided by family members. There are other differences also – it is female relatives that are most often called on to provide such care and it is family members, especially male family members, who are more likely to be asked for financial help or advice, while friends are used at least as often, and sometimes more, for emotional support and practical advice with personal problems (Willmott 1987, Wellman and Wortley 1990, Reynolds and Zontini 2006).

These differences between the care provided by family and friends are not simply 'natural'; rather, as we have argued in previous chapters, notions about obligations between parents and children are built up over the process of childrearing and gendered ideas about who should care for elderly people are embedded in social relationships and practices shared among a wider social group. These are processes that create, perhaps familial, often ethnically or class- and generation-specific, cultures of care. Reynolds and Zontini (2006) show that despite many similarities, the moral obligations between family members differed between Italian and Caribbean families. For example, in Caribbean families, 'fictive kin' were of greater importance and receiving care in the past was more important in obligating care-giving in the present. In contrast, in Italian families a norm of 'being obliged to demonstrate solidarity with aged family members' was more important (Reynolds and Zontini 2006: 23). Spencer and Pahl (2006) found that, although in some types of personal community there is a sharp division between the roles of family and friends, in others there is no clear division, with members of the personal community playing a variety of overlapping roles. They suggest that the latter may be particularly resilient to the disruptions of life changes, such as death of a partner or illness, and may help to ensure continuity of emotional and practical care in such circumstances. This emphasises both the significance of the *networks* of care relationships in a personal community and the wide range of expectations and practices of care that may be encountered.

So far, we have emphasised the ways in which distance affects the ability to provide 'hands-on', practical care. However, with strategies for communicating at a distance, especially through technological developments – letters, telephone and, more recently, email, texting and social networking sites on the web – there are a variety of ways in which people can maintain contact and exchange advice and emotional support frequently and interactively (Wellman 2001). These suggest that emotional support can be given without the need for co-presence (Spencer and Pahl 2006; Willmott 1987), and we have certainly seen a burgeoning in networking and communicating media that can provide just that. Nevertheless, having friends and/or family living nearby makes sharing activities and making contact at short notice easier than when friends or family are distant. Moving away from friends geographically is one way in which friendships can be lost. Living close to friends means that, if desired, frequent face-to-face meetings are possible. An interesting analysis by Belot and Ermisch (2006) of British data on single people aged 18–50 years suggests that having 'local friends' inhibits residential moves and that 'people attach a value to friends being reachable' (Belot and Ermisch 2006: 23).

Apart from practical care-giving, meeting face-to-face offers a number of advantages to the exchange of emotional care. For example, a wider range of emotional cues from the body language, appearance and facial expressions of protagonists can be assessed. Physical touch can be used to convey emotional concern and love; the tone of voice can give clues to feelings that are absent in text-based communication and may be difficult to judge in a telephone conversation. For most people in most situations, we suggest, mediated communication will be used to *maintain* a caring relationship that has already been established through meeting face-to-face or co-presence in the past. It is difficult to establish a caring relationship without such contact ever occurring. Reynolds and Zontini's (2006) study showed both how important such mediated communication is to maintaining family links but also that these links were periodically 'refreshed' by visits 'home'. Of course, there may be some settings where the characteristics of mediated communication (such as absence of body language, appearance and facial expression) could be an advantage – for example, the anonymity of contact with people on telephone help-lines. This may foster the feeling that what is told is not being judged, that intimate details will not be associated with the speaker or repeated to others who know the speaker.

Nevertheless, developments in communication technology are increasingly available to people generally and so it is likely that the need for co-presence in many situations will become less important. The advent of the internet and the mobile phone has created new virtual spaces of communication though which emotional support can be expressed. Such technologies allow people to create virtual 'maps' of each other's activities in space over time. They provide both methods of connecting with others but also of evading such connection. For example, we can avoid having to give immediate responses, and we can even hide behind alternative identities. Today, keeping up with friends via social networking sites has become the norm for younger people and is growing among older affluent people in Western countries (Wellman 2001).

Many people use the mobile phone to maintain social networks and this seems especially valuable for groups whose mobility is restricted by physical, social or financial constraints. For example, Lloyd Evans found that, in Britain, mobile phones are highly valued and used by some white working-class mothers isolated at home with young children. They may exchange 100 or more texts a day to 'chat' to friends (Lloyd-Evans, personal communication). Among children and teenagers, the use of these tools of communication may be constrained and monitored by parents but also used by young people to evade such surveillance (Valentine and Holloway 2001, Stevenson 2008). Lloyd-Evans and Bowlby (2007) found that young Asian teenagers in Britain who faced parental restrictions on their mobility and social contacts outside the home used mobile phones to create 'the street in my room' and to escape parental controls. It seems, however, that for the majority of young people, although phones or the internet may represent spaces largely free from parental or other adult surveillance – unlike the 'real' space of the street or school – they were used to organize and recall face-to-face social meetings rather than replace them (Green and Singleton 2009). Indeed, this seems to be an important outcome of the use of mobile phones and the internet for all adults: a trend that gives greater control to the individual in creating their patterns of social interaction (Wellman 2001, Hampton and Wellman 2003).

However, we should also note that the advent of such technologies creates problems for carers and care recipients. The ability to contact someone easily at any time may mean carers cannot escape from care demands, while the person being cared for may feel as if this is control and surveillance rather than care – as clearly is the case for some of the young people discussed above. As with any form of communication, there is the opportunity for abuse and verbal violence – the advent of bullying via emails and texts is an unpleasant reminder of this.

Timing care in a personal community

Chapter 3 has explored the ways in which care is bound up with time and the lifecourse. Here, we consider variation over our lifecourse in the networks of care in a personal community. It is well known that friendship is of particular significance early on and later in the lifecourse (Bukowski *et al.* 1996; Jerrome 1992, Scott and Wenger 1995), but it is also important to remember that the composition of personal communities shifts and changes over time.

Caring for and by other people requires time and is patterned in time – we may have daily or weekly or yearly routines of care – the daily tasks of childcare, the weekly phone call to a mother or Friday night at the pub, the annual visit from a friend. However, such routines are themselves often short-lived as changes over the lifecourse affect our priorities, possibilities and patterns of behaviour. Children grow up and leave home, parents age and die, friends move away, work demands wax and wane or take us to live in new places. Most people will be involved in a complex pattern of reciprocal care and support among members of their personal community, which varies across different timescales from the day-to-day to the lifecourse and which may be disrupted or transformed by major life events, especially those that involve residential movement over substantial distances. Alternatively, for others, networks of care and support may grow and develop in depth and complexity over time within a given place or may be sustained despite residential movement through mediated contacts, occasional visits and a belief in the importance of familial or friendship ties.

The variability of personal communities over time is well illustrated by Spencer and Pahl's (2006) study. They identified four patterns of making and losing 'friends' (who might be kin):

1 *Bounded* friendships patterns: those where the most important friends are made early on in life with relatively few changes thereafter. People with this pattern tended to have lived in the same area for a long time.
2 *Serial* patterns: when most friends are almost completely replaced at each new lifecourse stage. The people that displayed this pattern were highly geographically mobile and often had experienced major lifecourse disruptions.
3 *Evolving* friendship: retaining many early friends but also adding new ones when important changes in the lifecourse lead to new patterns of activity or a change of residence.
4 *Ruptured:* where some unexpected crisis, such as serious illness or a difficult divorce, disrupts both the functioning of individual friendships and the range of people who are now considered to be friends.

These four patterns offer ways to consider the significance of people's changing activities over time and space in their personal communities. They also provide contexts to forms of care and how care may be provided through a personal community.

In research on the support networks of older people in Wales and Liverpool, Scott and Wenger (1995) show both that there are five different types of support network found among the older people that they studied and that these may shift over time in response to such events as changes in health, the death of a spouse and the death of friends. The most common shifts were between the two dominant types of network: the local family dependent network (with close local family ties and a few friends and neighbours) and a locally integrated network (with close relationships with family, friends and neighbours). The importance of significant points in the lifecourse and associated changes in residence and social contacts are illustrated through the research of both Spencer and Pahl (2006) and Scott and Wenger (1995).

One of the central features of friendship is reciprocity. We have already discussed, in Chapter 2, the subtle and informal negotiation over time through which 'developing commitments' are established (Finch and Mason 1993). A further issue discussed in that chapter is the entrenchment of independence as an ideal and the denigration of dependency, so that the dependency inevitably involved in care exchange is seen as a weakness of the dependent person. In friendships, people often have to manage shifts in relative dependency over time as one or other member of the friendship pair or group becomes more dominantly a giver or a receiver. In order to care, we may also have to tell a friend an unpleasant truth – to say 'you were wrong' – an action that may lead to the loss of the friendship. In addition, care between friends may also involve instrumental calculations, matching the 'rewards' of care against its costs (see Rawlings (1992) for a discussion of similar issues in friendship more generally). These considerations emphasise that the care interdependencies that help to constitute so many social relationships reflect complex, confusing and contradictory emotions, and are laden with power and the possibility of abuse. Over time, care relationships may shift between dependence and independence, between acceptance and criticism, and between love and instrumentality, as the relationship is renegotiated. But what of the situation in which such a re-negotiation cannot take place – for example, when someone is terminally ill, dependent and needy? Pahl (2000) suggests that people are able to sustain such tensions if, at some previous period, the friendship had been strong and satisfactory to both parties. Thus, memories of past support and pleasure in each others' company can help sustain friends (and family as friends) through periods of difficulty, just as a hope of better times can sometimes also provide encouragement to keep caring. Sometimes, of course, the relationship cannot be sustained and caring is replaced by absence, neglect or abuse.

In Box 5.2, we explore changes in friendship relationships over time, the implications for care and the importance of friendship in moments of crisis. The friendship is strongly gendered and had been affected by the changes in interests both Nadezda and Maria have experienced as they have moved through the lifecourse. It has also been strained, and yet deepened, by Nadezda's knowledge of tensions in Maria's marriage.

Placing care in a personal community

Caring relationships are practiced in particular places and contexts. They are usually embedded within a wider network of relationships between members of the social group/s to which the participants belong and are often focused around particular places – for example, clubs, work, schools or neighbourhoods. For

Box 5.2 A Caring Friend: Prague, The Czech Republic

Maria is preparing to go out to spend the evening at her friend Nadezda's house, which is a few streets away. She is looking forward to seeing her – it will be good to talk about her worries about Agneta (see Box 3.2) with someone who will understand why she and Peter cannot possibly care for her. And she likes discussing the children with Nadezda who has two of her own, a few years younger than Maria's. They both work full-time and enjoy comparing the problems of dealing with children, husbands, paid work and housework. She has an evening with Nadezda about once a month – neither of them can afford to go out much and so they have organized these evenings at each other's houses, leaving either Peter or Nadezda's husband in charge of the children. It is fun – they have a bit of a laugh and a gossip about their other friends, along with some drinks.

Maria had known Nadezda in Brno as they went to the same primary school and had enjoyed each other's company, always getting into mischief. However, Nadezda and her parents moved to Prague when she was 14 years old, after her father was promoted by his company. Maria and Nadezda kept in touch with each other by letters and phone and the occasional visit back to Brno by Nadezda's family to see relatives. Maria looked forward to these visits to catch up on the gossip about each others lives and especially boyfriends. But when Maria was 19 years old, she met Peter and, while they were courting and newly married, she and Nadezda seemed to be less in touch with each other, especially as Nadezda began to get more involved in the political changes happening in Czechoslovakia. Maria did not pay much attention to these developments – she had been focused on her new life as a wife and, as she hoped, a mother. When Maria became pregnant, Nadezda was both a little envious and busy with her own, rather complex, love life and her full-time clerical job. When Maria and Peter moved to Prague, the friendship with Nadezda deepened again and the fact that Nadezda had married and now worked as an assistant in a nursery re-established a common core of interests.

Then there had been the terrible time recently when she had found that Peter was having an affair with a woman who was a secretary at the glass factory where he worked. She had been distraught – and with the health problems of the twins and her oldest boy going through a bad period at school, she was exhausted anyway. She had cried and screamed and hit Peter and told him to leave the house – and he had, he had left and she had been alone with the children and almost no money. Without Nadezda's support, she didn't know how she would have managed those 2 weeks when he had gone. But Nadezda had confronted Peter and shamed him into ending the affair and coming home.

After that, it had been difficult to get their friendship back on an even keel – she was so much indebted to Nadezda and Nadezda had seen the worst of Peter and the family so it had been hard for her to visit Maria's house. Also, it had been awkward to go back to keeping some form of privacy about her and Peter's relationship in their discussions. She had felt that Nadezda had rather enjoyed being the saviour of the household and had wanted to go on badmouthing Peter in a way that became unhelpful. After all, Nadezda's husband wasn't perfect even if he hadn't had an affair – he was a bit of a bore and very fussy about the way the housework was done. She and Peter shared more of the household chores and childcare than did Nadezda and

> her husband. But gradually things seemed to have got back to normal and she had
> been able to help Nadezda by babysitting and helping out when Nadezda's mother
> had fallen so ill with pneumonia and Nadezda had had to go away for a fortnight to
> care for her. Now it seemed they knew so much about each other, the good and the
> bad, that it would be hard to imagine life without the friendship.

example, the relationship between two girls at school may be embedded within a
wider friendship group who spend time together at break and after school, or the
relationship between two women in Africa who collect water together may be
embedded within a wider group of contacts between women who collect water
and share harvesting tasks. Their practices and expectations of caring friendship
are embedded within the practices and expectations of the group in the particular
'place' of the school, neighbourhood, well and village. Such places may vary in
the opportunities that they provide for caring relationships to flourish. The social
mixture of people, the physical environment, the temporal patterning of activities
may help or hinder the initiation and maintenance of caring friendships (Feld and
Carter 1998). The norms and patterns of behaviour of the group/s will influence
the form and style of the relationship.

The embeddedness of relationships is likely to be particularly important to care
– not only may the norms of the group affect whether or not care is given, they
may also help or hinder members of the group to share caring tasks. This is illustrated by a real and recent example of neighbouring that was told to one of us by
a friend – let us call him John. His father, who we will call Stephen, is retired and
has been recently widowed. Stephen had to have an operation that left him needing
practical help with shopping and minor assistance for several weeks. Both John
and his brother lived some distance away and were in full-time employment, which
made daily care for their father difficult. A network of neighbourhood friends came
to the rescue, organised by an old friend who had socialised with Stephen and his
wife in the past. A rota was agreed for shopping and for being 'on call' until John's
father was well again.

This example conjures up the idealised neighbourhood in which a network of
cross-cutting ties built up over time provides a secure system of care for members
of the neighbourhood who are in need. Such a system relies on shared norms of
behaviour regarding support from friends and neighbours and cross-cutting friendships that help to ensure that people live up to these expectations. But at a time in
the West when many people no longer have overlapping localised social contacts
built up from childhood or over a long period, is the significance of place vanish-
ing in a move to 'community without propinquity' (Webber 1964), which is made
more feasible by the rise of the internet?

It is worthwhile considering what 'local' might mean in the context of care.
'Localness' does seem to be important to caring that requires face-to-face interaction, but need not involve relationships within the 'neighbourhood' – understood
as an area of a few streets around a person's home – perhaps including local shops
(Lee 1968, Forrest 2000, Kearns and Parkinson 2001). A person's workplace or

leisure friends might live 'locally' but not within the residential neighbourhood. The term 'local' is very elastic and the distinguishing feature of local versus non-local friends is that they are close enough to maintain frequent or easy face-to-face contact. Thus, the meaning of 'local' will depend on transport costs and facilities. In contrast, people who are *not* 'friends' or 'family' but who can provide particular types of practical help need to live very close so that carrying out the tasks required is not too onerous. It is easy to feed a neighbour's cat for a week – asking a friend to drive half an hour to do so would seem, to most people, too great a demand.

Furthermore, it is important to distinguish between the emotional significance of members of a personal community and frequency of contact with them. For example, Wellman found in Toronto in the 1970s that if significance is measured by frequency of contact then it was *local* contacts (living within 1 mile) who were most important. If significance was measured in terms of the subjective 'import-ance' of the relationship, the significance of local contacts vanished. Nevertheless, although 'neighbours' may not be thought of as 'important' relationships, the care they gave was valued and interpreted differently – as instrumental rather than linked to being companions or confidantes. For example, people in Willmott's (1987) study talked about people who were 'just neighbours' rather than friends. These were people who lived very close by – within a few houses or across the street. Such people were useful – they provided help with issues such as keeping a key, keeping an eye on the house, small amounts of help with home maintenance and emergency help in a crisis. These are particular forms of care, creating a feeling of security and belonging that does not run deep but is nevertheless significant to people. When or if people move, such ties can be broken without mutual concern and fresh ties made in a new neighbourhood. Indeed, for many people, a deeper friendship with neighbours may not be desired for fear of losing privacy or of problems if the friendship founders. Similar low-intensity, but helpful, caring may be involved in many workplace relationships and between leisure friends. These relationships depend on an environment in which there is a feeling of trust in those who live nearby or who share the workplace or activity and the lack of such feelings is a serious problem in some neighbourhoods and work environments (Kearns and Parkinson 2001, Scharf *et al.* 2003, Young and Daniel 2003). For example, if you fear verbal attacks from neighbours or if violence occurs, you fear that other neigh-bours would not come to your aid; this creates a stressful living environment.

The specific importance of caring provided by people within the 'neighbour-hood' is likely to be linked to different periods in the lifecourse – thus those with small children, with elderly relatives or older people themselves may particularly value the intergenerational care provided by helpful neighbours even though these neighbours may not be close friends. The need to have a safe and secure local area or neighbourhood in which violence and threatening behaviour are rare, is particu-larly important to parents and children (Letiecq and Koblinsky 2004). In contrast, a lack of neighbourhood ties and high levels of trust in neighbours need not always be detrimental nor go along with a lack of close friendships or family to give care. There are places today, as in the past, where such neighbourly services and contacts seem not to exist. The areas of new-build gentrified flats that are found in many global cities today might be examples (Smith 2002, Boddy 2007, Davidson and Lees 2005). Many people living in these places use them simply as a place to sleep and they may find the care they need from local and non-local friends and family or from work colleagues and wish to live in isolation from neighbours. This is not to argue that there are not people who are socially isolated and who lack both neighbours and friends but simply to assert that caring friends and family need not live just round the corner.

This people scenario illustrates the importance of friends, neighbours and formal carers to practical help and the significance of time in a situation in which transport and technologies of communication are not well developed. Local networks have become an important source of support. Formal carers may also be seen as 'friends'. This story illustrates the impact of the stigma and fear of HIV/AIDS on family relationships and the importance of family privacy in some situations.

Box 5.3 Neighbours and Friends: Tanzania

Mary is on her way to see her neighbour, Patience. They have known one another for more than 20 years. Patience had moved to the village when she had married and they have been neighbours ever since. When Mary's daughter was dying, Patience had been very helpful. Mary had not liked to leave her daughter for a long time, and Patience had come and sat with her when Mary had to go out and work on her small-holding. That had been very good because none of Mary's relatives in the nearby town would come. They had blamed her daughter for being ill and would not visit. Patience had helped keep everyone's spirits up with her cheerful, if rather bossy, manner. Both of them were widows now and that was another thing they shared – the knowledge of what is was like to be getting old and to have lost your husband and for a child to have died before you. Patience's son had died some years back, so that was another bond. Over the years, they had worked together with other women when there were important farming tasks to be done and had exchanged small favours. Also, they had both borrowed money from one another in the past – small sums just to tide them over a temporary problem.

Nevertheless, Mary does not want to talk to Patience about her current worries about Joy and Grace – these are concerns she wants to keep to herself. These are family issues and Patience is a terrible gossip – everyone would know in no time what Mary is worried about. Agnes from the NGO in the neighbouring town had come to visit again yesterday, urging Mary to take Grace to the doctor to be tested to see if she needed medicine. But Mary does not see the point. Even if she got the free drugs Agnes has promised her, she has been told you have to eat very well if you take these medicines and she cannot afford to feed Grace, or any of them, well – and Grace does not seem to be too ill – it is probably all a fuss about nothing. It had been difficult though, trying to explain her feelings. Agnes had been so helpful when her daughter was ill and it was good that she still came to see the children – she had spent time with them when their mother was ill and visited after she died and the children liked her. Patience will try to find out why Agnes was visiting – she is bound to have noticed her – Mary will just have to be vague. And then there is Joy – Joy needs to start earning money to help the family but there are so few options for her. When a cousin had come to visit a month or so ago, she had mentioned Joy – she knows that he is in touch with relatives in the city, perhaps there will be an opportunity there – but so far she has heard nothing. And if Joy does go to the city, how will she, Mary, manage? She is certainly not talking to Patience about that; Patience always knows exactly how other people should handle things and is only too happy to tell them – Mary wants to make her own decisions.

But it's a good thing she is going to spend time with Patience, who always likes a good gossip and a lot of laughter. She will forget her worries while they are busy. Patience and she are both members of the same church and they occasionally go and clean there. This is what they are going to do this morning. They will probably meet some other women while they are there and it will be good to stop thinking about her own problems and hear about what everyone else is up to.

Settings for caring encounters in a personal community

'Placing' care can also be thought about in terms of the settings in which encounters between friends most often 'take place'. In Chapter 4, we have already talked about the importance of the home in the Western world today as a space in which emotional ties can be expressed and in which intimate physical and emotional caring practices can be enacted. The association of the home and the private sphere with intimacy and emotion has been argued to be a creation of the move towards modernity and affective individualism in the eighteenth and nineteenth centuries in Western societies (Oliker 1998). This association was also tied to a clear gendered division of social expectations between the 'male' sphere of the public and its emphasis on competition, and the pursuit of self-interest and the 'female' sphere of the 'private' in which intimacy, love and nurturance were expected to dominate, although the realities of this division are complex (Davidoff *et al.* 1976, Mackenzie 1989, McDowell 1999, Armstrong and Squires 2002).

Home in Western society became viewed as a site in which relations between female friends might be enacted and in which kin and mixed-gender activities were orchestrated by women. Men's friendships were expected to be performed more often in the public sphere – workplace, pub or club. In the pre-World War II and immediate post-war period, many researchers showed that this pattern was differentiated between working-class and middle class families – middle class men were likely to see friends in a variety of settings, including the home, whereas working-class men did not (Allen 1998). Allen has argued that the distinctive patterns of working-class gendered friendship practices in Britain and other Western societies in the 1930s–1950s are partly explained by the limited space and resources in people's houses and the limited funds available for socialising. Socialising outside the home in specific and limited settings allowed men (and women) to control their sociable expenditure – lack of funds could be dealt with by staying away from the setting, and the obligations of reciprocation limited to interactions within it (Allen 1998). For instance, meeting in the pub limited financial obligations to buying a round and meant the resources of the home were not involved. The 'friendship' could be considered as a relationship limited to the set-ting and so not involving potential obligations, personal commitments and 'care' outside that setting.

However, it is also the case that the practices of friendship help to *create* places as settings for interaction that are suitable for the forming and deepening of friend-ship ties and of forms of emotional care linked to friendship. In the more affluent times of today, with the development of strong social endorsement of the ideals of the companionate marriage and an increasing proportion of women in the work-place, diverse leisure sites – restaurants, cafés, gyms, sports centres, clubs – as well as the workplace itself have become settings for both gender-segregated and gender-integrated friendship practices. For example, a group of men and women may sing in a choir together and socialise afterwards at a local café or bar or a group of men who go to watch football together may socialise on journeys to and from the football ground as well as at the ground.

Friendships that cross class, race and gender boundaries, made at work or in a shared leisure activity (such as the football or choir-singing examples above) may be extended through going to the pub or for a meal together. Such meetings may loosen the tie between the friendship and a particular focus of activity. Meetings outside the home can preserve the idea that social differences linked to class, gen-der and race are not important to the friendship. Meetings in the home do seem often to signal the importance of the friendship as a relationship in its own right, independent of the shared activity that may have initiated it. Meetings in the home may be necessary to the development of *chosen-as-given* relationships. These may also signal that the status and resource differences evident in the furnishing and size of the home are either small or considered to be unimportant. Interestingly, the close identification of home with family may be de-stabilised by the extension of friendship practices into the space of the home. Roseneil and Budgeon (2004) provide a detailed discussion of three people with 'families of choice', whose domestic spaces were open to friends visiting frequently though an 'open door policy' and staying (sometimes for extended periods) or sharing the house. They maintain that, for these people, 'Space normatively constructed as 'private' and heterosexual is reconfigured as collective' (p. 150). We suggest that the blurred boundaries between friendship and family are at work here, loosening, but not destroying, the identification of 'home' with 'family'.

Settings for care encounters within the wider community: Volunteering

The nature and current status of volunteering

The dominance of the 'metaphor of family' in our everyday speech and thought risks under-estimating the importance of informal caring relationships based on a wider sense of responsibility to 'care' in some way for 'the community' or 'soci-ety'. Thus, considering the caring provided by volunteers raises the issue of why some people decide to care for 'strangers' and how volunteering organisations contribute to informal care-giving. It also problematises the divide between formal and informal care.

Informal volunteering is 'giving unpaid help to an individual' who is not a relative (Kitchen *et al.* 2006) and includes such activities as helping a neighbour. In contrast, *formal volunteering* entails people voluntarily allying themselves with an organisation that will co-ordinate them to carry out tasks to benefit individuals or groups or the environment, other than or in addition to close relatives (Low *et al.* 2007:10). Such 'work' is unpaid but involves formal arrangements – such as agreed hours of work and agreed methods of care. Many volunteer organisations also seek to ensure that their volunteers do not become too deeply personally involved in a 'friendship' relationship with their 'clients'. Thus, the caring work of volunteers has many similarities to paid formal care work. As in the case of paid care work, providing formal care may also lead to 'informal' friendship, emotional commitment and 'caring about'. It seems that formal volunteering is an activity that sits on a fuzzy boundary between informal and formal care.

Some formal volunteering is done to provide 'care' to people living in other countries – from the volunteer, for example, raising money for an international NGO through volunteering in a charity shop or doing unpaid administrative work for such a charity. People also donate money directly to such charities which, although not a volunteering activity itself, also reflects support for the volunteers and care for people 'at a distance'. This type of activity requires recognition of the needs of others who are not people such as members of one's family, friends, workmates or leisure friends, with whom the 'carer' has or had an everyday relationship. In Tronto's terms, this represents 'attentiveness' to the needs of others – i.e. finding out and 'noticing' the needs of other people (Tronto 1993). It also requires assuming responsibility for the need (see Chapter 2). That such activity is widespread suggests that caring 'attentiveness' and the recognition of responsibility for 'strangers' is a common feature of human societies; on the other hand, we know that many people do not engage in such activities.

The extent and composition of volunteering varies considerably between countries. Different countries (see below) have different numbers and proportions of volunteers engaged in what are termed 'service' and 'expressive' voluntary activities. *Service activities* mirror much state-provided welfare activity – for example, providing support to families with a disabled child, a drop-in centre for young people, or transport to outpatient hospital appointments. *Expressive activities* are those 'whose main purpose is the actualization of values or preferences, such as pursuit of artistic expression, preservation of cultural heritage or natural environment, political mobilization and advocacy, or the enhancement of the quality of life." (Salamon and Sokolowski 2001: 15).

The amount and type of formal volunteering activity depends first on the existence of social networks and organisations that are willing and allowed by the state and society to organise volunteering effort (Salamon and Sokolowski 2001). This, in turn, will depend on the type of welfare regime and its history of relations between social classes and key social institutions (Anheier and Salamon 2006). Where the state provides fairly effective formal care, volunteering in 'service' activities is less. For example, Salamon and Sokolowski (2001) estimate that, in social-democratic countries such as Sweden and Finland, there are high levels of volunteering but a large proportion (about 80%) is for 'expressive' activities. In Eastern Europe, the previously Communist regimes in which the state used to control and command the delivery of welfare have low levels of volunteering. In contrast, Britain and the United States, with liberal political regimes and lower levels of welfare spending than Scandinavia, have fairly high levels of volunteering, but more than half in 'service' activities; whereas 'corporatist' regimes such as Italy and The Netherlands, in which strong social groupings, recognised by the state, deliver welfare (e.g. the Church or labour associations) have only 'moderate' levels of volunteering.

Popular debates on care often suggest that that voluntary activity and informal 'community' care will be lower in the increasingly individualised and mobile society of prosperous Western nations than in poorer countries. However, the opposite appears to be the case. For example, Salamon and Sokolowski (2001) found that the less developed countries of Eastern Europe and Latin America showed far lower levels of volunteering than the more developed post-industrial countries that were studied. Thus, it seems that the ways in which care is expressed and the types of care-giving that are seen as socially legitimate will affect how care is practiced.

Spacing and timing volunteer care

It seems that volunteering varies between different types of welfare regime. However, there is variation in volunteering within given societies – not everyone volunteers and people's engagement in volunteering varies over their lifecourse. In order to explore this further, we will draw on the experience of England where volunteering is seen as a legitimate and socially approved activity and we find that more than half of people (59%) contacted in a recent government survey had been involved in 'formal volunteering' in the past year and, on average, formal volunteers had spent 11 hours volunteering in the previous 4 weeks (Low *et al.* 2007). This and other surveys show that women are considerably more likely than men to be involved in both formal and informal volunteering, thus re-emphasising the association between femininity and caring noted in earlier chapters. This difference is only partly the result of women's past lower level of involvement in paid work (Carlin 2001). Moreover, there are differences in the nature of the volunteering that men and women do – at least in England. Women are more likely to be involved in 'hands-on care', whereas men play a greater role in some aspects of organising voluntary activities (Bowlby and Lloyd-Evans 2007). Poorer groups are also less involved in formal volunteering and formal volunteering is also lower among ethnic minority groups.

Why then do people in England volunteer? Based on an in-depth study of volunteering in a deprived community, Hardill and Baines (2005, 2007) have suggested a useful fourfold categorisation of the motives for volunteering:

1   *Philanthropy* (volunteering to help others)
2   *Mutual aid* (volunteering to exchange help with others suffering from similar problems to oneself)
3   *'Getting by'* (volunteering to make friends, cope with bereavement or mental illness)
4   *'Getting on'* (volunteering to gain qualifications or experience)

In many cases, volunteers have more than one motive. In a UK study of a wide range of volunteering organisations in the town of Reading, in the south of England, Bowlby and Lloyd-Evans (2007) found that *'Getting By'* and *'Philanthropy'* were the most frequently cited motivations by both volunteers and those recruiting volunteers. It was also evident that, for some of those interviewed, volunteering was an important aspect of their whole way of life. For others, in contrast, volunteering was something done at a particular juncture in their lives that might not be repeated – for example, as a response to bereavement or helping out with the sports club that their child attended; Bowlby and Lloyd-Evans (2007) termed these two orientations *lifelong* and *lifestage* volunteering.

So how is it that some people adopt a lifelong orientation towards volunteering and caring about the needs of 'other', non-family strangers? Like other caring commitments, these seem to 'develop' in the course of people's upbringing or work experiences or spring from their commitment to particular religious or ideological beliefs (Bowlby and Lloyd-Evans 2007). For example, in a perceptive in-depth study of voluntary workers in two organisations in London, England, Taylor (2005) argues that attitudes to the voluntary or non-profit sector and to paid and unpaid work are an aspect of class-based *habitus* and must be understood in the context of the history of the development of the sector within Britain. Her study suggests that we cannot simply see participation in this form of 'caring' as a result of 'caring motives' – of some people being innately 'nicer' or more altruistic than others – but as the result of a set of social processes, operating over time in particular places, through which such motives are shaped and developed (as discussed in Chapters 3 and 4).

One aspect of caring and the ethic of care that has been much debated is how we come to decide for whom we should care. When it comes to volunteering, it seems that empathy with the situation of others who need some form of 'care' or 'help' is an important motivating factor not simply in deciding to volunteer but in deciding for which cause to volunteer. For example, Cloke *et al.* (2007), when interviewing people who did voluntary work for homeless people, found that some volunteers had themselves experienced homelessness, whereas others empathised with the situation of homeless people. In the Bowlby and Lloyd-Evans (2007) study, they found that, for some people, the desire to serve their 'local community' or 'community of interest' (e.g. other people interested in a sport or pastime – often, but not always, in its local manifestation) was central to their involvement. It appears then, that in formal volunteering, recognition of the claims of others requires that those 'others' are seen as sharing some commonality with the volunteer. The likelihood of such recognition resulting in 'caring' acts of unpaid work seems to relate to ideas about the obligations of members of society that are shaped over time through social relationships and, in particular, socio-spatial milieus.

Finding the time and space to do voluntary work can be difficult – just as with paid work, it has to be 'fitted in' with the demands of family, friends and paid work (Hardill and Baines 2005, 2007, Bowlby and Lloyd-Evans 2007). However, as already indicated, many volunteers participate in order to build networks of friends and companions. Bowlby and Lloyd-Evans (2007) found that many volunteers said that relationships between voluntary workers in their organisation were 'just like a family' – that 'metaphor of family' again! Some who had become volunteers as part of adjusting to bereavement, mental illness, leaving work or being away from home (*Getting by*) found such contacts with co-workers, as well as a sense of 'being useful', very important to their adjustment. The sense of doing work that the person feels is perceived as 'useful' by a wider group seems to us to be particularly important in understanding volunteering, but also care work more generally. Socially approved caring promotes a feeling of self-worth.

Spaces of volunteering

The activities of volunteering trace chains of relationships in time–space as volunteers gather together, as resources (people, materials, information) are assembled in order to carry out their work and as volunteers carry out their volunteer tasks. In particular, some volunteering activity has been conceptualised as creating 'spaces of care' – particular environments in which care-giving is prioritised (Conradson 2003). For example, Cloke *et al.* (2005) suggest that a soup kitchen for the homeless became a temporally specific 'space of care'. It was a time–space in which a network of social contacts between volunteers and homeless people and among the latter became possible. Thus, the 'care' involved was more complex and multi-faceted than simply the giving and receiving of food. However, they also note that, for other residents and for some homeless people and volunteers, this became a 'space of fear' in which violence might and sometime did erupt. Thus, 'spaces of care' may have concurrent multiple meanings that cannot be read off from their intended role but will depend on the actions within them and their interpretation by different people.

Consideration of spaces of care raises the question of how the relationships between the physical form of such spaces, their environmental characteristics and the social activities that constitute them affect the caring encounter. This question relates to the idea that some environments might be better shaped for caring and therapeutic relationships than others. Such a question is particularly pertinent in situations when spaces are designed for care-giving, but may also be of importance to the informal care-giving that operates in a variety of environments such as the workplace or the neighbourhood.

We have already noted that there are other 'spaces' of informal care outside the home. When friends meet and discuss their problems in the café in the local shopping or sports centre, they are establishing a short-lived 'space of care'. Public spaces offer the possibility of engagement with other people and hence the potential for care exchanges – helping someone cross a road, lifting a heavy bag for a tourist, even sharing thoughts on a problem with a fellow traveller. However, social codes, as well as the increasing state and private regulation of public spaces (Davis 1990, Fyfe 1998, Butler and Bowlby 1997), limit such encounters. Nevertheless, although these may be limited forms of care, like the neighbouring activities discussed earlier, they are important to people's feelings of trust, security and self-worth.

Resourcing care: Family, friends and volunteers

In conclusion, we briefly reflect on the significance of time and space in resourcing care. Caring, by definition, involves the use of resources. Some of these are the embodied resources of individual carer(s) – their health and strength, their practical, social and empathetic skills – but others are resources of money and material possessions. Societal resources are also central, as we have illustrated already in Chapter 1. Access to such resources for care will vary between different types of people and across time and space at a variety of temporal and spatial scales. But time and space are also themselves important resources for care – we need time to care and a place to care – and they are linked by technologies of mobility and communication, which affect the speed with which we can traverse space bodily or exchange messages across space. There are important social inequalities in access to time and space to care and to transport and communication media, which parallel the more familiar inequalities of class, gender, ethnicity and disability.

Lack of time can inhibit exchanges of volunteer care. For example, it is well established that rates of formal volunteering are lower among poorer groups (Low *et al.* 2007). This is likely to reflect a variety of factors, including the time demands of earning a living, perhaps working long hours on low pay and, for some, the competing demands of care for the family with limited financial means (Bowlby and Lloyd-Evans 2007). When it comes to friendship, Spencer and Pahl's study provided examples of people 'losing touch' at periods of their lives when the demands of family or paid work left them no time to meet together, as well as examples of friendships flourishing when time constraints were loosened (2006). The time demands of paid work and family fluctuate across the lifecourse and this is reflected in the changing rates of volunteering with age and shifts in patterns of friendship. Time as a resource affects the ability to care in the short term but also over the lifecourse as the demands of studying, training and paid work wax and wane. Women often are 'given' by society too much time to care and too little time for other activities.

Places and spaces for caring are also vital resources. Many forms of care require places with specific characteristics – for example, privacy, comfort, hygiene, social connotations of safety or control. As we have seen, lack of money and domestic space appears to influence friendship practices and practices of volunteering may be strongly affected by the availability of places to meet. We have also shown above how care between friends is linked to particular activities in particular places. Caring may also require that the carer can have a time and space to be away from care – for example, this may be very important to people caring for elderly relatives. Again, we note that women have often been assigned or restricted to spaces of care or that spaces of care have been understood socially to be feminine spaces – confining women in spaces of care and excluding men from them.

Resources that allow mobility and communication affect access to time and space for care. For example, having access to a car or to public transport may make it possible to visit a friend, whereas provision of transport may itself be a means of care. Transporting someone who is not able to drive to the shops, to the doctor or to see a friend is an act of care, but depends on the temporal availability of a driver and a car – and, of course, a whole infrastructure of roads, shops and services, which are absent in some countries. Access to the post, a phone or a computer for email and the internet can be vital in sustaining friendships – again, something that is well illustrated by some of Spencer and Pahl's respondents. Thus, inequalities in access to technologies for traversing space and communication – to transport, phone or computer – also create inequalities in care.

Summary

In this chapter, we have discussed the importance of networks of friendship relationships in providing practical and emotional care, emphasising the ways in which time and space are implicated in practices of friendship. We have shown both the importance of physical distance to some sorts of 'caring for' activities, but also that such distance may not matter to the exchange of emotional care through the use of a variety of communication media. We have also suggested that caring activities create 'spaces of care' and that the physical and cultural characteristics of such spaces matter to the caring interaction. We have argued that the social practices that constitute 'the family', 'friendship' and 'volunteering' will vary between societies with different welfare regimes and different levels of material resources. Hence, levels and ways of caring are not simply 'given' as 'natural' but are a product of particular social and economic circumstances. Or, put another way, they are 'achieved', not 'ascribed' (Sevenhuijsen 2000).

In the next chapter, we examine caring in the workplace – a venue in which friendship is important to informal care, but in which formal and informal caring is shaped by explicit State and employer policies, as well as implicit social expectations.

6 Working and Caring[1]

Introduction

Our focus now turns to interdependencies in paid work and care. We touched on some of the issues in earlier chapters (3, 4 and 5) but, given the prominence of paid work in the lives of most adults and households, it merits fuller examination. This chapter explores spatial and temporal perspectives on caring and working and the policies and practices associated with this.

The debate on work/care terminology

The debate on terminology concerning combining caring and working has been a lively one in recent years. The words and phrases used in or outside workplaces suggest ideas about informal care and working. They inform and contextualise policies and practices in workplaces, government and personal relationships, through the cultural norms and values that they promote.

'Work–life balance' is one of many terms that have evolved to describe the everyday and longer term challenges and opportunities of combining caring and working. Other terms include 'work-family', 'family friendly' and 'work–life reconciliation'. These various terms place a slightly different emphasis on the issues and, with the exception of family friendly, the starting point is paid work. Thus:

- 'Work–life balance' suggests that equilibrium is achievable, although, in reality, either work-life or home-life are likely to be compromised by the demands of the other.
- 'Work–life reconciliation' suggests that there are tensions between the two as the word 'reconcile' suggests adjustments to achieve a balance.
- 'Work-family' and' family friendly' bring families on to the agenda and are generally interpreted in terms of combining care for children or elderly relatives with paid work. Bringing families on the agenda, however, offers only a partial explanation of the relationship between informal caring and employment, as many forms of care take place in and around the workplace; for example, emotional support for colleagues experiencing tense or difficult times at work or in their personal lives and care outside the workplace may extend beyond the family – for example, to caring for friends or neighbours.

The use of the term 'family' restricts thinking and analysis to specific issues such as maternity or bereavement leave. A more neutral concept is work/life articulation (WLA) (Wall 2008). We interpret this term to mean the process of seeking to unite or join together paid work with other 'life' demands. However, we need to recognise that WLA could be interpreted as if work is somehow divorced from life and yet, for many people across the globe, paid work is part of life and interwoven with the everyday. An alternative is to combine this with work and family as WFA; this allows the exploration of the processes and practices of individuals, families and employers without any presumption about the outcomes. However, as we have argued, the word 'family' restricts the forms of care considered. We suggest the term work/care articulation (WCA). This term clearly indicates the key concepts of work (in this case, paid work) and care (in this case, informal care), which often includes organising or accessing formal care service provision or benefits as well.

The place of paid work in our lives

Although salaries or wages may not be the only source of household income, income from paid work is seen as critical to everyday, individual, and intergenerational survival and identities.[2] Paid work provides an avenue through which people can gain access to money and other resources, whether as employees, self-employed or as workers in receipt of welfare benefits. However, the relationship between paid work, income and resources varies across the world. For example, in the US, welfare provision by the government is limited and workers (and often their families) are dependent on benefits secured from employers, such as health insurance. In Europe, a more extensive welfare state regime ensures that government has a greater involvement in supporting income levels through the provision of benefits and services, including health services that are free at the point of access. In S-SA countries such as Tanzania, for example, the government argues that it cannot afford to back up household income. Welfare services are often provided, if at all, through funding provided by supranational organisations (for example, the International Monetary Fund (IMF) and World Bank), non-governmental organisations (charities such as Save the Children), various religious groups and through workers' own combined efforts. Household income itself may be generated from subsistence agriculture, a variety of work in the informal economy and/or formal paid work. Although 'productive' work can be viewed as being essential to generate household incomes in cash or in kind, how this blends with other resources and services differs – depending on historical, cultural and ideological factors, and economic regimes – and this does have a bearing on the ways in which working and caring inter-relate.

Paid work and societal development

Economic and social status is often assessed through types of employment, sector of employment and income levels (Pettinger *et al.* 2005). The formal economy generates company profits and wages, which are both taxed. A proportion of taxation not only finances formal care services but can be used to support informal care through, for example, tax allowances, welfare benefits or direct payments (Ungerson 2005). Global economic and financial institutions, such as the World Bank or IMF, promote waged work in a competitive labour market as the basis for development and growth (Parrenas 2005). Fundamental to this economic system is the generation of consumption through wages, and the advent of the interdependent global economy encourages global consumption of globally traded goods and services. However, there has been a recognition among supranational development organisations, such as the United Nations (UN) and International Labour Office (ILO) that economic and societal development will not happen by simply promoting any type of paid employment: paid work has to have social meaning and value. The result of this thinking has been the Decent Work Agenda led by the ILO, the overarching aim of which is to 'Promote decent work as a key component of national development strategies' (ILO 2006). By decent work is meant:

> ... opportunities for work that is productive and delivers a fair income, security in the workplace and social protection for families, better prospects for personal development and social integration, freedom for people to express their concerns, organise and participate in the decisions that affect their lives and equality of opportunity and treatment for all women and men.
>
> (ILO 2007: 15)

Indeed, the Decent Work Agenda (ILO 2007: 12) is seen as central to improving economic equality between men and women and as 'one of the best means of empowering women to protect themselves from HIV infection and of containing the impact of HIV/AIDS on children and households'. All parties to the African Regional Meeting on this topic in the 2007 meeting recognised that promoting opportunities for women from largely low-waged less productive work to better paid and more productive work will be a challenge, all the more so in times of economic constraint.

At the time of writing this book, most governments and many businesses and employers are grappling with the consequences of a global economic recession. Evolving with some speed in the second half of 2008, the effects of this recession are likely to deepen and impact on employment trends for 2–3 years hence. In Europe and North America, the effects of this recession has hit three groups of workers: first, unemployment is on the rise among professional groups such as lawyers, accountants, architects – all professions in which women have make notable in-roads. Second, as a consequence of the recession, there has been a marked impact on many service sectors, with a resultant rise in unemployment among those in low-paid and part-time work, often women. Last, the pool of migrant workers, that had become increasingly important in some economies, has become destabilised, especially in Western Europe. Limited rights in some host countries mean that they can be dismissed and sent home without recourse; and some migrants are voting with their feet to return home or travel to other countries, as the economic advantages of working in the host country erode.

The processes of WCA will be more challenging as employers expect more from workers, in both commitment and labour, and in turn, workers find it hard to refuse overtime or changes to work schedules. In the context of economic recession, negotiations over changes to work patterns to accommodate caring responsibilities become more complex and contested. Commentators are speculating about the impact of recession on management attitudes. Organisations that represent employers across the EU and in other economies (for example, the USA, Latin America, Australia, China and Malaysia) have called for a halt to further measures to extend work/care legislation as the current economic recession intensifies (International Monetary Fund 2008). Such views and economic tensions may result in policy clashes between employers and governments. For example, despite requests from the Confederation of British Industry (CBI) that work-family legislation should not be changed, in April 2009 the UK government extended rights to request flexible working to parents of all children up to the age of 16 years (this was previously only for children under the age of 6 years, or if the child was disabled and 18 years or under). The debate surrounding this change was notable for the evident tensions over the continued pressures on parents to combine caring and working, and business desire to cut employment costs in an economic recession. Nevertheless, an extension to legislation, although welcomed by many workers, trade unions and professional associations, may not result in greater flexibility. In the context of recession, with rising levels of unemployment, it is likely that individualised negotiations on working and caring within the workplace will replace the use of policies and legislation. In these negotiations, factors such as gender, age and the state of working relationships are likely to be important. The woman with two children aged under 12 years, who gets on well with her manager, may find it relatively straightforward to negotiate a change to working hours and patterns. A male colleague with a working wife and one child aged under 5 years, who recently complained about his line manager's poor communication skills, may find his request is investigated. His line manager asks why his wife cannot organise flexible hours to accommodate after-school care. Presumptions about who should care, and for whom, and the state of working relations, are coming into play as the request for flexible working is considered.

In the rest of this chapter, we first address how time and space affect the combination of working and caring. We then explore how working and caring are represented through images and ideas. Understanding the issues faced by people trying to combine working and caring requires an understanding of the economic changes that are transforming the workplace, and so we next turn to examine how working lives have changed, including the growth in paid care work and the evolution of markets in care. In the final part of the chapter, we draw upon data from two research projects undertaken by teams in which two of the authors have been involved.[3] Reflecting findings from these projects and relevant literature, we explore practices of flexible working and control over work time to aid what we have termed WCA.

Temporal and spatial perspectives on caring and working

In previous chapters, we identified three dimensions of time that are particularly relevant to working and caring – namely, daily scheduling, employment planning and work in adult years, and the context of the lifespan or lifecourse. These are not mutually exclusive.

Box 6.1 Getting to the Training Course: Prague, The Czech Republic

In Prague, Peter has been offered a place on a training course that could enhance his chances for a better job in the glass factory. Given the threat of redundancies that has been hanging over everyone at work, this has been excellent news for him. But he is worried about taking up the place on the course since the timing is dreadful – it takes place only 2 days after his grandmother will have moved in to stay with them long term. He and Maria are hoping that they will be able to persuade her to move to a residential home near to them once she has made the move from her own home and village. But he knows that, in the short term, having her at home will make life very difficult for everyone. The course takes place over a whole week and is residential, and Maria will also be out at work for much of the time. Given the recent tensions in his marriage and the chronic condition of the teenage twins, both of whom suffer from severe asthma, he is concerned about Maria's reaction when he tells her about the course. It had been very difficult to persuade Maria to have Agneta in their home – she does not have the close bond that he has with Agneta. It was only because he had arranged for some care input for Agneta from the local municipality, including the provision of one hot meal a day, and transport to a nearby social care centre, that Maria had been persuaded. He hopes that this, combined with informal support for Maria and Agneta from neighbours, will be enough during the week that he will be away. At the same time, Peter is concerned about the teenage children, wondering how Maria will manage one son who is being very moody and unreliable at the moment. Before he can go to the course, he feels there are a range of arrangements to make. He has already spent a lot of time talking and organising Agneta's care from the municipality, but he is anxious that things may go wrong in the first few days. Now he must also talk to his friends and neighbours about the week he will be away. And he has to arrange things at work too – ensuring cover for some of his work commitments. Nevertheless, he hopes that the pressures of organising attendance at the course will be compensated by better job opportunities. In the long run, Peter speculates, the whole family could gain if he does well on this training course.

In the scenario depicted in Box 6.1, the negotiation of just one event reveals how caring interdependencies can affect all family members and bring together the everyday and the long term. 'Care' is part of these everyday exchanges; it is woven into the narratives of each person's lifecourse; it traverses the past, present and future, as well as the boundaries between work and home, employment and leisure:

different understandings of time bear on our lives simultaneously: the clock time of work schedules is constantly challenged and undermined by non-commodified times such as memory, or expressive, or caring time.

(Halford and Leonard 2006: 661)

Spatial dimensions do not merely provide a "frame" or "container" for lived experiences, but, rather, act as a tool of thought and action (Lefebvre 1991: 26). Peter, in the example above, is traversing the physical and mental spaces of his home and neighbourhood, thinking about how his grandmother will adapt to the new space of Peter and Maria's home, the hotel where the course takes place, the need to work through feelings and plans and keep in touch with the family through his telephone calls and texts. Rose (1993:28) asserts that spatial and temporal analysis needs to explore the 'emotional, the passionate, the disruptive, and the feelings of relations with others.' There are many and individual ways of experiencing space; for example, Maria may prefer a telephone call to a text, Agneta may prefer services to come to her rather than to go to a centre for lunch or she may feel happy to leave their unfamiliar, crowded, untidy home to be with people of her own age. As Pile and Thrift (1995: 29) comment, the discursive experience of everyday lives is 'dependant to some degree on the immediate resources available to [*the person*] at the moment they show up in time and space.' This is true for both Peter, Maria and Agneta, albeit their resources and everyday lives differ while inter-connecting.

Images and ideas

In Chapters 2 and 3, we noted how ideas and images of care draw upon memories, often of childhood experiences, and popular discourses and representations. These ideas and images may stand in contrast to what happens in everyday practices. Dominant images of caring and working in the West are gendered and focus on adult working women who, as mothers, are combining paid work with childcare. Yet, although many working women may experience this, households with children are now in a minority; for example, across much of the EU, at any one time, only a third of households contain dependent children and around one in ten have children under five years (Alber *et al.* 2008). Classic images include the working mother with young children struggling to get them to school before going to work, taking time out of the workplace when a call comes from the school with news that one of the children is ill and should be taken home, and organising childcare over the school holidays. In developing countries, the image of the mother in the rural village looking after children, foraging for firewood, walking miles to collect water, milling corn and preparing meals still prevails, although in many such countries the urban population has been increasing rapidly and some women's lives are changing accordingly.

Within employing organisations across the globe, the images of care are epitomised by human resource departments and their everyday practices of 'doing gender' (McKie *et al.* 1999). Staff are overwhelming female, working with care-related staff issues, and polices that are implicitly gendered. In practical and emotional terms, women in HR represent powerful dimensions of what being female and caring at work is about, for they 'care' for others whilst ensuring that staffing resources aid the attainment of organisational goals (Hearn and Parkin 2001).

Policy documents, academic reports and information leaflets on flexible working and work-life issues are peppered with pictorial images of women with children, often white and middle class. Men, ethnic minority groups and the impaired are among the individuals and groups that are generally absent from debates and materials at all levels and yet many are actively negotiating caring and working. For example, findings from research by Brandth and Kvande (2002) on fathers negotiating parental leave in Norway found varied practices among men. Drawing on survey data and interviews with 30 couples, Brandth and Kvande (2002: 189–190) identified how fathers choose different responses to parental leave opportunities:

- Those who want to get as much time as possible with their children, termed fathers with 'limit-setting practice'
- In complete contrast, those who place work first; 'unrestrained practice'
- Fathers who took parental leave as it had been 'reserved' for them
- 'Tradition-bound' fathers for whom masculinities in the work environment and the demands for flexibility rendered parental leave problematic.

Constructions of mothering and fathering in the workplace were considered by Kugelberg (2006), who undertook an anthropological study in one workplace. The analysis of data indicated that the 'articulations of motherhood and fatherhood [are] expressions of contesting discourses in the local discourse order at one company. … The recognition of mothers' special needs both legitimated and motivated discrimination in the perspective of the company discourse' (Kugelberg 2006: 168). Rather than recognising parenting, the gendered constructions of mothering and fathering infused discourses and practices. Hochschild (2003) has argued that, in capitalist workplaces, the trend to a presence and long hours culture, which is considered to be critical to demonstrating a commitment in many workplaces, renders parenting problematic. For mothers, there is the double jeopardy of pressures associated with gender, caring and working, and the gendered nature of domestic labour at home.

There is an image 'default setting', as Ransome (2008) asserts, in which full-time paid employment is seen as the surest way of achieving full citizenship and that, were it not for the inconvenience of dependants of one kind or another, everybody would prefer to be engaged in full-time paid employment. Interestingly, Eurostat (2008a) databanks on the number of employed persons wishing to change the organisation of their working lives and care responsibilities show that 30% of females aged 15–64 years (who have caring responsibilities) wish to work and reduce care time. Care can be both a delight and a drudgery; a responsibility and a challenge.

Care work may be done or indeed received by all paid workers, whether or not they have dependent children, elderly relatives, live alone or with others.

Demographic trends (not least of which is the increase in longevity in some areas, or early mortality due to disease in other areas) and increases in employment participation have brought about an increase in paid workers who exchange care with relatives and friends. Eurostat (2008d) databanks show that of those employed married men and women using some form of childcare service, just over a quarter (26%) were using unpaid relatives/neighbours/friends. In more deprived areas, whether pre- or post-industrial, parent's work commitments can mean children having to take on informal caring (think of children caring for a disabled parent in the UK or children caring for siblings when their parents have succumbed to AIDS in S-SA (Evans and Becker 2009)). The growth in child-headed households and 'street families' in S-SA has led to organisations providing care programmes that are designed not just to create leadership and life/organisational skills, but also to facilitate openings into 'legal' paid work such as recycling (HopeHIV 2009). Heymann *et al.* (2007), in a study on extended family caring for children orphaned by AIDS, found that these care-givers spent fewer hours care-giving to their own children and other family members. Twenty five per cent reported having to take unpaid leave to meet such sick children's needs. Families help to provide adequate care but, for orphans and households headed by orphans, there are particular challenges in surviving economically. Increased levels of social supports and improvements in working conditions can help, but are often difficult to gain.

In affluent countries, there is increased attention to care of the elderly but, despite documented trends to lower fertility rates, increasing longevity and solo living, the idea that combining caring and working is about managing childcare continues to dominate. Such images and ideas limit the potential for recognising, debating and responding to the myriad ways in which we engage with caring and working over our lives. Across industrialised and post-industrial societies, solo living is on the increase. For example, as a result of longevity, divorce, separation and personal choice, a third of households in the UK are single-person, 14% of whom are of pensionable age (Office of National Statistics 2003). This compares with 26% of households being single-person in the USA (USA Census Bureau 2003) and 17% of African-headed households in South Africa (South African Census 2001). As we have suggested in Chapter 5, single people may be closely involved with caring for or being cared for by friends or relatives who do not live with them.

Across the globe, engagement in any form of employment is predicated on informal care work; my partner might make sure I eat regularly or have clean clothes to wear so that I am fit, well and presentable when I go to work; my work colleague might offer me emotional and practical help when I confide in her the bullying I have had from my manager. In any working day, people engage in care relations and this can incorporate formal and informal forms of care, and bring people into contact with a range of organisational policies and procedures. For example:

- A clerical worker may telephone his elderly mother in the middle of the day to check that all is well, confirm that paid care workers came in earlier in the day to bathe and dress her, and that the formal care was acceptable. Company policy states that mobile phones should be switched off and personal calls made at break times. This worker has been anxious all morning waiting for an appropriate time to step out of the office to make this call.

- The head of the marketing department takes time to have a coffee with a colleague who is separating from her husband. She offers her colleague practical and emotional support. As a consequence, the head of marketing calls home to say that she will be late. There are work tasks that she couldn't get round to and must complete before going home. Time to care for a colleague has implications for herself and her family. Her late arrival home irritates her partner and children, but when she explains the circumstances they all express sympathy.

Over the last century, governments across the world have created health, welfare and education services and benefits, although in many cases only minimal welfare services are available. Services and benefits differ between countries on the basis of history, culture and resources. Nevertheless, there are common features that include policies based on families/households formed around an adult heterosexual partnership with the male in full-time employment and the woman a carer and nurturer, possibly engaged in part-time work, but with caring for others as a priority. Many families and households do not equate to this model; whether in downtown Los Angeles or downtown Johannesburg, the luxury of a mother devoted to full-time family care is rarely achieved, even if desired. In more agrarian societies, childcare and livelihood work is likely to be managed concurrently, especially when welfare benefits are absent. In these cases, as mentioned above, it is not unusual for children, at an early age, to be drawn into both formal work as well as care for siblings (White 2002, Kielland and Tovo 2006, Lloyd-Evans 2008).

As discussed in Chapter 2, the notion of independence tends to be seen as an ideal state of being in post-industrial societies, is often highly individualised and has intensified in recent decades. The growth in consumer societies has led to increased living costs and, by the 1970s, most Western households needed two wages to ensure what was considered to be a 'reasonable' standard of living. Consumerism and consumption patterns promoted material goods as essential to socio-economic status and well-being. This, coupled with welfare systems that offered better long-term benefits to those in employment than to those not in paid work, has resulted in a de-valuation of care, informal carers and paid care work. Ironically, the same outcome can be found in those countries that provide little in the way of welfare, with informal care unpaid and subsumed within a feminised, undervalued home setting. Cost containment has been a key motivator for governments in addressing formal and informal types of care. What has become known as the nuclear family continues to dominate economic and welfare policies and service developments, including, where they are available, education, housing, social security, health and social care (Carling *et al.* 2002).

Paid work: Old concerns, new perspectives

Interdependence, although critical to human flourishing, is opaque, assumed, de-valued and predicated on the sacrifices of some, mostly women, for others – largely, children, elders and partners (Groenhout 2004). As discussed earlier, many Western governments have developed welfare state regimes to support the smooth-running of economies. Welfare state regimes were established to aid workers plan for retirement, periods of illness and ensure a minimum level of support for dependants. The EU, for example, has implemented a range of strategies and services to support adults to engage in paid work, including education and training and social security (Saraceno, 2008). Mutual dependency among countries, across free-market economies, has grown, supported by supranational organisations such as the IMF and World Bank. Welfare state regimes and economic prosperity impact on consumption and consumerism. In some countries awareness that health care or education is available at no or relatively low costs has encouraged households to spend more on consumer goods and services and thus enhanced economic growth.

In recent years, migrant workers have become crucial to plugging care gaps in – usually wealthy – countries and, in so doing, plug the economic welfare gaps in the countries that they leave behind. For example, workers from the Philippines help to underpin care services in a number of economies (Arab states, the EU, other Asian countries), but the Philippines' own informal care sector is also highly dependent on income that is sent home by migrant workers (Parrenas 2005). Patterns of migration are subject to change, and at a pace that makes the moulding of caring and working hard to manage. One recent example is the movement of workers across Europe from east to west on the accession of countries such as Poland and Bulgaria to the EU. When recession hit countries in the north and west of the EU, many of the new migrants chose to return home: the economic advantages of migrating had evaporated. Many of these migrant workers were employed in care jobs – work that local people could not or would not undertake (Galgóczi *et al.* 2009).

Changes in economies since the 1950s have led to changes in production. There has been a shift to service work in the West (Peck and Wai-chung Yeung 2005) and a new international division of labour that has encouraged the growth of manufacturing in poorer countries as well as the growth of migrant labour (Castree *et al.* 2003). These shifts have led to changes in the gendering and racialisation of paid work in different ways in different countries. Such trends have led to new challenges for the provision of formal care and combining informal care with paid work. In the West, given the costs of welfare services (not least of which is education) and competition from economies in which labour is cheaper, the EU and other post-industrial countries emphasise knowledge as a competitive component in an era of global markets. Rodrigies (2004) defined the 'knowledge economy' as economic activity that emphasises information, ideas and the potential for innovation. Knowledge industries include information technologies, finance and banking, health, education, and research and development; in fact, any sector in which information and ideas are prized and developed across all levels of education. This drive towards the knowledge economy has led to pressure for improvements in educational performance. Interestingly, this may be working in favour of women's employment as, in many EU countries, more young women than men are entering university, intending to train for professional employment, which is generally paid above the average and imperative to the knowledge industries and economies (Saraceno, 2008).

Post-industrial societies are not alone in this shift to knowledge-based economies. Many Asian countries (e.g. India, China) have made or started to make similar shifts and others, it could be argued, have been in the vanguard (in some aspects, for example, information technology) for a number of years (e.g. Japan, Korea). The movement to a knowledge-based economy driven by supranational organisations such as the EU and World Bank, and promoted by the higher education sector globally, may or may not lead to high-paid knowledge work. An increasing number of graduates may find themselves working in low-paid, insecure jobs, as there are not the available posts in the professional jobs and knowledge industries for graduates. These varied changes will impact on incomes and pensions, and thus care practices and services, highlighting the global inter-connections of economies and work opportunities.

In other parts of the world, poverty, debt, corruption, civil conflict or natural disasters have had an impact on economic development and opportunities for paid work (Edgell 2005, Parrenas 2005). In S-SA, the migration of rural workers (many in the face of the impact of the aforementioned problems) to cities and towns, both within and outside of their own countries, has left behind an often impoverished countryside, with the old, young and infirm having to redefine both their work and care expectations and roles. But more than that, Adepoju (2008: 1), writing about female migrants in S-SA, points to a change in migration where 'a significant share of these women is made up of migrants who move independently to fulfil their own economic needs: they are not simply joining a husband or other family member.' He goes on to point out that the gendered divisions of family labour are breaking down, especially in rural areas where the lack of traditional male labour in rural areas has meant new roles emerging for women, '… many families came to rely on women and their farming activities for day to day support. These women became the de-facto resource managers and decision-makers …' Furthermore, educated women are seeking positions abroad rather than working at home: for example, nurses and doctors being recruited from Nigeria to work in Saudi Arabia (Adepoju 2008).

We said earlier that images of paid work that bring to mind an adult male working full-time with a partner, children and possibly other relatives or friends to support, have been challenged and even overturned in most work sectors in post-industrial countries. Nevertheless, the feminisation of some professions, the segregation of women and men in different sectors of the economy, and the lower rates of pay for women, is evidence of an ongoing gender inequality and inequity in the workplace. In less prosperous countries, many women struggle to ensure personal and family livelihoods in situations in which they bear the major burden of informal care but still have fewer political and legal rights than men. We argue, along with others, that perceived and actual female obligations associated with formal and informal care work underpin such inequalities (Himmelweit and Land 2008). In capitalist market economies, caring skills have a low wage rate placed on them, even though formal health, welfare and social services are highly dependent on such skills. In other transitional or agrarian economies, caring skills are also required, demanded, yet still undervalued in terms of social status and political power. Cultural contexts and beliefs have an impact too and, in many African, Chinese and Asian communities, there are more deeply held notions of cross-generational support for young and old. However, in many areas, the traditions and necessities of working away from home constrain 'care' to the remote – that is, financial support and others provide the immediate practical tasks and offer emotional support (Adepoju 2008, Parrenas 2005). The growth of free-market economies, with the focus on engagement in paid work, places tensions on presumptions to care, and many who want to care for relatives and friends find that they can no longer do so while others may be making active decisions not to do so. Traditional values and networks do adapt, but current changes suggest that informal care networks will be strained, with those needing care having to resort to statutory or charitable support. Stigma and negativity may impact on those in receipt of such care, as well as those who could not offer informal/familial care (Sullivan and Lewis 2001).

Paid care work

Although this book is about informal care, we have made it clear that formal and informal care inter-weave and that informal carers often depend on care services and paid care workers, as well as the reverse. Paid care work includes nursing and allied professions, social and personal care assistants, nursery and after-school care services. The carer and cared-for forge knowledge of each other and create emotional ties (Qureshi 1990). These range from shared joy at progress, appreciation for each other as people, to concern and anxiety over care situations, to frustration and, sometimes, anger over perceived behaviours.

In the UK, four out of five paid carers are women and, in the USA, 89% of direct care workers (e.g. personal care assistants, health care aides, home care aides) are women (Smith and Baughman 2007). Figures from the UK 2001 census illuminate trends in unpaid care related to ethnicity. The White Irish, Bangladeshi, Pakistani and White British groups had the highest rates of caring, spending 50 hours a week or more in the role of caring. Indian, Pakistani, Bangladeshi and Other Asian groups had the second highest rates, spending 20–49 hours a week caring. These figures reflect the combination of cultural mores, the proportion in older age groups and the relative health status (National Statistics 2005). There is no figure for gender and care in S-SA and the closest that can be found is for those who work in community and personal services in South Africa; 48% are male and two-thirds of all employees in this category are Black African (Statistics South Africa 2006). The gendered and racialised nature of employment, still premised on assumptions about the 'naturalness' of femininities and care skills, is mirrored across the world.

Education, employment and formal/informal care policies and services continue to reflect and reinforce the gendered nature of paid care work (Himmelweit and Land 2008). Although there are initiatives to promote jobs and careers in the care sector to boys and men, low pay, poor employment conditions (often on temporary or fixed-term contracts) and the intense nature of the work (physical and emotional), have done little to promote paid care work as a chosen (male) employment option. Lupton (2006: 120) explored why some men enter what he termed 'female-concentrated occupations' – that is, occupations that are overwhelmingly associated with some form of care work or care relationship. He found a confluence of gender and social class. Men were aware of the challenges to their identity by working in female-concentrated work, but took up work opportunities as these could offer potential for mobility and security. Working-class men were disproportionately found in lower-status jobs mainly occupied by women. In this context, middle-class men may be able to 'escape less-valued occupations on account of the advantages of their gender' and move upwards in a company, whereas working-class men may not 'realise this advantage' because of the confluence of social class and gender (Lupton 2006: 122). The search for work among those with limited opportunities appears to lead men from working-class backgrounds into female-concentrated, generally low-paid, occupations. Thus, paid care work continues to have highly gendered images, with men taking up paid work in care only when other employment commonly associated with masculinity is not readily available.

Women who are both paid and unpaid carers face a double jeopardy in terms of current and future opportunities and income. Interdependency among members of families, communities and workplaces 'devalues care and imposes severe economic costs on the (mostly) women who provide it' (Himmelweit and Land 2008: 2), not least of which is low income post-retirement. Indeed, the UK governmental enquiry, Valuing and Supporting Carers (House of Commons Work and Pensions Committee 2008: 11), concluded that most informal carers are of working age but experience a range of 'opportunity penalties' in relation to engagement in paid work. As the participation of women in labour markets increases, and all workers seek to maximise pay and conditions, a double deficit is evolving – namely, of not enough paid care workers, *or* relatives and friends to provide care. Add to this those caring for children and providing informal care on a short-term basis for another adult at home and in the workplace, and the implications of informal care work are dramatic. The consequences of these trends are to place ever greater pressures on all those – male and female, young and old – who are in need of care or trying to combine working and caring. Indeed, the conclusions of the European Family Care project's Pan-European report called for 'The development of comprehensive labour market policies to include 'caring as a lifetime resource' within the context of reconciling work and family life. e.g. part-time work for both men and women with full pension and insurance credits for specified periods of time devoted to the care of children, dependent adults and older dependents' (Mestheneous and Triantafillou 2005).

Markets in care

The promotion of the concept of 'choice' in care services in many Western countries has resulted in the development of a mixed economy (private, third and public sectors) in care services. A long-term shift to market-orientated provision, within the broad orbit of welfare states, has grown over the past 20 years. For example, in the UK, about 70% of social and personal care is provided by private sector companies, mostly small to medium enterprises, and these are businesses that need to make a profit to survive. Given that 80% of the costs for these companies are salaries, the wages for care workers are constantly under review. It is in this context that migrants with limited or no employment rights provide a potentially tempting pool of low-cost workers for care providers. However, such a switch in labour provision has implications for the experience of care, in that language, cultural, age and gender differences are factors in establishing care relationships and negotiating caring and working among families, friends, informal and formal care services. For example, an older person with limited hearing may find it hard to understand a carer for whom English is a second language and who therefore speaks with an unfamiliar cadence. In the USA, the Office of Minority Health have produced National Standards for Culturally and Linguistically Appropriate Services in Health Care (US Department of Health and Human Services 2001). Following on from this, Talamantes and Aranda (2004: 17) drew attention to the importance of cultural competency in the provision of all types of care: 'As the caregiving community continues to grow nationwide, the diversity of caregivers and caregiving needs and situations will also expand. The better informed and prepared that providers are to address caregivers' needs from a socio-cultural perspective, the more likely we will be able to see more favourable outcomes in service provision.'

In developed economies, the growth in private sector provision of care was, in part, a result of financial constraints imposed by cuts in resources by most governments in the EU, North America, Australasia and Latin America. The outsourcing of care services from the public to private sector has helped to limit costs for governments, but increased the costs to service users who are often asked to pay in full or part for formal care, and also created a mixed economy of care. By contrast, in developing economies, private sector care services are often established as part of donor aid programmes. Public sector provision is limited, as neo-liberal theories of development through free-market trade encourage minimal state service development. Across the world, the provision of care services by not-for-profit organisations is on the increase. More commonly referred to as charities, voluntary sector or the Third Sector organisations, they may be based on philanthropic, political, social or religious beliefs. Third sector organisations may also ration service provision, in part due to finite resources but also, sometimes, due to their mission, which may favour a particular group or community.

Some providers draw from political theories, which prize choice in markets as a method of aiding user involvement, user responsibility and confidence. User involvement is about the participation of people with an interest or role in a service.

Choice, many assert, allows both the cared-for and the carer to have control over shaping the provision of care. A market in care services has led to debates on the quality and regulation of formal care services. Some commentators and users consider the private sector better able to deliver 'quality' care, whereas others are suspicious of the profit motive when associated with caring for vulnerable people. Related debates on public and third sector provision are peppered with questions, such as: are care services run for the user or to suit service providers? One response to these questions has been the introduction of what are known in the UK as Individual Care Budgets. The idea behind individual budgets is that people who need social care and associated services have the power to decide the nature of the services they need and to pay for these direct. Similar schemes are in evidence across the EU and states of the USA, often promoted by social movements such as disability rights group. This can provide freedom from the emotional pressures of informal care and offer independence and autonomy to people in need of care who can be abused and patronised. Individual Care Budgets are not without problems. Those in need of care may not wish to have the responsibility that goes with direct payment and the level of payment available is low. For governments and service providers, however, this can help to lessen pressures in public sector services, although it does require a system of monitoring to ensure quality control and a regular audit of budgets (Watson *et al.* 2004, Bondi 2008).

Regardless of how formal care is sourced and financed, informal carers are active in the care market as negotiators of care packages for dependants, or part-providers of those 'packages'. However, care packages or care task lists prescribe the content and time of personal care work, thus allowing limited opportunity for the day-to-day readjustment of care and the provision of emotional care. Crucially, this inflexibility may also constrain the ability of informal carers to access paid work at all or may dictate the type of paid work that can be accessed – for example, it may be limited to certain hours per day or certain days in the week. Given the importance of external work not just in the economic sense but in the sense of social participation and support, the informal carer who wants to maintain an external work presence can, in effect, become trapped by the terms of the delivery of the care package rather than supported and liberated. Although care packages are most readily associated with personal home care for the elderly or chronically sick, other professional groups (for example, nurses, podiatrists, residential home staff, social workers) have work-based competencies, content guides and schedules that promote particular methods of, and timing for, the delivery of care. Getting through delivering the relevant bits of care packages in the time allotted may be driving formal care delivery, but that (we might argue) is a commonality between providing informal and formal care in today's working society – care has its time-slots.

The development of markets in formal, paid care work has an effect on both employment in care work but also on how people can stitch together the patchwork quilt of formal and informal care for family, friends or work colleagues. Market-style mechanisms are promoted as effective ways to redress the balance of power between providers, service users and informal carers, but they are no guarantees of real value for money and high-quality care.

Care in the workplace

Care is evident in many employee-focused policies and practices in the workplace. A manager may use flexible working policies and procedures to address the work difficulties of a colleague who is about to take on sole custody of children following separation. A trade union representative may alert another worker, who is voicing concerns about the behaviour of a fellow worker, to company policies and union advice on bullying and grievance procedures. So, in many different ways, care is produced by and defined through policies to support workers. We now briefly explore whether and how policies to provide flexible working and workers' desire to control work time operate to facilitate WCA.

Flexible working

The major emphasis in workplace policies and practices in Western economies has been on work-*family* articulation. This includes maternity and parental leave and flexible working. Legislation offers rights to maternity and paternity leave in most countries and, although this can be complex to follow, and result in lowered incomes during the leave period, there are minimum rights. Access to flexible working, however, is less clear. Here, we use the example of UK legislation on flexible working to examine how policies concerned with WCA link to practices of care (Office of Public Sector Information 2009). Common practices can include:

- Part-time: working less than the standard full-time hours
- Flexi-time: negotiating the hours to work each day or week to enable non-work responsibilities and activities
- Annualised hours: hours are agreed and worked over the year
- Compressed hours: working your agreed hours over fewer days
- Staggered hours: different starting, break and finishing times for employees in the same workplace. Often, these patterns can be negotiated among colleagues
- Job sharing: the working hours and task of one post shared among two people
- Working from a location other than the office.

This list is not exhaustive and varied types of flexible working may be combined. In the case of the UK, anyone can ask their employer for flexible work arrangements, but the law provides some employees with the statutory *right* to request a flexible working pattern. Employees (but not agency workers or those in the armed forces) who have worked for an employer for 26 weeks continuously before applying, have the statutory right to ask this if they:

- Have a child under 16 years or a disabled child under 18 years who receives Disability Living Allowance

- Are responsible for the child as a parent/guardian/special guardian/foster parent/private foster carer or as the holder of a residence order
- Are the spouse, partner or civil partner of one of these and are applying to care for the child
- Are a carer who cares, or expects to be caring, for an adult who is a spouse, partner, civil partner or relative; or who, although not related to you, lives at the same address as you.

Under the law, an employer must seriously consider any application, but these can be rejected if there is what are termed 'good business reasons' for doing so.

In most economies, women workers continue to be the group most likely to apply for, and be granted, flexible working. Policies and practices can both create and re-enforce gender and age ideas about caring and working. This is not to say that men do not wish to care (albeit their engagement in care is less than that of women), but access to 'care' policies can be restricted by social, cultural and organisational norms (Brandth and Kvande 2002, Lupton 2006).

These issues were highlighted in a research project, involving two of the authors, in which flexible working policies and practices in a range of workplaces were examined.[4] Interviews were conducted in 2008, with 87 workers, who were employed in 15 different organisations. Themes in the data illuminated how the processes of requesting, negotiating and managing flexible working were largely individualised and framed by the nature of the relationship between employee and line manager. In the following paragraphs, we use excerpts from interviews to illustrate employee perceptions and experiences of policies of flexible working.

Interviewees were consistent in noting that the 'onus was on management to grant flexible working, and staff to justify the request and account for the implications for others' (quote from Jane, in her 40s, voluntary sector organisation). Requests that involved women with care responsibilities for children and older relatives were said to be 'favoured' (quote from John, in his 30s, IT company) and rarely denied. There was an obligation, it was suggested, for employers to recognise the gendered nature of caring. This recognition, however, could have drawbacks as managers and colleagues expressed frustrations at the everyday implications. These could include additional work load and responsibilities for colleagues and scheduling issues for managers trying to provide, for example, a service for customers over a specified period of the day or week. Workers who did not project the classic image of apologetic embarrassment for the request could find themselves being refused, suggesting some stereotyping in terms of request and response.

What interviewees termed 'presentism' (the focus upon being present in the workplace) dominates working patterns despite the growth in home and remote working. This brings its own pressures for informal carers who may need to work from home (or part-time at a location) as their only option to participate in employment. For example, someone working from home, regardless of their informal care responsibilities, may be viewed with suspicion (are they really doing as much as we are in the office?) and envy (I'd love to work in a more relaxed way and not have to trail into work). 'Presentism' also means being part of the visible day-to-day 'working club' of employees, with all the rights and responsibilities of that club, including the possibility of offering support to other workers and being offered such support in adversity. But, like all clubs, there is a limit or tipping point in relation to the minimum 'presence' required to be a recognised and valued member. A danger of 'Presentism' is that it can marginalise and devalue informal carers' contributions to work.

Reciprocity and trust were cited as 'important components of successful flexible working practices' (quote from Mary, in her 30s, banking), but the focus on the relationship between worker and line manager can result in allegations of favouritism and the naming of people as 'good workers going along with what management say' or 'sucking up and being too friendly' (quote from Peter, in his 50s, public sector). Economic downturn has affected attitudes towards flexible working, with many of the employees interviewed noting an increased reluctance on the part of themselves or others to request a change in work patterns. People are concerned about job security and keen to remain part of the 'working club'. As a consequence, the organisation of care among family and friends, and the payment for care by formal services, will have enhanced relevance to the daily juggling of caring and working. In this research project, business needs were spoken of 'as paramount', which may reflect the tendency for the power imbalance between the carer/worker and the line manager to shift towards management in times of economic restraint. Interviewees in this project knew of and had experience or witnessed the use of flexible working policies. Some people, however, avoid using policies and it is to the experiences of this group of workers we now turn.

Controlling work time to aid work–care articulation

Across the world, the food retail sector is a major employer of women. Many of these jobs are low-paid and part-time but are favoured by workers who need to, or would like to, work near to home. The association of women with food provision in households, service sector and care work more generally, reinforces gender segregation in employment (Edgell 2005). Women are moulding their paid work around caring responsibilities: for example, being close to children and relatives can be a factor in the choice of job and workplace.

Women working in low-paid, part-time jobs in the food retail sector should be an obvious group of workers keen to request flexible working but, in recent research, this presumption has been challenged[5] (Backett-Milburn *et al.* 2008). Data demonstrated that women valued the ability to retain control over their existing work time and patterns. For example, rather than opt to change to flexible working patterns, they would rather negotiate a swap of shifts with colleagues. Women did not walk out of their workplace in order to accommodate caring responsibilities, unless it was an emergency. Personal control over working time was a key goal and, as a consequence, some women resisted promotion to roles with increased responsibilities that might jeopardise that element of control. For low-paid women, there was a trade-off between meeting care responsibilities, deriving income to aid household budgets and retaining the ability to be flexible with working time.

The articulation of work and care was different, however, for those working in supervisory grades. There was a general expectation for them to work flexibly to suit the needs of the business, simply because of their designation. For example, supervisors considered themselves responsible for staffing shops and ensuring that opening hours were met, and they spoke graphically of the day-to-day implications for their family life of having to cover shifts at short notice. They found it more challenging than shop workers to assimilate the domains of work and home. However, they were quite clear on the gains they personally made by taking this level of job: interestingly, increased monetary gain was rarely mentioned as a motivator – most had chosen the added responsibility to fulfill an identity 'gap' in their lives, such as children leaving home, a need for stimulation, to provide an additional social outlet or an escape from care responsibilities.

> No, I definitely won't give up my job. I am not giving up anything else for nobody and that's including my mother. I know it might sound selfish but I have done a lot and I am not doing it again. Me and my husband is my priority and I like my job.
>
> (Supervisor, female, aged 47 years)

In summary, jobs within the food retail sector are an example of work that is relatively fluid and perceived to be adaptable to women's lives. For many, their current job was secondary to family life. Being and remaining a shop worker was an 'active choice'.

Workplaces as part of care networks: The case of HIV/AIDS

In some countries, the advent of HIV/AIDS has triggered a new type of care within workplaces, albeit one borne largely out of economic necessity. The diminution or loss of labour through workers' illness will reduce the profitability of businesses. Initial reactions to what was happening in, for example, parts of the USA, was to protect the business by discriminatory practices such as pre-employment health screening, denying training opportunities, reassigning workers, limiting promotion opportunities, and simply dismissing HIV-positive workers regardless of their current ability to do the work (ILO 2007: 11). However, the almost overwhelming reality of how HIV/AIDS permeated some societies, and communities, and therefore the available and future workforce, is forcing employers to recognise the interconnected nature of work and wider society.

Employers have now become actively involved in trying to secure their workforce as a productive entity and employers' organisations have become an active part of creating work-related strategic plans. First, at the macro level, through organisational collaboration – such as the Central and West African Strategic Plan led by the Cameroon Employers Organisation, but including International Labour Organization, International Organisation of Employers, the Pan African Employers Confederation, Joint United Nations Programme on Aids and Groupement Inter-Patronal du Cameroon. The focus includes organising counselling for those affected and protecting the rights of those affected. Second, through enterprise-level interventions such as SHARE (a Saving Lives, Protecting Jobs initiative), where 15 enterprises in Ethiopia have developed HIV/AIDS workplace policies including focal points, where people within the enterprise can go to, and a committee to run various programmes, including peer education. Supportive environments are the new work mechanisms.

Trades Unions are also developing care initiatives to both educate and support the workforce through a new concept of 'teacher unions'. For example, the International Federation of Chemical, Energy, Mine and General Workers Union has a project in the mining industry of Ethiopia to educate union leaders and activists about HIV/AIDS and, through them, to promote greater awareness and lead prevention campaigns in the workplace and mining communities (ICEM 2009). ICEM recognises the need to reduce the stigma and discrimination among high-risk but economically valuable workers, and the need to negotiate agreements with employers and thus protect workers and families and the wider community.

Individual workers are also recognising the need to take their own action to protect their abilities to care for themselves and families in a work environment where social protection schemes such as health insurance are not the norm. In the Democratic Republic of Congo (DRC), teachers at one Catholic school, struggling to pay for family health care at times of illness, got together to form an association whereby people would pay into a fund that could then be drawn upon in times of need to access health care (and, importantly, good-quality health care). With the help of the Africa ILO office, what was a simple and very localised scheme has now extended to other teaching networks in DRC and influenced the creation of a National Programme for the Promotion of Health Associations (ILO 2007).

Our different examples show how care has become a vehicle for economic survival, be it the employer trying to maintain a productive workforce, or the trade union trying to educate and protect workers or workers protecting themselves. Care within and through work is no longer an optional extra in these circumstances; it is becoming a central part of learning to live and work in the shadow of HIV/AIDS.

Informal care in the workplace

So far, we have talked about policies to allow workers to exchange informal care with people outside the workplace in the home or in the community. But it is also the case that workers may provide informal care for one another. Caring practices have always taken place in work. Colleagues may help one another out or show concern for one another in a wide variety of ways. In workplaces, repeated social exchanges offer the opportunity for emotional interactions and these seemingly minor acts of care can help to ease the experience of paid work. The absence of these interactions can create an unhappy and stressed environment. Through such minor acts of care as volunteering information, noticing a fellow worker's mood and offering sympathy, finding ways to improve communication and creating loyalties and a myriad of other thoughtful actions, caring spaces can be created in the workplace.

A variety of researchers have shown the significance of friendship to work relations both in gaining a job and to the everyday interactions within the workplace (Pollert 1981, Cavendish 1982, Westwood 1984, Marshall 1986, Stephenson and Stewart 2001). Friendships may also draw on or create relationships outside work. For example, Pettinger (2005: 46) discusses how friendships between workers in a retail store drew on family relationships, as well as 'age, gender, position in the workplace hierarchy and membership of particular departments'. These friendships helped people to work together as a team, involved the exchange of confidences and provided emotional support. Although Pettinger (2005) concludes that these relationships were not always positive (sometimes involving back biting, ill-natured gossip and even violence), they did, in general, facilitate the day-to-day process of working and sometimes provided important emotional support.

Box 6.2 Supporting a Colleague at a Time of Bereavement: Orange Country, California, USA

In Orange County, Nancy, John's carer, learns that the mother of a colleague has died. She calls John to say she will be late in arriving at his home as she wants to see Rita first. The manager of the care agency is with Rita when Nancy arrives, talking about Rita's request for time off to go to the funeral in Mexico. This will require the re-allocation of work and Nancy willingly offers to help. Rita had become more than a colleague, a friend, and one who would do the same for her in these circumstances. Over the last year, they have helped one another out at work a few times and shared their feelings about the hardships of their lives. However, Nancy is wary of the manager who she feels is suspicious that she is giving 'extra' care to John. There is always pressure in the home to increase the amount of work done for each client in the time allotted and Jayne, the manager, is ever-vigilant about keeping costs down. While she is pleased when clients are happy, she is opposed to workers becoming too close to their clients – she says it is bad to get involved and 'only leads to trouble'. Nancy does not agree, but she fears Jayne as she knows that Jayne is well aware that her papers are dubious. Nothing has been said but they both know that Nancy is vulnerable. So she is anxious on both grounds of friendship and fear to oblige over Rita's absence.

Of course, there is an up side – she will earn some extra money to send home and that is always welcome. Nevertheless, she will be very busy while Rita is away – she will have to do evening as well as day shifts, as well as a couple of night shifts in the nursing home attached to the complex. She hates working there – she only does it occasionally and the regular staff look down on 'interlopers' such as herself – they make sure they get the hardest work. Many of them are qualified nurses and some of them seem to dislike Mexican Americans such as herself – she has overheard some remarks about *wet-backs* and *border bunnies* about the cleaners who work there, which she found quite upsetting. She is sure they say similar things about herself but she dare not complain – she does not want to be known as a trouble-maker and she does not want to draw attention to herself.

After the meeting with Rita, she goes over to work at John's apartment. He is pleased to see her and wants to chat, but she explains she has to rush off. He is not happy when she tells him that she will be doing a lot of extra work over the next

> few days and won't be able to spend much time with him. She hopes he won't complain – that would draw attention to the fact that she does spend more time than she is supposed to looking after him. But she is keen to support Rita and has to make it clear to John that Rita's need is the greatest at the moment.

The people scenario in Box 6.2 illustrates the importance of friendship in the workplace. It also considers the intensification and regulation of care work to contain costs, combined with the problems of the insecure legal status of migrant workers. Racism in the workplace, combined with the conflicting demands of care for a workplace friend and care for a client, make Nancy's choice of what to do seem complex but support for her friend is prioritised. Workplaces also do not exist in isolation from the wider social, economic and political contexts in a country or multi-national company. As Halford and Leonard (2006: 74–75) put it: 'workplaces are highly specific yet this specificity is wrought from social, cultural and economic processes operating at global and national [scales] as well as in the locale'. A long-established body of literature has shown how workplace relationships interact with local life outside paid work. For example, at one extreme, in their classic study *Coal is our Life* (1969), Dennis *et al.* show how a gender-segregated pattern of friendship and domestic work outside the mine was tied to the exigencies of the masculinised mining labour process. Although this may be a highly particular example, it serves to remind us that gendered expectations of caring, linked to ideas of family and home, can be reinforced or developed in the workplace and also brought into the workplace. The example we have given above of how female workers in a retail store informally swapped shifts in order to allow each other to respond to domestic caring demands is perhaps a more commonplace occurrence (Backett-Milburn *et al.* 2008). Here, care for one another took place on the shop floor and workplace relationships (rather than policies) facilitated care outside it.

In low-income countries, workplaces for many people are either their own small-holdings or farms or plantations. They may also be what are termed sweatshops, where there is minimal or no employment rights and very low pay, or factories in which Health and Safety and Human Resource policies are minimal (Castree *et al.* 2003, Momsen 1991). Moreover, in low-income countries, it is estimated that about 80% of employment is in the informal sector and that the informal sector accounts for 40–60% of urban employment (Castree *et al.* 2003: 226). Informal labour is work that is conducted outside the 'formal economy', such as 'unpaid work in family businesses, paid work where the worker has no fixed employer, and paid work where the employer evades the rules and regulations of normal economic activity' (Castree *et al.* 2003: 226). Such informal work is often enmeshed in family relationships and gendered social and spatial practices. For example, the location and nature of the activities of street traders and scavengers are often differentiated by gender and sometimes also by ethnicity (Lloyd-Evans and Potter 1998, Momsen 1991). In her study of women's employment in garment production in Ecuador, Lawson notes how men's work is largely formal and situated away from the home, whereas women's work is in the 'informal sector' and carried out at home. For men, success in paid work was seen as an individual achievement; for many of the women, paid work was 'defined primarily in terms of family and their duty and responsibility to support siblings, parents, and husbands through paid work that does not interfere with their domestic roles' (Lawson 1999: 221). Women thus understood their paid work in terms of caring roles and this simultaneously contributed to a weak position in the labour market but also 'Home for them, is a site where masculinist forms of power are overcome with a subversive domestic, mother focused politics that invokes the power of being central to the family' (Lawson 1999: 225).

In this section, we have shown how care in the workplace relates both to care exchanged with people within the workplace and people outside. It can be linked to formal policies, as in the case of flexible working; to juggling informal relationships at home and work, as in the case of the retail workers; to creating networks of care focused on the workplace, as in the case of HIV/AIDS in Africa; and to informal relationships with co-workers, which are often influenced by ideas of status and care relationships outside the workplace.

Box 6.3 Working Futures: Tanzania and New York

In New York, Ellen's daughter Lauren is thinking about her future. Her Mom has just come back from visiting her granddad and has spent a lot of time talking to her dad about how frail her granddad has become. Ellen is irritated because she is anxious to talk about going to college. They had had a session at high school 2 days ago to discuss going to college and she is feeling very enthusiastic about the possibilities. Of course, she doesn't really know what she will study – there is a year and a bit yet until she graduates from high school. She knows her parents are worried about the money it will cost for her and her brother to go to college. Her parents want them both to go to a State University, but she has set her heart on going to somewhere more exciting, perhaps Colorado – she is keen on skiing and snowboarding – or maybe California where her granddad lives. She wonders how much it will all cost – could she work at the same time and help pay her fees and living costs? She doesn't really know how much money is involved, or indeed how much money her parents earn. She is hoping she will be able to major in something to do with Business and Finance and get a well-paid job. She fancies a life in the centre of New York – not in the dreary suburb her family live in. She won't be like her parents, always seeming rushed and worried about work. She will live in New York and her parents will stay here, not like her granddad, they wouldn't want to go off and live far away, she thinks, they will stay where they are and she will visit them sometimes – she can't imagine them getting old though, they are in very good health, they will be around for ages.

In Tanzania, Joy is thinking about her future. How will she be able to earn some money to help out her grandmother and her brother and sister? She knows she has not done well enough at her school to be able to go secondary school. She has heard that the NGO in town has sponsored some young women to learn tailoring and dressmaking – that would be a good way of earning money – but she would have to get the finance to buy a sewing machine and she doesn't see how she will be able to manage that. Yesterday, Mary had had a letter from a relative in the city asking if Joy would be interested in coming to live with them and help with housework and looking after their children. They say they would pay her a small wage so, since they would feed and house her, she should be able to send money home to Mary. She knows this is probably what she will do but she is putting off making the final decision. It will be good to go and live in the city but she is not very hopeful about living with her relatives. She expects she will have to work hard and she doesn't know them, so has no idea whether they will be kind to her. It will be exciting to be back in the city where she lived with her mum, but she will miss her grandmother and Grace and Abel. But then, if she doesn't go she, won't be able to help them. But how will her grandmother manage without her help? Joy worries that her grandmother's health won't last for long – she seems tough, but Joy can see that she is finding the work on the smallholding more difficult than before. And Abel isn't big and strong enough to help with some of the tasks – and it is important he continues school. Joy is undecided, yet she knows she has few options if she is to help the family survive.

Ideas about working futures vary markedly across the globe. Although paid work is critical to both the lives and futures of Ellen and Joy, it has very different meanings and implications, given the context in which they reflect on working futures. In the concluding section, we explore how we might bring together these, and other seemingly diverse strands, within the framework of organisation carescapes.

Organisations, work and care

Our frameworks of caring and carescapes offer analytical possibilities for exploring informal care in and around employing organisations (McKie *et al.*, 2008). The employing organisation is a purposive entity in which policies and practices operate, and employers and employees can both 'care about' and 'care for' others. The caring done, however, through an employing organisation is a by-product of meeting the dominant goals of profit-making in the private sector or output goals in the public and third sector. Employing organisations generally put in place policies of 'care' in response to pressures from the state, the workforce, Trade Unions, professional organisations and government agencies, to enhance recruitment and retention. 'Moral' commitments may also be a factor – for example, the paternalist approach of many nineteenth-century employers, the principles adopted by some small independent employers and the avowed commitment to corporate social responsibility of some modern corporations. Such moral orientations, as well as state policies, employees' expectations and trade union and professional organisation demands will themselves be linked to the sorts of moral frameworks that are accepted in society at large and, in particular, to the value accorded to practices of caring for and caring about others. So, we can envisage employing organisations trying to realise particular aims and goals relating to 'caring' for their employees by actively selecting their paths through a map or a terrain that includes legislation, an economic context, company finances and goals, and the needs of employees as these shift with demographic trends. Once again, this 'map' will incorporate processes operating over a range of different temporalities and spatialities.

We can also explore the level of the individual employee. Here, whether we think about the situation of a manager, a secretary or a part-time shop-floor worker, the individual can be thought of facing a similar 'map' of caring possibilities to any individual informal carer. This map, however, will incorporate not only their personal caring obligations and expectations (for example, their need to care for an ageing mother or to be cared for by a partner), but also the caring obligations and expectations placed on them within the workplace. These overlapping domains are illustrated in Figure 6.1. The structure and practices of the employing organisation (its climate and culture) will form a central and changing context for planning, following and revising their caring 'routes'. Analysis of practices of care within organisations must focus both on interactions between the employing organisation and supranational organisations, the state, the labour market and civil society, as well as the individual worker and interactions between workers and the organisation.

The concept of organisation carescapes was developed to direct research to analysing the genesis and operation of formal 'care policies'; the implementation of policies and practices of care within the workplace; experiences of care within the workplace and their impact on care beyond the workplace; the organisation cultures and, in particular, its cultures of care.[6] Organisation carescapes are not static: thus the planned 'routes' of the employing organisation (policies and practices) must sometimes be changed or amended in response to shifts in public policies (e.g. the introduction of disability rights legislation, and flexible working guidelines) or changes in their labour market competitiveness. In addition, for individual employees, planned routes will change as a result of the actions of their employers or personal events such as the arrival of a child. Often, an event rather than a managed transition necessitates action by employers and workers. Adopting an organisation carescapes approach thus focuses attention on the following issues:

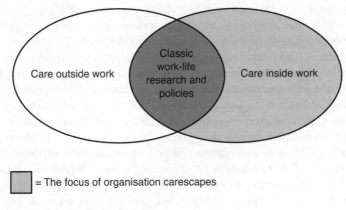

= The focus of organisation carescapes

Figure 6.1 Overlapping Spheres of Care.

- What are the formal 'care policies' of the employing organisation? That is, those policies that either demand caring behaviours of workers (e.g. mentoring, sharing tasks) or are designed to ensure the psychological and physical health and well-being of workers (e.g. bullying and harassment).
- How are policies implemented in practice? Do policies inform practices? If so, how? If not, why not?
- Who uses policies, how, when and why? Who holds discretion over their implementation and how do they make decisions on how policies are implemented?
- How do workers experience these policies and practices? Do they feel they treat workers fairly, are transparent and justifiable? How do they affect working practices and care outside the workplace?
- What types of informal care relationships are present in the workplace? Who benefits and who loses from them? How do they affect working practices and care outside the workplace?
- How do the above come together to create cultures of care in a particular employing organisation?

In the concluding chapter, we reflect on how the frameworks of caringscapes, carescapes and organisation carescapes can aid individuals, policy-makers and organisations in identifying and supporting informal care and WCA.

Summary

Paid work plays a prominent role in the lives of many people and, in this chapter, we have identified a number of ways in which paid work and care intertwine. In many countries and economies, paid work is critical to individual and familial identities but, at times, the tensions between informal care and paid work give rise to anxieties and stresses. Workers may care for co-workers or customers, for children, relatives and friends while holding down a job. Their representatives in a trade union, professional association or business organisation, as well as governments and supranational organisations, may be involved in developing policies to address such issues as workplace bullying, unsafe working practices and WCA, and so enhance the potential for safer, 'caring' workplaces.

Providing care services is also a growing source of employment as markets in care work are opened up. Formal and informal types of care, however, remain gendered. The practical and emotional skills associated with all types of care have a low status and attract low pay. Yet care work, formal and informal, is generally highly valued by those receiving, offering and giving care. The cared for, and carer, gain affirmation that enhances their human flourishing (Paul and Miller 1999). Early on in this chapter, we quoted Pile and Thrift's (1995: 29) comment that the experience of everyday lives is 'dependant to some degree on the immediate resources available to [*the person*] at the moment they show up in time and space' to draw attention to the fluid and dynamic ways that temporal and spatial perspectives collide. Thus, WCA is multi-faceted, takes place across the varied dimensions of time and space, inside and outside the workplace, with colleagues, managers, family members, relatives and neighbours. In the final chapter, we return to the analytical framework of caringscapes and explore how this, and the related concepts of carescapes and *organisational carescapes*, highlight the significance of time–space to the organisation and understanding of care relationships.

Notes

1 We would like to acknowledge and thank colleagues who have helped to inform and develop our ideas and research: Laura Airey, Kathryn Backett-Milburn, Fatima Malik, Jeff Hearn, Gill Hogg, Marjut Jyrkinen and Andrew Smith.

2 Household income may be defined as the combined income of all household members from all sources, including wages, commissions, bonuses, welfare benefits and other retirement benefits, unemployment compensation, disability, interest from bank accounts, dividends from investments and remittances from family members working away from home.

3 The two projects are: (1) Organisations Carescapes: Policies and Practices of Care in Business Organisations, *McKie, L., Bowlby, S., Hogg, G., Smith, A.* Economic and Social Research Council, 2005–2009; (2) Gender Related Work-life Balance and Well-being in Scottish Food Retail Businesses, *McKie, L., Backett-Milburn, K., Hogg, G. and Airey, L.* European Social Fund, 2003–2006. For further details, see www. organisationsworkandcare.org. Accessed 28 October 2009.

4 Organisations Carescapes: Policies and Practices of Care in Business Organisations, *McKie, L., Bowlby, S., Hogg, G., Smith, A.* Economic and Social Research Council, 2005–2009. All names of interviewees are pseudonyms.

5 Gender Related Work-Life Balance and Well-Being in Scottish Food Retail Businesses, *McKie, L., Backett-Milburn, K., Hogg, G. and Airey, L.* European Social Fund, 2003–2006.

6 The framework of organisation carescapes evolved through discussions with Jeff Hearn, Management and Organisation Studies, Hanken School of Economics, Helsinki. We are indebted to him. Gill Hogg, Department of Management and Languages was also critical to conceptual and research developments.

Part III

7 Visions of Care

Introduction

In this final chapter, we consider the potential application of caringscapes and carescapes in the arenas of research, policy-making and business. To set the scene for this task, we open with a résumé of key ideas and debates that were introduced in earlier chapters. At the outset of the book, we introduced our ideas on time and space, together with the frameworks of caringscapes and carescapes. We started by accepting the premise that caring interdependency is vital to human flourishing (Paul and Miller 1999, Groenhout 2004). Our understandings, practices and experiences of care change over time and space as we learn about care in a variety of relationships and settings over our lives. A contradiction was identified: informal care is vital to human flourishing but is often taken for granted and marginalised. Drawing on the philosophical, sociological and geographical work of Melucci (1996) and Adam (2000) on time, and that of Hagerstrand (1978), Giddens (1984) and Massey (2002) on space, we offered the notion of the terrain – the imagery of a landscape – one that shifts with changes in life possibilities. Our ideas of movement and flows in time and space provide the basis of the frameworks of:

- Caringscapes, which assume that an individual's practices and emotions of care are shaped and reshaped over the lifecourse, through the interplay of social processes operating in time and space; and
- Carescapes, which offer a wider focus on change; change in the policy and service contexts that impact on the doing of both formal and informal care. In carescapes, we again seek to analyse the ways in which such polices and services are shaped by particular time–space relationships and processes.

Thus, the caringscape framework offers an analytical focus on *individual* caring behaviours. This approach sees individual behaviours as influenced by the policy and service contexts – that is, the carescape within which they are situated. Individual caring practices, understandings, expectations and feelings will be altered in response to changes in the policy and service environment, but this environment is not the subject of analysis. The concept of carescapes was developed by us to allow movement from a focus on individual caring behaviours to analysis of the development and implementation of the range of formal and informal policies and services concerned with care. Carescapes encompass varied forms of informal and formal care and interdependences that inter-weave across relationships, organisations and settings, and over the lifecourse.

The 'doing of care' across the world and over time shows many similarities and yet differences. Family and household members, friendships, work and neighbourhood networks are important relationships through which we learn to care and live with care and practice individual caringscapes. In Part I, we emphasised that there are also differences in carescapes – important differences between communities and countries in the cultural, economic and social contexts for care; differences that are reflected in the historical evolution of welfare regimes. These differences, and their potential impact on individual caringscapes, were illustrated through the devices of our three Geographical Zones and our fictional People Scenarios. In Part I, we also explored key concepts relating to informal care. We examined understandings of informal care and the distinction between 'caring for' and 'caring about'. We drew attention to the importance of the social construction of the notions of 'dependence' and 'independence', of emotions and processes of reciprocity, and tacit negotiation in the practice of informal caring.

We discussed and used examples to illustrate the importance of time to caring throughout Part II. Key issues explored included: memories and anticipations of caring; exchanges of care between the generations; the need to organise caring activities through multiple temporalities; and the need to synchronise and order caring activities. We also emphasised the significance of space, place and spatial scale in shaping and reflecting caring behaviours using the examples of home, school and neighbourhood. Both time and space relationships were brought together to explore the importance of networks or chains of caring relationships outside the family. Finally, we examined the relationship between care and paid work – taking the opportunity to explore the significance of care polices within the workplace and to introduce the idea of 'organisation carescapes'. A crucial idea that we introduced is that informal care relationships are not confined to the spaces or times of 'home' and 'family' activities, but are found also at work and in relationships in the 'community'. Throughout both Part I and Part II, we noted gendered inequality in the social allocation of care tasks, although we also noted that age and ethnicity are important dimensions of inequities in (in)formal care practices.

In this final chapter, we take the opportunity to consolidate ideas and offer ways in which the linked frameworks of caring and carescapes might be used in research, policy and business practice. Caringscapes was developed a number of years ago and has generated debate on the spatial and temporal aspects of doing care among a range of audiences. Carescapes is a more recent development and lends itself to the analysis of policy and service perspectives. We have termed both of these linked frameworks because, to understand the impact of policies and services, you need an appreciation of individual caringscapes.

Past and present use of caringscapes and carescapes

We offered the frameworks of caringscapes and carescapes as analytical tools and, in recent years, these concepts have been adopted, adapted and critiqued by researchers working on varied themes and topics such as:

- Families, parenting and institutions

  1 Reflecting on motherhood as an activity (Maher 2005)
  2 Changing families, changing food (Fisher 2006)
  3 Parents and children working towards partnership (Crozier and Reay 2005)
  4 Care in post-divorce families (Haugen 2007)

- Paid employment and care work

  1 Risk in dual-earner and working lone-parent households (Sarre 2007)
  2 Confronting the challenges of work (Parry *et al.* 2005)
  3 Working patterns of employees without childcare responsibilities (Roberts 2004)
  4 Constructing health and sickness in the context of motherhood and paid work (Cunningham-Burley *et al.* 2006)

- Health and social care

  1 Understanding the reproduction of health care (Andrew and Evans 2008)
  2 Gendered nature of sleep disruption among couples with children (Venn *et al.* 2008)

- Ethics, relationships and citizenship

  1 Moral and ethical issues in geography (Barnett and Land 2007)
  2 Affective equality and love labour (Lynch 2007)
  3 Care as a key concept in social analysis (Philips 2007)

Although it is pleasing for academics to find their work having an impact on debate and research, a more important finding is that caringscapes is generally used to illuminate the multi-faceted nature of care practices and care relations in a range of settings. Thus, our focus on time–space dimensions has been recognised and is considered to be relevant in the broader analysis of care and social issues and problems. Each of the authors cited above is an academic and, although many are active in bridging the worlds of academia, policy and practice, their use of caringscapes varies; it is adopted and adapted as they consider relevant and justifiable. Carescapes has yet to be widely considered. For us, a challenge is how we would apply these overlapping frameworks and explore the various dimensions of doing care, experiencing care, and organising care across settings and relationships over time and space.

Let's talk about life

Within the book, the People Scenarios from the old and new Europe, the USA and S-SA illustrate similarities, differences, and change in care tasks and emotions. This device has allowed us to draw out the dynamic ways in which interdependencies and care inter-weave through time and space. One example is the scenario constructed around the character of John, a widow in his 80s, living thousands of miles away from his daughter, in a gated community in California. Nancy, an illegal migrant from Mexico, works as his carer. Over time, they became dependent on each other for emotional support. This led to mixed feelings among his children, especially his daughter who was relieved that John was experiencing good quality care but also felt guilty that she could not support her father in this way. In Chapter 6, we left John missing the amount of attention he usually receives from Nancy. She was rushing in and out while covering shifts for a friend who returned to Mexico for her mother's funeral.

A month on and Nancy has returned to Mexico. John has just heard she has decided not to return for the time being. On arrival home to attend a family wedding, Nancy found her son ill. His condition is curable but will take time to settle. She is worried about her son and upset about John. Her son needs her but how will John manage without her? John was easy to work for and they got on well but her son is the priority now. Thankfully, John sent a reference for Nancy, which helped her to find a part-time job near the family home. She is keen, however, to try and get back to the USA, as she knows she can earn much more there and the family will need all the income it can get to cover medical bills. Meanwhile, the manager of the agency that provides carers for the community that John lives in has contacted his daughter Ellen who lives in New York. She talks with Ellen about the options, including the potential that Nancy might return in a few months time.

In this scenario, the caringscape encompasses:

Current context

- Nancy is in Mexico where she is working.
- She was an illegal migrant to the USA.
- Nancy is keen to return as soon as she can to earn a higher salary.
- John lives thousands of miles from his children.
- Mobility problems mean care needs will increase.
- John has reasonable resources to pay for care.
- The care agency have people who can replace Nancy and meet immediate needs. But the agency manager and John's daughter know that he got a psychological boost from Nancy's visits.

Memories, anticipations and speculations

- John has seen many friends and neighbours put up with indifferent, even rude, carers.

- He wants someone who will talk to him as an adult with a brain and be interested in more than the required care tasks.
- Might Nancy return? She wants to, but is this wishful thinking on the part of them both?
- The care agency manger would like patterns of care to settle into a routine.
- Recruitment of workers and managing a change in carers is time-consuming and can be draining for all concerned.

The web of obligations between John and Nancy is evident. A practical example is the reference that John sent to help Nancy secure a job. Emotions are also evident as each express anxieties and wish to return to the previous working arrangements and friendship. Obligations are imbued with reciprocity and not just between Nancy and John. The manager of the care agency, and John's daughter Ellen, explore temporary solutions to care work, recognising how the formal provision of care was infused with the important informal aspects, which in the case of John and Nancy were thankfully positive and conducive to the well-being of all concerned. Such concerns also bring into play ethical concerns about the quality of care and how quality and costs may be balanced. In insurance-based health care systems, these debates can raise a range of cost concerns, not least of which is the anticipation of care needs and costs over an unknown period of time.

Carescape

Continuing with the analysis of John and Nancy's story, a **carescape** could be expressed as the following policy and service dimensions:

- The overarching policy context.
- Recognition of the emotional and practical needs of clients and workers.
- Management of care at a distance through informing workers and family members of clients.
- Assessment of current temporary care provision and/or temporary loss of care provision.
- Consideration of costs.
- Discussing and agreeing a plan.
- Ensuring that this is monitored and reviewed.

The points noted above offer a guide to possible approaches, questions and issues for research. Furthermore, carescapes is a framework that draws attention to the implementation and workings of policies and services. Although the caringscapes of both John and Nancy are focused around the topic of care support for John, the word 'policy' or examples of specific services are not cited above. Each issue raised, however, requires engagement with varied policies or services.

Moving forward ...

Keen to share our ideas, we have introduced and debated these 'core' frameworks with diverse audiences, including policy-makers and practitioners in business, health and social care, and third-sector organisations concerned with support for carers and the cared-for. So, what of more practical applications of caring and carescapes? The response from non-academics has ranged from interest, to bemusement, to bafflement. Policy-makers drawn from various types and sizes of organisations across the private, public and third sector have expressed interest in these frameworks and many have commented that reflecting on these has encouraged consideration of a broader range of evidence to inform policies and planning related to care practices and relationships. But the suggestion that caringscapes and carescapes might offer frameworks for analysis and longer term planning was met with surprise. Critics considered these frameworks too complex to apply in any practical way. So, our challenge became to illustrate how the frameworks can provide a useful tool for those concerned with the shaping or implementation of policy to think about the problems they confront.

We start by offering a number of assertions to identify the contents of caring and carescapes. These are drawn from our theoretical and empirical work. Under each assertion are a series of questions, and addressing these will require various combinations of empirical data, ethical considerations and decision-making. These assertions and questions are not exhaustive. In raising these questions, we are uncomfortably aware that they could be used to justify a type of social engineering that is far from our intention; rather, we wish to illuminate the taken-for-granted in relation to informal care and put into perspective the need to address and not assume.

Assertion 1: Informal caring is a social / relational activity embedded in notions of obligation and reciprocity

Questions include:

- What are the important caring relationships that exist in the relevant policy/ service provision context?
- How do those involved feel about the caring relationships that they are involved in?
- What notions of obligation and reciprocity underpin these relationships?
- Who does most of the caring work?
- Are there inequalities of power in those relationships? How could these inequalities be reduced?

Assertion 2: Informal caring is an ethical activity involving notions of normative behaviour and desirable or 'appropriate' social relationships

Questions include:

- What are the values underpinning caring relationships in the particular context? Or – if there is an absence of care – what ethical values are absent?
- What do those involved think about the ethical basis of their actions? Are these ethical values ones that should be supported by policy-makers?
- Are they consonant with an 'ethic of care'? Are these ethical values supported or undermined by the social context within which the policy-maker/service provider is operating?

Assertion 3: Informal caring often involves relationships of unequal power – especially inequalities of class, gender, race and (dis)ability

Questions include:

- Are there systematic social patterns in the caring relationships relevant to the policy/provision context?
- Are some types of people usually the cared-for and others the carers?
- What types of belief or access to resources underpin these inequalities?
- Are there systematic differences in the resources for caring available to people on the basis of race, class, gender or (dis)ability? If so, how could these inequalities be reduced?
- How do those involved feel about any inequalities in the caring relationships?

Assertion 4: Informal caring is an embodied activity in which co-presence, bodily separation and mediated forms of communication affect the caring encounter

Questions include:

- What types of caring relationship are present or possible via mediated forms of communication and through co-presence?
- How do the different types of caring encounter affect the various participants?
- Could or should new types of caring relationship be enabled through access to new forms of communication technology?
- How do those involved feel about the different forms of caring encounter?

Assertion 5: The performance of informal caring necessarily involves processes that connect across time–space

Questions include:

- How do the informal caring relationships of interest operate across time–space? Are they confined to particular places and, if so, how are these places socially defined? Are they confined to particular times or periods in people's lives and how are these socially defined?
- What is the effect of this time–space specificity – is it helpful and appropriate or unhelpful and inappropriate to the operation of informal care in the policy/provision context? Do the relationships depend on links to the past or future in particular places (for example, to shared past or future experiences in a given context)?
- How do those involved feel about the timing and placing of the caring relationships in which they are involved? Could or should changes be encouraged in the time–space specificity of these relationships?

Assertion 6: The performance of informal caring involves a person using resources – people, ideas, material objects, as well as time and space to care – accessed through particular places and spaces at particular times

Questions include:

- What resources are used by those involved in informal caring relevant to the policy/provision context?
- Do people feel that they lack adequate resources to care?
- From what places do these resources come? From what types of 'supplier': 'the family', 'friends', private individuals, firms, state organisations, voluntary bodies?
- In what legal or social jurisdictions are these suppliers to be found?
- Is their supply limited to particular places? Are there spatial limits to their supply – borders or boundaries? What time scales govern the supply of these resources? Are they available at any time or is their supply limited to particular times?
- In what ways do these resources affect the nature of the caring performed? Is access to these resources available to all?
- Could access to these resources be improved for those who lack access?

Assertion 7: The performance of informal caring involves a person reflecting on or enacting aspects of past informal caring relationships and/or anticipating future caring relationships

Questions include:

- In what ways do the practices and meanings of care relevant to the policy/provision context depend on past 'learning' of care behaviours and beliefs? How individually specific is this learning?
- Are there common patterns of past learning that appear to be important to current practices? Does this suggest that changes should or could be made to policy in order to change these patterns?
- How does anticipation of future caring relationships affect people's behaviour? Are these anticipations realised? If not, is this a problem?
- Are there ways that information on future opportunities and resources would be helpful to people's development of lifecourse paths?

Assertion 8: The performance of informal caring involves a person reflecting on and/or anticipating how informal caring relationships link to other actual or anticipated aspects of their lives

Questions include:

- How do people involved in the particular policy/provision context see the role of different aspects of informal caring within their lives?
- How do they think or find these different aspects affect their working careers, their lifecourse hopes and decisions, their everyday behaviours?
- Are different aspects of informal care experienced as a central organising feature of life, as taken-for-granted elements of life, as obligations and involvements that should be minimised or maximised – or in some alternative way?

These various dimensions encourage us to explore the nature of the informal caring relationships that a person is, has been, or expects to be, involved in; when and where these relationships were, are or might be enacted; and the part played by different people in the relationships. It requires recognition of the wide variety of people, spaces and occasions on which care might be exchanged so that it should encourage practitioners to think beyond the obvious categories of family members or women when identifying caring exchanges and move the focus to the:

- Contested aspects of these relationships and the power relations involved
- Moral expectations that a person, team or department has about care
- Connectivities across time and space
- Place and space constraints and opportunities
- Relationships between spaces of care and other spaces and flows
- Implications of different forms of communication across space and between individuals
- Individuals' subjective assessments of their situation at centre-stage
- Informal caring as a continuously evolving and changing element in people's lives

Although these assertions and questions offer insights on how a research or ethical agenda on informal care might evolve, the question remains as to what value could the frameworks offer to policy-makers, practitioners, and those considering care policies and practices in employing organisations.

So what? A matrix to address a change in business practice

Overleaf, in the matrix *Dimensions of Carescapes*, we have refined each of the eight assertions listed above. Below, we work through dimension 1 – obligations and reciprocity – in detail. The focus here is on understanding the current nature of the relationship between obligations and reciprocity, the past nature of this relationship, and how to move from analysis to consensually adjust policies and practices. Take, for example, a major retailer with an ethical trading policy. This has just been challenged by staff who have requested a change in the African company supplying uniforms. Staff have become aware that the wages and conditions of the workers making the garments are poor. Furthermore, they are concerned that this is not the image that they or their company should be associated with and have asked the trade union to approach the company to take action. On hearing this, the retailer realises that they must address this if they are not to suffer a backlash from the workers, the union, the public and the shareholders. However, they face a dilemma – yes, the wages and conditions are not good but, if they take away the contract, the workers could lose what little they have and the supplier is the major source of work in the town. The retailer wants to consider the options and try to get an agreed way forward. As part of this process, they want to focus on the care impacts, in tandem with business economics and if possible to balance the two by resetting the contract. As part of this process, they need to understand the current relationship that they have with their supplier.

The *Dimensions of Caringscapes* matrix would help to illuminate the key aspects of the relationship and point to gaps and areas for adjustment. It is not a case of working through all the dimensions but of selecting those that are germane to the issue. In this case, the most likely useful dimensions are: obligation and reciprocity, dimension 1; ethical activity, dimension 2; power relations, dimension 3; co-presence and mediated communication, dimension 4; past and future care relations, dimension 7. It is important to remember that addressing these involves three relevant parties: the retail company, the supplier, and their workers or representatives. Ideally, each should contribute to the process, and in the case of this example, modern technology can facilitate communication between continents. It becomes a matter of ethos and values, and of coordination and access.

Continuing with the example of the retail company and the ethical dilemmas on the working conditions for staff in a supply company, how might we work through dimension 1 – namely, what notions of obligation and reciprocity underpin the relationship? Taking Dimension 1 we now work through the potentially competing perspectives of the retailer, supplier and workers.

Matrix 7.1 Dimension of Carescapes Matrix

Dimension 1	Focus	Development Questions
Obligations and Reciprocity	Create Maintain Adjust Understand	What notions of o/r underpin the relationship?[1] How is the current o/r relationship viewed? What are the consequences of the current o/r relationship? What needs to be addressed? e.g. inequalities; support mechanisms, attitudes How will this be addressed? What outcomes are desired?

Dimension 2	Focus	Development Questions
Ethical Activity	Create Maintain Adjust	What are the ethical values underpinning the relationship? What ethical values are absent? Are the ethical values being used appropriate to the context? What needs to be addressed? How will this be addressed? What outcomes are desired?

Dimension 3	Focus	Development Questions
Power Relationships/ Inequalities	Maintain Adjust Understand	What type of 'care' relationship exists? Who gains and loses what from the relationship? What limits are there to participants changing the relationship? What issues underpin the relationship (past, current and anticipated future)? What is the effect on 'care' delivered and received? What needs to be addressed? How will this be addressed? What outcomes are desired?

Dimension 4	Focus	Development Questions
Co-presence and mediated communication[2]	Create Maintain Adjust Understand	What are the current types of co-present relationship? What are the current types of mediated communication? What are the perceived and actual benefits and dis-benefits for those involved? What needs to be addressed? How will this be addressed? What outcomes are desired?

(continued)

Dimension 5	Focus	Development Questions
Connections across time, space and place	Create Maintain Adjust Understand	Are the caring relationships confined to particular spaces and places? What are the consequences of this? Are they confined to particular time periods? What are the consequences of this? Do the relationships depend on past, current or future links to people or resources? In what places and over what spatial scales are these past, present or future links to people and resources? What are the consequences of this? What needs to be addressed? How will this be addressed? What are the desired outcomes?

Dimension 6	Focus	Development Questions
Resources through time, space and place	Create Maintain Adjust Understand	What resources are used in the care relationship? What care resources are flexible through time, space and place? What care resources are rigid through time, space and place? What is the balance between these in the context under consideration? What are the benefits and dis-benefits of the current mix? What needs to be addressed? How will this be addressed? What are the desired outcomes?

Dimension 7	Focus	Development Questions
Past experiences and future anticipations	Create Maintain Adjust Understand	In what ways do the practices and meanings of care depend on past 'learned' behaviours and beliefs? Are there common patterns of past learning that appear to be important to current practices? How does anticipation of future caring relationships affect people's behaviour? What needs to be addressed? How will this be addressed? What are the desired outcomes?

Dimension 8	Focus	Development Questions
Linkages to actual and anticipated lives	Create Maintain Adjust Understand	How are the different aspects of informal care experienced: central organising feature of life; taken-for-granted elements of life; obligations and involvements to be minimised or maximised; some alternative way? What are the current consequences of this? What are the future anticipations in terms of the identified experiences? What are the implications of this? What needs to be addressed: current and anticipated? How will it be addressed? What are the desired outcomes: current and future?

Notes
1 o/r, obligations and/or reciprocity
2 Co-presence refers to being in the same place and mediated communication to communication other than face-to-face communication such as via letter, telephone or internet connection

UK Retailer: As far as the retailer is concerned, they are in a commercial relationship with the supplier. The supplier was told that the retailer operated an ethical trading policy and it was a condition of the contract that workers receive a fair wage and work in reasonable conditions. In the first year of the contract, a representative was sent out on three occasions to make sure that the contract was operating correctly both from a business and ethical stance, but since then the only visit had been to contract them to make a new style of uniform.

African Supplier: Knew that the retailer had an ethical trading policy but is unclear as to what that really means and feels that there are limits on any sense of obligation to provide what the retailer deems are decent wages and working conditions. As far as the supplier is concerned, the workers have the best conditions of any company in the town and are paid the local rate.

African Workers: They have no idea about the nature of the commercial contract; to them, it is just another piece of work. They are not sure that the retailer has any obligation to them or vice versa, other than getting the work done and getting paid. They would like better working conditions and better pay, but actually having the work is more important to them as job opportunities in the town are few and far between.

How is the current relationship viewed?

UK Retailer: As a positive one in that the goods are delivered on time, to specification and price. The workers were being paid the same rate as similar employees doing similar work in nearby countries. Early site visits had suggested that all was well in relation to wages and conditions, but the last site visit had been more than 3 years ago. Analysis of the relationship showed that it was predicated on functional matters and obligations and reciprocities – and the ethical contract – had been subsumed in other matters.

African Supplier: Felt that the relationship was very good in that the retailer always paid on time and gave them a platform of steady work. Beyond that, the supplier had not really considered the obligations/reciprocity relationship, particularly in relation to the idea that the retailer could have ethical obligations to the supplier.

African Workers: Had no idea of the relationship with the retailer other than that the work kept coming and, therefore, by default, it must have been okay. They have no notion that the retailer might have influence over their working conditions or wages.

What are the consequences of the current relationship?

UK Retailer: Realizes that they actually know little or nothing about their supplier's current operating conditions and have no feel for either the pressures that the supplier may be under concerning wages and conditions across their business that might be affecting the terms of this agreement: the corners that might be being cut for profit or survival; they know nothing about the workers themselves and their needs, not just monetary needs but health, family, education etc. The obligations and reciprocities that they thought were in place and functioning seem to have stalled. Indeed, are these still germane? The relationship as it stands cannot continue as the ethical obligations do not seem to be being met.

African Supplier: For the supplier, the relationship is fine and they are fulfilling their ethical part of the contract: the workers are getting paid the going local rate and the working conditions are actually quite good compared with some other local companies. Yes, they would like to be paid more money per unit of item made, but are wary of jeopardizing the contract. There is little or no money for the supplier to start developing other services for the workers.

African Workers: For them, there are no discernible consequences as the retailer, to them, is just another customer who would probably have little or no interest in their lives so they are surprised to be part of this process. Maybe they are missing an opportunity to get help in terms of their pay and conditions from an influential customer, but they too are wary of stirring up a hornet's nest.

What needs to be addressed?

UK Retailer: Clearly, the obligations and reciprocities surrounding this contract need to be reset. The retailer needs a clearer understanding of the actual working conditions and the needs of the workers and to look at these in terms of how they can help through the ethical part of the contract. They realise that they have been too focused on the obligations part of the equation and not enough on the reciprocity. They need to look carefully at the supplier's operating context both with themselves and more widely: is there something they could help with? Certainly, if they expect more to be paid to the workers, they have to think carefully about how that can be done without creating waves in the local economic environment. The best opportunity might be to look at the working conditions and see what they could assist with: for example, many of the workers have no health insurance and the supplier cannot afford to run such a scheme. Is there some potential to set up such a scheme by using some of the joint profits? It has become obvious that the workers have little or no knowledge of ethical contracts and what that means for them. Better communication and a more involved approach needs to be developed to prevent this situation from happening again. They need to look carefully at what the workers need and what can be done to support them at work.

African Supplier: Wants clarification of what the retailer expects from them. They also want the retailer to advise and help them if the retailer wants to push the ethical component of the contract in these difficult economic times.

African Workers: They want more information to understand these types of contracts and what it should mean for them – that is, how they can use this to better their working lives.

How might the issues identified be addressed? This could include:

• Sending a senior representative out to listen and learn from the supplier and the workers about their working conditions and economic context.
• Re-setting the contract.

- Setting up annual conversations with the supplier on a jointly agreed development agenda.
- Exploring the idea of a company insurance scheme.
- Giving the workers clear and easily understood information in their own languages about what they should expect from their employer and the retailer (as customer) in terms of the ethical contract.

Possible outcomes might be:

- A consensually agreed ethical contract that is feasible and flexible.
- A review procedure to enable the contract to be sustained.
- A health insurance scheme for all workers in the supplier company.

The example has only worked through one dimension of the potential dimensions for this problem but the process for each is similar. From the data collected across the relevant dimensions, a common core of issues to be addressed can be elicited across the dimensions, as well as specific agendas to address within each dimension. Furthermore, it takes into account the understandings and adjustments of each party – retailer, supplier, workers – so there is more likelihood of realistic and agreed change. This follows the principles of triangulating data to strengthen analysis and outcomes – namely, examining different data relating to the same issue to check that the varied data sources are largely telling the same story. It also follows the principles of 'pluralistic evaluation' – that is, evaluation that recognises that differing parties to an issue may have differing criteria for assessment of success and the results to create solutions follow (Smith and Cantley 1985; Moss *et al.* 2008). Too often, the focus is on the agenda agreed for action, leaving other issues to one side. As a result, some may feel aggrieved or marginalised and discontent can fester. It is vital to recognise differing agendas and criteria for evaluation of all parties, if a sustainable way forward is to be achieved.

Final words

Throughout this book, we have demonstrated and emphasised the significance of interdependencies of care over the lifecourse. Caring activities at particular moments in a person's life are not isolated from the social connections and activities in which they were involved before, or from those that are expected to come after. Nor are they divorced from the economic and cultural contexts within which they act that facilitate and constrain their actions. In so doing, we have tried to move forward research, policy and practice, and avoid the tendency to focus on particular *types* of care. Too often, care is viewed in isolation from earlier and later experiences of interdependencies and the giving and receiving of care. Through the devices of Geographical Zones and People Scenarios, we have illustrated that there is as much that unites as divides the nature and practice of care across the world. Care is part of the everyday exchanges and narratives of each person's lifecourse: it is dynamic and flows across times and through spaces.

Bibliography

Adam, B. (1990) *Time and Social Theory*. Cambridge: Polity Press.

Adam, B. (1995) *Timewatch: the Social Analysis of Time*. Cambridge: Polity Press.

Adam, B. (1998) *Timescapes of Modernity. The Environment and Invisible Hazards*. London: Routledge.

Adam, B. (2000) The temporal gaze: the challenge for social theory in the context of GM food. *British Journal of Sociology* 51:125–142.

Adam, B. (2006) Time. *Theory, Culture and Society* 23:119–126.

Adepoju, A. (2008) *Migration in Sub-Saharan Africa*. Uppsala: Nordic Africa Institute.

Airey, L., McKie, L., and Backett-Milburn, K. (2007) Women's experiences of combining eldercare and paid work in the Scottish food retail sector. *Health Sociology Review* 16(4):292–305.

Alber, J., Fahey, T. and Saraceno, C. (2008) *Handbook of Quality of Life in the Enlarged European Union*. London: Routledge.

Allen, G. (1998) Friendship and the private sphere, in R. G. Adams, and G. Allen (eds) *Placing Friendship in Context*. Cambridge: Cambridge University Press.

Amoateng, A. Y., Heaton T. B. and Kalule-Sabiti, I. (2007) Living arrangements in South Africa, in A. Y. Amoateng and T. B. Heaton (eds) *Families and Households in Post-Apartheid South Africa*. Cape Town: HSRC Press.

Anderson, R. and Bury, M. (eds) (1988) *Living with Chronic Illness: the experience of patients and their families*. London: Unwin Hyman.

Andrew, G. and Evans, J. (2008) Understanding the reproduction of health care: Towards geographies in health care work. *Progress in Human Geography* 32(6):759–780.

Angus J., Kontos P., Dyck I., McKeever P. and Poland B. (2005) The personal significance of home: habitus and the experience of receiving long-term home care. *Sociology of Health and Illness* 27(2):161–187.

Anheier, H. K. and Salamon, L. M. (2006) The non-profit sector in comparative perspective, in W. W. Powell and R. Steinberg (eds) *The Nonprofit sector–A Research Handbook*. Yale University Press: Yale, USA.

Arber, S. and Gilbert, N. (1989) Men: the forgotten carers. *Sociology* 23(1):111–118.

Arber, S. and Ginn, J. (1999) Gender differences in informal caring, in A. Graham (ed.) *The Sociology of the Family. A Reader*. Oxford: Blackwell.

Armstrong, F. (1999) Inclusion, curriculum and the struggle for space in school, *International Journal of Inclusive Education* 3(1):75–87.

Armstrong, C. and Squires, J. (2002) Beyond the public/private dichotomy: Relational space and sexual inequalities. *Contemporary Political Theory* 1:261–283.

Arts, W. and Gelissen, J. (2002) Three worlds of welfare capitalism or more? A state-of-the art report. *Journal of European Social Policy* 12:137–158.

Ashton, M. (2008) *The Family Car: The Relational Geographies of In-Car Space.* Unpublished PhD, Department of Geography, University of Reading, UK.

Atkinson, T., Cantillon, B., Marlier, E. and Nolan, B. (2009) *Social Indicators: The EU and Social Inclusion.* Oxford: Oxford University Press.

Backett-Milburn, K., Airey, L., McKie, L. and Hogg, G. (2008) Families come first: Low paid women working in the food retail sector. *Sociological Review* 56(3): 474–496.

Balbo, L. and Nowotny, H. (eds) (1986) *Time to Care in Tomorrow's Welfare System.* Vienna: Eurosocial.

Barnett, C., Cloke, P., Clarke, N. and Malpass, A. (2005) Consuming ethics: Articulating the subjects and spaces of ethical consumption. *Antipode* 37(1): 23–45.

Barnett, C. and Land, D. (2007) Geographies of generosity. *Geoforum* 38(6): 1065–1075.

Beck, U. and Beck-Gernsheim, E. (2002) *Individualization.* London: Sage.

Belgrave, M. and Brown, L. (1997) *Beyond a Dollar Value: The Cost of Informal Care of Older People.* Auckland: Massey University.

Belot, M. and Ermisch, J. (July 2006) *Friendship Ties and Geographical Mobility, Evidence from the BHPS,* IESR Working Paper 2006–33. Colchester: University of Essex.

Bendelow, G. and Williams, S. J. (1997) (eds) *Emotions in Social Life: Social Theories and Contemporary Issues.* London: Routledge.

Benn, M. (1998) *Madonna and Child. Towards the New Politics of Motherhood.* London: Jonathan Cape.

Bernardes, J. (1987) *Family Studies: An Introduction.* London: Routledge.

Blunt, A. (2005) 'Cultural geography: cultural geographies of home'. *Progress in Human Geography* 29(4): 505–515.

Boddy, M. (2007) Designer neighbourhoods: new-build residential development in nonmetropolitan UK cities – the case of Bristol. *Environment and Planning A* 39(1): 86–105.

Boler, T. (2008) *Strengthening the role of schools as centres for care and support.* Mexico, UNESCO AIDS Conference. www.unesco.org. Accessed 24 April 2009.

Bondi, L. and Domosh, M. (1998) On the contours of public space: A tale of three women. *Antipode.* 30(3): 270–289.

Bondi, L. (2008) On the relational dynamics of caring: A psychotherapeutic approach to emotional and power dimensions of women's care work. *Gender, Place and Culture* 15(3): 249–265.

Bould, S. (2003) Caring neighborhoods bringing up the kids together. *Journal of Family Issues* 24(4): 427–447.

Bourdieu, P. and Wacquant, L. J. D. (1992) *An Invitation to Reflexive Sociology.* Cambridge: Polity Press.

Bowlby, S., Gregory, S. and McKie, L. (1997) "Doing home": patriarchy, caring, and space. *Women's Studies International Forum* 20(3): 343–350.

Bowlby, S. and Lloyd-Evans, S. (2007) *Valuing Volunteering: A Study in Greater Reading.* Reading: University of Reading, UK.

Brandth, B. and Kvande, E. (2002) Reflexive fathers: Negotiating parental leave and working life. *Gender, Work and Organization* 9(2): 1186–11203.

Brannen, J. (2005) Time and the negotiation of work-family boundaries: Autonomy or illusion? *Time & Society* 14(1): 113–131.

Brannen, J. (2006) Cultures of intergenerational transmission in four-generation families. *The Sociological Review* 54(1): 133–154.

Brown, M. (2003) Hospice and the spatial paradoxes of terminal care. *Environment and Planning A* 35: 833–851.

Bukowski, W. M., Newcomb, A. F. and Hartup, W. W. (1996) *The Company They Keep: Friendship in Childhood and Adolescence*. Cambridge: Cambridge University Press.

Bury, M. (1982) Chronic illness as biographical disruption. *Sociology of Health and Illness* 4: 167–182.

Butler, R. and Bowlby, S. (1997) Bodies and spaces: An exploration of disabled people's experiences of public space. *Environment and Planning D: Society and Space* 15: 411–433.

Carlin, P. S. (2001) Evidence on the volunteer labor supply of married women. *Southern Economic Journal* 67(4): 801–824.

Carling, A., Duncan, S. and Edwards, R. (2002) *Analysing Families. Morality and Rationality in Policy and Practice*. London: Routledge.

Carsten, J. and Hugh-Jones, S. (1995) *About the House: Levi-Strauss and Beyond*. Cambridge: Cambridge University Press.

Carsten, J. (ed.) (2000) *Cultures of Relatedness: New Approaches to the Study of Kinship*. Cambridge: Cambridge University Press.

Castells, M. (1997) *The Power of Identity*. Oxford: Blackwell.

Castree, N., Coe, N., Ward, K. and Samers, M. (2003) *Spaces of Work: Global Capitalism and Geographies of Labour*. London: Sage.

Cavendish, R. (1982) *Women on the Line*. London: Routledge and Kegan Paul.

Charles, N. (2000) *Feminism, the State and Social Policy*. London: Macmillan.

Cheal, D. (1991) *Family and the State of Theory*. Hemel Hempstead: Harvester.

Cheal, D. (1999) The one and the many: Modernity and postmodernity, in G. Allen (ed.) *The Sociology of the Family. A Reader*. Oxford: Blackwell.

Christensen, P. and O'Brien, M. (eds) (2002) *Children in the City: Home, neighbourhood and community*. London: Routledge.

Central Intelligence Agency (2008) World Fact Book. Washington: Central Intelligence Agency.

Ciscel, D. H., Sharp, D. C. and Heath, J. A. (2000) Family work trends and practices 1071–1991. *Journal of Family and Economic Issues* 21(1): 21–36.

Clinton, H. (1996) *It Takes a Village to Raise a Child*. New York: Simon & Schuster.

Cloke, P., Johnsen, S. and May, J. (2005) Exploring ethos? Discourses of 'charity' in the provision of emergency services for homeless people. *Environment and Planning A* 37: 385–402.

Cloke, P., Johnsen, S. and May, J. (2007) Ethical citizenship? Volunteers and the ethics of providing services for homeless people. *Geoforum* 38(6): 1089–1101.

Coleman, J. (1988) Social capital in the creation of human capital. *American Journal of Sociology* 94(Suppl): S95–S120.

Connolly, S. and Gregson, N. (2008) *The Pay Risks from Part-time Employment: Life-time earnings of British women*. Unpublished Paper, School of Economics, University of East Anglia and Department of Economics, University of Oxford.

Conradson, D. (2003) Spaces of care in the city: the place of a community drop-in centre. *Social and Cultural Geography* 4(4): 507–524.

Cosaro, W. A. (1997) *The Sociology of Childhood*. Thousand Oaks: University of California Press.

Cottingham, J. (2000) Caring at a distance: (Im)partiality, moral motivation and the ethics of representation – partiality, distance and moral obligation. *Ethics, Place and Environment* 3(1): 309–313.

Cox, R. and Narula, R. (2003) Playing happy families: Rules and relationships in au pair employing households in London, England. *Gender Place and Culture* 10: 333–344.

Crossley, N. (1998) Emotion and communicative action: Habermas, linguistic philosophy and existentialism, in G. Bendelow and S. J. Williams (eds) *Emotions in Social Life. Critical Themes and Contemporary Issues*. London: Routledge.

Crozier, G. and Reay, D. (eds) (2005) *Activating Participation: Parents and teachers working towards partnership*. Stoke-on-Trent: Trentham Books.

Cunningham-Burley, S., Backett-Milburn, K. and Kemmer, D. (2006) Constructing health and sickness in the context of motherhood and paid work. *Sociology of Health and Illness* 28(4): 385–409.

Daly, K. J. (2001) Deconstructing family time: from ideology to lived experience. *Journal of Marriage and Family* 63: 238–294.

Daniel, P. and Ivatts, J. (1998) *Children and Social Policy*. London: Macmillan.

Davidoff, L., L'Esperance, J. and Newby, H. (1976) Landscapes with figures: home and community in English society, in J. Mitchell and A. Oakley (eds) *The Rights and Wrongs of Women*. Penguin: Harmondsworth.

Davidson, M. and Lees, L. (2005) New build gentrification and London's riverside renaissance. *Environment and Planning A* 37: 1165–1190.

Davis, M. (1990) *City of Quartz: excavating the future in Los Angeles*. London: Verso.

Davis, S. and Meyer, C. (1999) *Blur: The Speed of Change in the Connected Economy*. New York: Warner Books.

Deacon, B. (2007) *Global Social Policy and Governance*. London: Sage.

Dennis, N., Henriques, F. and Slaughter, C. (1969) *Coal is our Life*. 2nd edition. London: Routledge Kegan & Paul.

Dewilde, C. (2003) A life-course perspective on social exclusion and poverty. *British Journal of Sociology* 54(1): 109–128.

Domínguez, S. and Watkins, C. (2003) Creating networks for survival and mobility: Social capital among African-American and Latin-American low-income mothers. *Social Problems* 50(1): 111–135.

Drew, E. P., Emerek, R. and Mahon, E. (eds) (1998) *Women, Work and the Family in Europe*. London: Routledge.

Dryfoos, J. G. (1994) *Full Service Schools: A revolution in health and social services for children, youth and families*. San Francisco: Jossey-Bass Inc.

Duflo, E. (2003) Grandmothers and granddaughters: Old-age pensions and intrahousehold allocation in South Africa. *World Bank Economic Review* 17(1): 1–25.

Duncan, S. (2005) Mothering, class and rationality. *The Sociological Review* 53(1): 50–76.

Duncan, S. and Edwards, R. (1999) *Lone Mothers, Paid Work and Gendered Moral Rationalities*. Basingstoke: Macmillan.

Duncan, S., Edwards, R., Alldred P. and Reynolds, T. (2003) Motherhood, paid work, and partnering: values and theories. *Work, Employment and Society* 17(2): 309–330.

Duvdevany, I., Buchbinder, E. and Yaacov, I. (2008) Accepting disability: The parenting experience of fathers with spinal cord injury (SCI). *Qualitative Health Research* 18(8): 1021–1033.

Dyck, I. (2005) Feminist geography, the 'everyday', and local-global relations: hidden spaces of place-making. *Canadian Geographer* 49(3): 233–243.

de Valk, H. A. G. and Schans, D. (2008) They ought to do this for their parents: perceptions of filial obligations among immigrant and Dutch older people. *Ageing and Society* 28(1): 49–66.

Edgell, S. (2005) *The Sociology of Work: Continuity and Change in Paid and Unpaid Work.* London: Sage.

Ehrenreich, B. and Hochschild, R. (2002) *Global Woman: Nannies, maids and sex workers in the new economy.* London: Granta Books.

Elias, N. (1982) *The Civilising Process.* Oxford: Blackwell.

Equality and Human Rights Commission (2009) Working better: Fathers, family and work. http://www.equalityhumanrights.com/media-centre/fathers-struggling-to-balance-work-and-family/. Accessed 20 October 2009.

Ermarth, E. (1998) Time and neutrality: Media of modernity in a postmodern world. *Cultural Values* 2(2/3): 355–367.

Esping-Anderson, G. (1993) *The Three Worlds of Welfare Capitalism.* Princeton: Princeton University Press.

Eurostat (2003a) *Comparable Statistics in the Area of Care of Dependent Adults in the European Union: A Feasibility Study.* Brussels: Eurostat. Accessed 18 February 2009.

Eurostat (2003b) *Comparable Statistics in the Area of Care of Vulnerable Children in the European Union: A Feasibility Study.* Brussels: Eurostat. Accessed 21 February 2009.

Eurostat (2005) *Statistics in Focus: Population and Social Conditions – EU Labour Force Survey Principle Results.* Brussels: Eurostat. http://epp.eurostat.ec.europa.eu/cache/ITY_OFFPUB/KS-NK-06-013/EN/KS-NK-06-013-EN.PDF. Accessed 12 February 2009.

Eurostat (2008a) *Europe in Figures: Eurostat 2008 Yearbook – Living Conditions and Welfare.* Brussels: Eurostat. Accessed 27 February 2009.

Eurostat (2008b) *The Lives of Men and Women. A Statistical Portrait.* Brussels: Eurostat. Accessed 9 February 2009.

Eurostat (2008c) *Thematic Data: Main type of childcare used by employed persons for own/ spouse's children up to 14 while working.* Brussels: Eurostat. www.eurostat.ec.europa.eu/extraction/retrieve/en/theme3. Accessed 1 March 2009.

Eurostat (2008d) *Thematic Data: The number of employed persons wishing to change the organization of their working lives and care responsibilities.* Brussels: Eurostat. www.eurostat.ec.europa.eu/extraction/retrieve/en/theme3. Accessed 1 March 2009.

Evans, R. and Becker, S. (2009) *Children Caring for Parents with HIV and AIDS: Global Issues and Policy Responses.* Bristol: The Policy Press.

Feder Kittay, E. and Feder, E. K. (eds) (2002) *The Subject of Care. Feminist Perspectives on Dependency.* Lanham, Maryland: Roman and Littlefield.

Feld, S. and Carter, W. C. (1998) Foci of activity as changing contexts for friendship, in R. G. Adams and G. Allen (eds) *Placing Friendship in Context.* Cambridge: Cambridge University Press.

Finch, J. (1989) *Family Obligations and Social Change.* Cambridge: Polity Press.

Finch, J. and Mason, J. (1993) *Negotiating Family Responsibilities.* London: Routledge.

Finch, J. and Mason, J. (1999) Obligations of kinship in contemporary Britain: Is there normative agreement?, in G. Allan (ed.) *The Sociology of the Family. A Reader.* Oxford: Blackwell.

Fine, G. (1996) *Kitchens: The Culture of Restaurant Work.* Berkeley: University of California Press.

Fink, J. (ed.) (2004) *Care, Personal Lives and Social Policy.* Oxford: Blackwell.

Fisher, P. (2006) Making healthy families: Changing families, changing food. Working Paper. Sheffield: University of Sheffield.

Folbre, N. and Bittman, M. (2004) *Family Time: The social organization of care.* London: Routledge.

Forbat, L. (2005) *Talking about Care: Two sides to the story.* Bristol: The Policy Press.

Forrest, R. S. (2000) *Does Neighbourhood Still Matter in a Globalised World*, Occasional Paper Series No. 5. Bristol: University of Bristol.

Forrest, R. and Kearns, A. (2001) Social cohesion, social capital and the neighbourhood, social cohesion, social capital and the neighbourhood. *Urban Studies* 38(12): 2125–2143.

Frank, A. (1991). *At The Will of the Body: Reflections on illness*. Boston: Houghton Mifflin.

Fraser, N. and Gordon, L. (2002) A Genealogy of dependency: Tracing a keyword of the U.S. Welfare State, in Feder Kittay, E. and Feder, E. K. (eds) *The Subject of Care: Feminist Perspectives on Dependency*, Lanham, MD: Rowman and Littlefield.

Fultz, E., Rick, M. and Steinhilber, S. (eds) (2003) *The Gender Dimensions of Social Security Refore in Central and Eastern Europe: Case Studies of The Czech Republic, Hungary and Poland*. Geneva: International Labour Office.

Fyfe, N. R. (1998) *Images of the Street: Planning, Identity, and Control in Public Space*. London: Routledge.

Galgóczi, B., Leschke, J. and Watt, A. (2009) *Intra-EU Labour Migration: Flows, Effects and Policy Responses*. Brussels: European Trade Union Institute.

Gershuny, J. (2000) *Changing Times: Work and Leisure in Postindustrial Society*. Oxford: Oxford University Press.

Giddens, A. (1979) *Central Problems in Social Theory: Action, structure and contradiction on social analysis*. Berkeley: University of California Press.

Giddens, A. (1984) *The Constitution of Society. Outline of the Theory of Structuration*. Cambridge: Polity Press.

Giddens, A. (1991) *Modernity and Self Identity*. Cambridge: Polity Press.

Giddens, A. (1992) *The Transformation of Intimacy: Sexuality, love and eroticism in modern societies*. Cambridge: Polity Press in association with Blackwell Publishers, Oxford.

Gierveld, J. D. J. and Dykstra, P.A. (2008) Virtue is its own reward? Support giving in the family and loneliness in middle and old age, *Aging and Society* 28: 271–287.

Gilligan, C. (1982) *In a Different Voice: Psychological theory and women's development*. Cambridge, Mass: Harvard University Press.

Gillis, J. (1996) Making time for family: the invention of family time(s) and the reinvention of family history. *The Journal of Family History* 21: 4–21.

Gittins, D. (1997) *The Child in Question*. London: Palgrave Macmillan.

Godfrey, M., Townsend, J. and Denby, T. (2004) *Building a Good Life for Older People in Local Communities: The experience of ageing in time and place*. York: Joseph Rowntree Foundation. www.jrf.org.uk/knowledge/findings/socialcare/014.asp. Accessed 28 October 2009.

Goffman, E. (1959) *The Presentation of Self in Everyday Life*. New York: Doubleday.

Goodman M. R. and Rao S. P. (2007) Grandparents raising grandchildren in a US–Mexico border community. *Qualitative Health Research* 17(8): 1117–1136.

Gough, I., Wood, G., Barrientos, A., Bevan, P., Davis P. and Room, G. (2004) *Insecurity and Welfare Regimes in Asia, Africa, and Latin America: Social policy in development contexts*. Cambridge: Cambridge University Press.

Goulbourne, H. and Chamberlain, M. (eds) (2001) *Caribbean Families in the Trans-Atlantic World*. London: Macmillan.

Graham, H. (1983) Caring: A labour of love, in J. Finch and D. Groves (eds) *A Labour of Love: Women, work and caring*. London: Routledge and Kegan Paul.

Graham, H. (1991) The concept of caring in feminist research: the case of domestic service. *Sociology* 25: 61–78.

Gram-Hansen, K. and Bech-Danielsen, C. (2004) House, home and identity from a consumption perspective. *Housing Theory and Society* 21(1): 17–26.

Green, E. and Singleton, C. (2009) Mobile connections: an exploration of the place of mobile phones in friendship relations. *Sociological Review* 57(1): 125–144.

Gregory, S. (2000) *Food, Caring and Illness in the Family Setting*. Unpublished Ph.D. Guildford: University of Surrey.

Gregory, S. (2005) Living with chronic illness in the family setting. *Sociology of Health and Illness* 27(3): 370–390.

Groenhout, R. E. (2004) *Connected Lives: Human nature and an ethics of care*. Lanham, Maryland: Roman and Littlefield.

Gurney, C. (1997) "… Half of me was satisfied": making sense of home through episodic ethnographies. *Women's Studies International Forum* 20(3): 373–386.

Hagerstrand, T. (1970) What about people in Regional Science? *Papers in Regional Science* 24(1): 7–21.

Hagerstrand, T. (1978) Survival and arena: on the life histories of individuals in relation to their geographical environment, in T. Carlstein, D. Parkes and N. Thrift (eds) *Timing Space and Spacing Time*. Volume 2, Human Activity and Time-Geography. London: Edward Arnold.

Hakim, C. (2000) *Work-Lifestyle Choices in the 21st Century: Preference theory*. Oxford: Oxford University Press.

Hakim, C. (2002) *Models of the Family in Modern Societies: Ideals and realities*, Aldershot: Ashgate.

Halford, S. and Leonard, P. (2006) Place, space and time: contextualizing workplace subjectivities. *Organizational Studies* 27: 657–676.

Hampton, K. and Wellman, B. (2003) Neighboring in Netville: How the internet supports community and social capital in a wired suburb. *City and Community* 2(4): 277–311.

Hand, M. and Shove, E. (2004) Orchestrating concepts: kitchen dynamics and regime change in *Good Housekeeping* and *Ideal Home*, 1922–2002. *Home Cultures* 1: 235–256.

Hanson, S. and Pratt, G. (1995) *Gender, Work and Space*. Routledge: New York.

Hanson Thiem, C. (2008) Thinking through education: the geographies of contemporary educational restructuring. *Progress in Human Geography* 33: 154–173.

Harden, J. (2000) There's no place like home: the public/private distinction in children's theorizing of risk and safety. *Childhood* 7(1): 43–59.

Hardill, I. and Baines, S. (2005*) Making a difference: Voluntary action in a community beset by economic decline, Policy Brief*. Nottingham Trent University/University of Newcastle upon Tyne.

Hardill, I. and Baines, S. (2007) Volunteering for all? Explaining patterns of volunteering and identifying strategies to promote it. *Policy and Politics* 35(3): 395–412.

Haugen, G. (2007) Caring children: exploring care in post-divorce families. *Sociological Review* 55(4): 653–670.

Healy, S. (2008) Caring for ethics and the politics of health care reform in the United States. *Gender, Place and Culture* 15(3): 267–284.

Healy, J. and Yarrow, S. (1997) *Family matters: parents living with children in old age*. Bristol: The Policy Press..

Hearn, J. and Parkin, W. (2001) *Gender, Sexuality and Violence in Organizations: The unspoken forces of organization violations*. London: Sage.

Held, V. (2007) *The Ethics of Care*. Oxford: Oxford University Press.

Hepworth, M. (1998) Ageing and emotions, in G. Bendelow and S. J. Williams (eds) *Emotions in Social Life: Critical themes and contemporary issues*. London, Routledge.

Heymann, J., Earle, A., Rajaraman, D., Miller, C. and Bogen, K. (2007) Extended family caring for children orphaned by AIDS: balancing essential work and caregiving in high HIV prevalence nations. *Aids Care* 19(3): P337–345.

Hill Collins, P. (2000) *Black Feminist Thought*. 2nd edition. London: Routledge.

Himmelweit, S. and Land, H. (2008) *Reducing Gender Inequalities to Create a Sustainable Care System*. York: Joseph Rowntree Foundation.

Hochschild, A. (1983) *The Managed Heart: Commercialization of human feeling*, Berkeley: University of California Press.

Hochschild, A. (1989) *The Second Shift: Working parents and the revolution at home*. Berkley: University of California Press.

Hochschild, A. (2003) *The Commercialization of Intimate Life: Notes from home and work*. Berkeley: University of California Press.

Hochschild, A. and Machung, A. (1989) *The Second Shift: Working families and the revolution at home*. London: Piatkus.

Hockey, J. and James, A. (1993) *Growing Up and Growing Old: Aging and dependency in the life course*. London: Sage.

Holt, L. (2007) Children's sociospatial (re)production of disability within primary school playgrounds. *Environment and Planning D: Society and Space* 25: 783–802.

HopeHIV (2009) *Africa's Generation of Hope*. London: website http://www.hopehiv.org/. Accessed 22 May 2009.

House of Commons Work and Pensions Committee (2008) *Valuing and Supporting Carers*. London: The Stationary Office.

Human Resources Department (2009) *Strategy to Develop the Human Resources of the Tanzanian Population*. http://www.tanzania.go.tz/human.html. Accessed 25 May 2009.

International Federation of Chemical, Energy, Mining and General Workers Unions (2009) *HIV/AIDs Bulletin*, No. 43. Geneva: ICEM.

International Labour Office (2006) *Report of Working Party on the Social Dimensions of Globalization, 297th Session*. Geneva: ILO.

International Labour Office (2007) *Decent Work Agenda Africa 2007–2015*. Report of the 11th African Regional Meeting. Addis Ababa: ILO.

International Labour Office (2008) *Global Employment Trends*. Geneva: ILO.

International Labour Office (2009) *8th European Regional Meeting: Facts on Social Protection in Europe and Central Asia*. Geneva: ILO.

International Monetary Fund (2008) *World Economic Outlook. Financial Stress, Downturns and Recoveries*. Washington DC: International Monetary Fund.

International Organization for Migration (2005) World Migration Trends Report, IOM.

International Social Security Association. (2008) *Country Profiles*. www.issa.int/aiss/observatory/country. Accessed 4 April 2009.

James, A., Jenks, C. and Prout A (1998) *Theorizing Childhood*. Teachers College Press: Vermont.

James, A. and Prout, A. (eds) (1990) *Constructing and Reconstructing Childhood: Contemporary issues in the sociology of childhood*. London and Philadelphia: Falmer Press.

Jamieson, L. (1998) *Intimacy. Personal Relationships in Modern Societies*. Cambridge: Polity Press.

Jamieson, L. (2005) Boundaries of intimacy, in McKie, L and Cunningham-Burley, S (eds) *Families and Society: Boundaries and Relationships*. Bristol: Policy Press.

Jarvis, H. (2005) Moving to London Time: Household co-ordination and the infrastructure of everyday life. *Time and Society* 14(1): 133–154.

Jendrek, M. P. (1993) Grandparents who parent their grandchildren: effects on lifestyle. *Journal of Marriage and the Family* 55(3): 609–621.

Jerrome, D. (1992) *Good Company*. Edinburgh: Edinburgh University Press.

Karsten, L. (2003) Children's use of public space: the gendered world of the playground. *Childhood* 10: 457–473.

Katz, C. (1993) Growing girls/closing circles: Limits on the spaces of knowing in rural Sudan and US Cities, in C. Katz and J. Monk (eds) *Full Circles Geographies of Women over the Life Course*. London: Routledge.

Kearns, A. and Parkinson, M. (2001) The significance of neighbourhood. *Urban Studies* 38(12): 2103–2110.

Kielland, A. and Tovo, M. (2006) *Children at Work: Child Labour Practices in Africa*. London: Lynne Rienner.

King, R., Warnes, A. M. and Williams, A. M. (1998) International retirement migration in Europe. *International Journal of Population Geography* 4(2): 91–111.

Kitchen, S., Michaelson, J., Wood, N. and John, P. (2006) *2005 Citizenship Survey: Active Communities Topic Report*. London: Department for Communities & Local Government.

Kugelberg, C. (2006) Constructing the deviant other: mothering and fathering at the workplace. *Gender, Work and Organization* 13(2): 152–173.

Lawson, V. (1999) Tailoring is a profession; Seamstressing is just work! *Environment and Planning A* 30:209–227.

Lee, T. (1968) Urban neighbourhood as a social-spatial schema. *Human Relations* 21(3): 241.

Lee-Treweek, G. (1996) Emotion work, order and emotional power in care assistant work, in V. James and J. Gabe (eds). *Health and the Sociology of Emotions*. Oxford: Blackwell.

Lefebvre, H. (1991) *The Production of Space*. Oxford: Blackwell.

Letiecq, B., Bailey, S. and Porterfield, F. (2008) "We have no rights, we get no help": The legal and policy dilemmas facing grandparent caregivers. *Journal of Family Issues* 29(8): 995–1012.

Letiecq, B. L. and Koblinsky, S. A. (2004) Parenting in violent neighbourhoods: African American fathers share strategies for keeping children safe. *Journal of Family Issues* 25(6): 715–734.

Lewis, J. (1992) Gender and the development of welfare regimes. *Journal of European Social Policy* 18(4): 595–573.

Lewis, J. (1997) Gender and welfare regimes: further thoughts. *Social Politics: International Studies in Gender, State and Society* 4(2): 160–177.

Little, J. and Austin, P. (1996) Women and the rural idyll. *Journal of Rural Studies* 12(2): 101–111.

Llewellyn, M. (2004) Designed by women and designing women: gender, planning and the geographies of the kitchen in Britain, 1917–46. *Cultural Geographies* 11: 42–60.

Lloyd-Evans, S. (2008) Child Labour, in V. Desai and R. B. Potter (eds) *The Companion to Development Studies*. Chapter 4.9. London: Hodder Education; 225–229.

Lloyd-Evans, S. and Bowlby, S. R. (2007) *Spaces and Territories in the City: Perspectives from Pakistani Youth in the UK*. Paper presented at The Annual Conference of the Association of American Geographers, Boston, USA.

Lloyd-Evans, S. and Potter, R. (1998) *The City in the Developing World*. Harlow: Pearson Education.

Longino, C. F. and Bradley, D. E. (2003) A first look at retirement migration trends in 2000. *The Gerontologist* 13(6): 904–907.

Low, N., Butt, S., Ellis Paine, A. and Davis Smith, J. (2007) *Helping Out: A national survey of volunteering and charitable giving*. Prepared for the Office of the Third Sector, Cabinet Office of the National Centre for Social Research and the Institute for Volunteering Research, URN/07/Z6. http://www.cabonetoffice.gov.uk/third_sector/research_and_statistics/third_sector_research/helping_out.aspx. Accessed 20 November 2009.

Lucchini, R. (1996) The street and its image. *Childhood* 3(2): 235–246.

Lupton, B. (2006) Explaining men's entry into female concentrated occupations: issues of masculinity and social class. *Gender, Work and Organization* 13(2): 120–126.

Lynch, K. (2007) Love labour as a distinct and non-commodifiable for of care labour. *Sociological Review* 55(3): 550–570.

Mackenzie, S. (1989) *Visible Histories: Women and environments in a post-war British city*. Montreal: McGill Queen's University Press.

McDowell, L. (1998) *Gender, Identity and Place*. Cambridge: Polity Press.

McDowell, L. (1999) *Gender, Identity and Place: Understanding feminist geographies*. Minneapolis: University of Minnesota Press.

McDowell, L., Ray, K., Perrons, D., Fagan, C. and Ward, K. (2005) Women's paid work and moral economies of care. *Social and Cultural Geography* 6(2): 219–235.

McDowell, L., Ward, K., Fagan, C., Perrons, D. and Ray, K. (2006) Connecting time and space: the significance of transformations in women's work in the city. *International Journal of Urban and Regional Research* 30(1):141–158.

McKie, L., Bowlby, S. and Gregory, S. (1999) Connecting gender, power and the household, in L. McKie, S. Bowlby and S. Gregory (eds) *Gender, Power and the Household*. London: Macmillan.

McKie, L., Gregory, S. and Bowlby, S. (2002) Shadow times: the temporal and spatial frameworks and experiences of caring and working. *Sociology* 36(4): 897–924.

McKie, L., Hearn, J., Bowlby, S., Hogg, G. and Smith, A. (2008) Organisations Carescapes: Researching Organisations, Work and Care. *Hanken Published Papers*. Helsinki: Hanken School of Economics.

McKie, L., Hogg, G., Rew, Z., Airey, L. and Backett-Milburn, K. (2010) Time for Work: Combining Caring and Working in Food Retail, *Industrial Relations Journal*, forthcoming.

Maher, J. (2005) A mother by trade: Australian women reflecting mothering as activity, not identity. *Australian Feminist Studies* 46: 17–30.

Mallett, S. (2004) Understanding home: a critical review of the literature. *The Sociological Review* 52: 62–89.

Marshall, G. (1986) The workplace culture of a licensed restaurant. *Theory, Culture and Society* 3(1): 33–48.

Massey, D. (2002) *For Space*. London: Sage.

Massey, D. and Thrift, N. (2003) The passion of place, in R. Johnston and M. Williams (eds) *A Century of British Geography*. Oxford: Published for the British Academy by Oxford University Press.

Melucci, A. (1996) *The Playing Self: Person and Meaning in the Planetary Society*. Cambridge: Cambridge University Press.

Messkoub, M. (2008) Social security and population ageing in sub-Saharan Africa. *Development Issues* 10(2): 16–18.

Mestheneous, E. and Triantafillou, J. (2005) *Supporting Family Carers of Older People in Europe. The Pan-European Background Report*. Münster: LIT-Verlag.

Milligan, C. (2005) From home to 'home': situating emotions within the caregiving experience. *Environment and Planning A* 37: 2105–2120.

Milligan, C. (2008a) *Caring for Older People in New Zealand: Informal carers' experiences of the transition of care from the home to residential care*. Lancaster: Institute for Health Research, Lancaster University. http://www.lancs.ac.uk/users/ihr/staff/christinemilligan. htm. Accessed February 26 2009.

Milligan, C. (2008b) *The Spatial and Ethical Dimensions of New Care Technologies – Who Cares Where?* Paper presented at Durham International Workshop on Care of the Body: Spaces of Practice, Durham University, September 2008.

Mills, M. (2000) Providing space for time. The impact of temporality on life course research. *Time and Society* 9(1): 91–127.

Momsen, J. (1991) *Women and Development in the Third World*. London: Routledge.

Momsen, J. H. (2004) *Gender and Development*. London: Routledge.

Montgomery, C. M., Hosegood, V., Busza, J. and Timæus, I. M. (2005) Men's involvement in the South African family: Engendering change in the AIDS era. *Social Science and Medicine*, (62)10: 2411–2419.

Mordoch, E. and Hall, W. A. (2008) Children's perceptions of living with a parent with a mental illness: finding the rhythm and maintaining the frame. *Qualitative Health Research* 18: 1127.

Morgan, D. (1996) *Family Connections. An Introduction to Family Studies*. Cambridge: Polity Press.

Morrisens, A. and Sainsbury, D. (2005) Migrants' social rights, ethnicity and welfare regimes. *Journal of Social Policy* 34(4): 637–660.

Moser, C. (1989) Gender planning in the Third World: meeting practical and strategic gender needs. *World Development* 17(11): 1799.

Moss, C., Walsh, K., Jordan, Z. and MacDonald, L. (2008) The impact of practice development in an emergency department: a pluralistic evaluation. *Practice Development in Health Care* 7(2): 93–107.

Muzzetto, L. (2006) Time and meaning in Alfred Schütz. *Time and Society* 15(1): 5–31.

National Alliance for Caregiving (2005) *Young Caregivers in the US: Findings from a National Survey*. Bethseda MD: National Alliance for Caregiving in collaboration with United Hospital Fund.

National Centre for Social Research (2000) *Trends in Attitudes to Health Care 1983–1999: Report Based on Results from the British Social Attitudes Surveys*. London: National Centre for Social Research.

National Statistics (2005) *UK Census 2001*. London: Stationary Office. http://www.statistics.gov.uk/census2001/census2001.asp. Accessed 7 June 2009.

Nespor, J. (1997) *Tangled Up in School: Politics, space, bodies and signs in the educational process*. Philadelphia: Lawrence Erlbaum Associates.

Noddings, N. (1986) *Caring – A feminine approach to ethics and moral education*. Berkeley: University of California Press.

Noddings, N. (2002) *Starting at Home: Caring and social policy*. Berkeley: University of California Press.

O'Brien, M., Jones, D. and Sloan, D. (2000) Children's independent spatial mobility in the urban public realm. *Childhood* 7(3): 257–277.

Office of Economic Cooperation and Development (2001) *An Overview of ECEC Systems in the Participating Countries*. Paris: OECD.

Office of National Statistics (2003) *Households*. London: Office of National Statistics. http://www.statistics.gov.uk/cci/nugget.asp?id=350. Accessed 7 June 2009.

Office of Public Sector Information (2009) *The Flexible Working (Eligibility, Complaints and Remedies) (Amendment) Regulations*. http://www.opsi.gov.uk/si/si2009/ uksi_20090595_en_1. Accessed 7 June 2009.

Oleson, V. and Bone, D. (1998) Emotions in rationalizing organizations: conceptual notes from professional nursing in the USA, in G. Bendelow and S. J. Williams (eds) *Emotions in Social Life: Critical themes and contemporary issues*. London: Routledge.

Oliker, S. J. (1998) The modernization of friendship, individualism, intimacy, and gender in the nineteenth century, in R. G. Adams and G. Allen (1998) (eds) *Placing Friendship in Context*. Cambridge: Cambridge University Press.

Orloff (1996) *Gender and the Welfare State*. Institute for Research on Poverty. Discussion Paper no. 1082–96. Wisconsin: University of Wisconsin–Madison.

Oxford Dictionaries (2008) *Concise Oxford English Dictionary*. 11th edition. Oxford: Oxford University Press.

Pahl, R. (2000) *On Friendship*. Cambridge: Polity Press.

Palm, R. and Pred, A. (1974) *A Time-Geographic Perspective on Problems of Inequality for Women*. Institute of Urban and Regional Development, Working paper 236. Berkeley: University of California.

Parker, R. (1981) Tending and social policy, in E. Goldberg and S. Hatch (eds) *A New Look at the Personal Social Services*. London: Policy Studies Institute.

Parrenas, R. S. (2001) *Servants of Globalization: Women, migration, and domestic work*. Palo Alto, CA: Stanford University Press.

Parrenas, R. (2005) *Children of Global Migration. Transnational Families and Gendered Woes*. Palo Alto, CA: Stanford University Press.

Parry, J., Taylor, R., Pettinger, L. and Glucksmann, M. (eds) (2005) *A New Sociology of Work?* (Sociological Review Monograph) Oxford: Blackwell Publishing.

Paul, J. and Miller, F. D. (1999) *Human Flourishing*. Cambridge: Cambridge University Press.

Peck, J. and Wai-chung Yeung, H. (eds) (2005) *Remaking the Global Economy*. London: Sage.

Pettinger, L. (2005) Friends, relations and colleagues: the blurred boundaries of the workplace, in J. Parry, R. Taylor, L. Pettinger, and M. Glucksmann (eds) *A New Socialogy of Work?* Oxford, Blackwell Publishing.

Philips, J. (2007) *Care. Key Concepts*. Oxford: Polity Press.

Phillips, J., Bernard, M. and Chittenden, M. (2002) *Juggling Work and Care: The experiences of working carers of older adults*. Bristol: The Policy Press.

Pile, S. and Thrift, N. (eds) (1995) *Mapping the Subject: Geographies of cultural transformation*. London: Routledge.

Pollert, A. (1981) *Girls, Wives, Factory Lives*. London: Macmillan.

Portes, A. (1998) Social Capital: Its origins and applications in contemporary sociology. *Annual Review of Sociology* 24: 1–24.

Powell, J. L. (2006) *Social Theory and Aging*. Oxford: Rowman and Littlefield.

Pratt, G. (1998) Inscribing domestic work on Filipina bodies, in H. Nast and S. Pile (eds) *Places Through the Body*. London: Routledge.

Prout, A. (ed.) (2000) *The Body, Childhood and Society*. London: Macmillan.

Putnam, R. (2000) *Bowling Alone: The collapse and revival of American community*. New York: Simon and Schuster.

Qureshi, H. (1990) Boundaries between formal and informal care-giving work, in C. Ungerson (ed.) *Gender and Caring: Work and welfare in Britain and Scandinavia*. London: Harvester Wheatsheaf.

Radio Prague (2007) www.radio.cz/en/article/89547 (21 March 2007).

Ransome, P. (2008) The boundary problem in work-life balance studies: theorizing the total responsibility burden, in C. Warhurst, D. Eikhof and A. Haunschild (eds) *Work Less, Live More? A Critical Analysis of the Work-Life Boundary*. Basingstoke: Palgrave Macmillan.

Rawlings, W. K. (1992) *Friendship Matters: Communication, dialectics, and the life course*. New York: Aldine de Gruyter.

Reimer, S. and Leslie, D. (2004) Identity, consumption, and the home. *Home Cultures* 1: 187–208.

Reynolds, T. and Zontini, E. (2006) *A Comparative Study Of Care and Provision Across Caribbean and Italian Transnational Families*. Families & Social Capital ESRC Research Group Working Paper No. 16. http://www.lsbu.ac.uk/families/workingpapers/familieswp16.pdf. Accessed 28 October 2009.

Ribbens, J. (1994) *Mothers and their Children: A feminist sociology of childrearing*. London: Sage.

Roberts, E. (2004) *'Me Time': Life temporality and customized working patterns of employees without childcare responsibilities*. Leeds: Leeds University Business School.

Rodrigies, M. (2004) *Knowledge-Based Economy and Competitiveness*. Report 3 European Commission's Advisory Group on Social Sciences and the Humanities in the European Research Area, Brussels: European Commission.

Rose, G. (1993) *Feminism and Geography: The limits of geographical knowledge*. Cambridge: Polity Press.

Roseneil, S. and Budgeon, S. (2004) Cultures of intimacy and care beyond the 'family': personal life and social change in the early 21st century. *Current Sociology* 52(2): 135–159.

Rosenthal, C., Martin-Matthews, A. and Keefe, J. (2007) Care management and care provision for older relatives amongst employed informal care-givers. *Ageing and Society* 27: 755–778.

Rudd, K. (2006) Faith in Politics. *The Monthly*, No 17. http://www.themonthly.com.au/node/300. Accessed 28 October 2009.

Russell, C. (2007) What do older women and men want? Gender differences in the 'lived experience' of ageing. *Current Sociology* 55(2): 173–192.

Saegert, S. (1980) Masculine Cities and Feminine Suburbs: Polarized Ideas, Contradictory Realities. *Signs*, (5)3, Supplement, Women and the American City, S96–S111.

Salamon, L. M. and Sokolowski, W. (2001) Volunteering in a Cross-National Perspective: Evidence From 24 Countries. *Working Papers of the Johns Hopkins Comparative Nonprofit Sector Project*, no. 40. Baltimore: The Johns Hopkins Center for Civil Society Studies.

Saraceno, C. (2008) *Families, Ageing and Social Policy: Generational solidarity in European welfare states* (Globalization and Welfare Series). London: Edward Elgar.

Sarre, S. (2007) *Risk in Dual-earner and Working Lone Parent Households: Parents and young people's perceptions*. Social Contexts and Responses to Risk Research Network, Working Paper. London: London School of Economics.

Scanzoni, J. H. (2001) Reconnecting household and community: an alternative strategy for theory and policy. *Journal of Family Issues* 22: 243–264.

Scharf, T., Phillipson, C. and Smith, A. (2003) *Older People's Perceptions of the Neighbourhood: Evidence from socially deprived urban areas*. Sociological Research Online.

Scott, K. A. (2002) "You want to be a Girl and not my Friend", African-American/Black girls' play activities with and without boys. *Childhood* 9(4): 397–414.

Scott, A. and Wenger, G. C. (1995) Gender and social support networks in later life, in

S. Arber and J. Ginn (eds) *Connecting Gender and Aging*. Buckingham: Open University Press.

Scottish Office (1998) *New Community Schools Project*. Edinburgh: The Stationary Office.

Sen, A. (2001) *Development as Freedom*. Oxford: Oxford University Press.

Sevenhuijsen, S. (1998) *Citizenship and the Ethics of Care: Feminist Considerations on Justice, Morality and Politics*. London: Routledge.

Sevenhuijsen, S. (2000) Caring in the third way: the reflection between obligation, responsibility and care in the third way discourse. *Critical Social Policy* 20(1): 5–37.

Sharp, J. P., Routledge, P., Philo C. and Paddison, R. (2000) Entanglements of power: geographies of domination/resistance, in J. P. Sharp, P. Routledge, C. Philo and R. Paddison (eds) *Entanglements of Power: Geographies of domination/resistance*. London: Routledge.

Silk, J. (1998) Caring at a distance. *Ethics, Place and Environment* 1(2): 165–182.

Silk, J. (2000) Caring at a distance: (Im)partiality, moral motivation and the ethics of representation – Introduction. *Ethics, Place and Environment* 3(1): 303–309.

Smith, D. (1998) How far should we care? On the spatial scope of beneficence. *Progress in Human Geography* 22(15): 15–38.

Smith, D. (1999) Geography and ethics: how far should we go? *Progress in Human Geography* 23(1): 119–125.

Smith, N. (2002) The urbanization of neoliberalism: theoretical debates, new globalism, new urbanism – gentrification as global urban strategy. *Antipode* 34(3): 427–445.

Smith, K. and Baughman, R. (2007) Caring for America's aging population: a profile of the direct-care workforce. New York: *Monthly Labor Review* 20–26.

Smith, F. and Barker, J. (2000) Contested spaces: children's experiences of out of school care in England and Wales. *Childhood* 7(3): 315–333.

Smith, G. and Cantley, C. (1985) *Assessing Health Care: A study in organisational evaluation*. Buckingham: Open University Press.

Somerville, P. (1992) Homelessness and the meaning of home: rooflessness or rootlessness. *International Journal of Urban and Regional Research* 16: 528–539.

Southerton, D. (2006) Analysing the temporal organization of daily life: social constraints, practices and their allocation. *Sociology* 40: 435–454.

Spencer, L. and Pahl, R. (2006) *Rethinking Friendship: Hidden solidarities today*. Princeton and Oxford: Princeton University Press.

Spilsbury, J. C. (2005) "We don't really get to go out in the front yard" – children's home range and neighbourhood. *Children's Geographies* (3)1: 79–99.

Stacey, M. (1988) *The Sociology of Health and Healing*. London: Unwin Hyman.

Statistics South Africa (2001) *A Survey of Time Use Survey of South African Men and Women*. www.statssa.gov.za. Accessed 23 March 2009.

Statistics South Africa (2001) Census. www.statssa.gove.za/census2001. Accessed 2 April 2009.

Statistics South Africa (2006) *South African Labour Force Survey*. www.statssa.gov.za. Accessed 25 March 2009.

Stephens, J. (1999) A fight for her time: challenges facing professional mothers, in L. McKie, S. Bowlby and S. Gregory (eds) *Gender, Power and the Household*. Basingstoke: Macmillan.

Stephenson, C. and Stewart, P. (2001) The Whispering Shadow: Collectivism and individualism at Ikeda-Hoover and Nissan UK. *Sociological Research Online* 6(3). http://www.socresonline.org.uk/6/3/stephenson.html. Accessed 28 October 2009.

Stevenson, O. (2008) *From Public Policy to Family Practices: A study of children and their families use of Information and Communication Technology.* Unpublished PhD. Leeds: Department of Geography, University of Leeds.

Sullivan, O. (2001) The division of domestic labour: twenty years of change? *Sociology* 34(3): 437–456.

Sullivan, O. (2006) *Changing Gender Relations, Changing Families: Tracing the pace of change over time* (Gender Lens Series). New York: Rowman & Littlefield.

Sullivan, C. and Lewis, S. (2001) Home-based telework, gender, and the synchronization of work and family: perspectives of teleworkers and their co-residents. *Gender, Work and Organization* 8(2): 123–145.

Tabboni, S. (2001) The idea of social time in Norbert Elias. *Time and Society* 10(1): 5–27.

Talamantes, M. and Aranda, M. (2004) *Cultural Competency in Working with Latino Family Caregivers. San Francisco: National Center on Caregiving.*

Tanzanian Government (2009) Human Resources Department. *Strategy to Develop the Human Resources of the Tanzanian Population.* http://www.tanzania.go.tz/human.html. Accessed 25 May 2009.

Taylor, R. (2005) Rethinking voluntary work, in L. Pettinger, J. Parry, R. Taylor and M. Glucksmann (eds) *A New Sociology of Work?* Oxford: Blackwell.

Taylor, L., Seeley J. T. and Kajurac, E. (1966) Informal care for illness in rural southwest Uganda: the central role that women play. *Health Transition Review* 6: 49–56.

Thrift, N. (1983) On determination of social action in space and time (Environment and Planning D. Society and Space), reprinted in N. Thrift (1996) *Spatial Formations.* London: Sage.

Thrift, N. (1996) *Spatial Formations.* Thousand Oaks, CA: Sage.

Thrift, N. (2006) Space. *Theory, Culture Society* 23: 2–3, 139–155.

Thomas, C. (1993) De-constructing concepts of care. *Sociology* 27(4): 649–669.

Thomas, C. (1995) Domestic labour and health: bringing it all back home. *Sociology of Health and Illness* 17: 323–352.

Thomas, M. E. (2005) "I think it's just natural": the spatiality of racial segregation in a US high school, *Environment and Planning A* 37: 1233–1248.

Thomson, S. (2005) 'Territorialising' the primary school playground: deconstructing the geography of playtime. *Children's Geographies* 3(1): 63–78.

Tronto, J. C. (1987) Beyond Gender Difference to a Theory of Care, *Signs* 12(4): 644–663.

Tronto, J. C. (1993) *Moral Boundaries: A political argument for an ethic of care.* London: Routledge.

Turner, J. H. and Stets, J. E. (2005) *The Sociology of Emotions.* Cambridge: Cambridge University Press.

Twigg, J. (1999) The spatial ordering of care: public and private in bathing support at home. *Sociology of Health and Illness* 21(4): 381–400.

Twigg, J. (2000) *Bathing: The Body and Community Care.* London: Routledge.

Ungerson, C. (1983) Why do women care?, in J. Finch and D. Groves (eds) *A Labour of Love: Women, work and caring.* London: Routledge and Kegan Paul.

Ungerson, C. (1990) *Gender and Caring: Work and welfare in Britain and Scandinavia.* Hemel Hempstead, UK: Harvester Wheatsheaf.

Ungerson, C. (2005) Care, work and feeling. *Sociological Review* 53(SUPP/2): 188–203.

United Nations (2000) *Millennium Development Goals.* New York: UN.

United Nations (2002) *Expert Group On Sustainable Development Indicators.* New York: UN.

United Nations (2008) *Millennium Development Goals Review*. New York: UN.

United Nations Children's Fund (2006) *Child Friendly Schools: Quality of Education*. New York: UNICEF.

United Nations Children's Fund (2008) *The State of the World's Children*. New York: UNICEF.

United Nations Children's Fund (2009) *Learning Plus Initiative: Schools as Centres for Care and Support*. New York: UNICEF.

US Bureau of Labour Statistics (2007) *American Time Use Survey*. www.bls.gov. Accessed 22 March 2009.

US Census Bureau (2000) *Population Profile of the United States: 2000*. People at Risk: Health Insurance Coverage. http://www.census.gov/population/www/pop-profile/files/2000/chap15.pdf. Accessed 28 October 2009.

US Census Bureau (2003) *2001 American Community Survey*. Washington DC: US Census Bureau.

US Census Bureau (2004) *Population Profile of the United States*. Washington DC: US Census Bureau.

US Census Bureau (2007) *Current Population Reports: Income, Poverty and Health Insurance Coverage in the United States*. Washington DC: US Census Bureau.

US Department of Health and Human Services (2001) *National Standards for Culturally and Linguistically Appropriate Services in Health Care*, Office of Minority Health, Final Report. Washington DC, U.S. Department of Health and Human Services.

Valentine, G. (1997) A safe place to grow up? Parenting, perceptions of children's safety and the rural idyll. *Journal of Rural Studies* 13(2): 137–148.

Valentine, G. and Holloway, S. (2000) Spatiality and the new social studies of childhood. *Sociology* 34: 763.

Valentine, G. and Holloway, S. (2001) On-line Dangers?: Geographies of parents' fears for children's safety in cyberspace. *Professional Geographer* 53(1): 71–83.

van Blerk, L. and Ansell, N. (2007) Alternative care giving in the context of HIV/AIDS in southern Africa: complex strategies for care. *Journal for International Development* 19: 865–884.

VanEvery, J. (1995) *Heterosexual Women Changing the Family: Refusing to be a wife!* London: Taylor and Francis.

VanEvery, J. (1996) Sinking into his arms … . arms in his sink: heterosexuality and feminism revisited, in L. Adkins and V. Merchant (eds) *Sexualizing the Social: Power and the organization of sexuality*. Basingstoke: Macmillan.

VanEvery, J. (1997) Understanding gendered inequality: reconceptualizing housework. *Women's Studies International Forum* Special Issue 20(3): 397–410.

Venn, S., Arber, S., Meadows, R. and Hislop, J. (2008) The fourth shift: exploring the gendered nature of sleep disruption among couples with children. *British Journal of Sociology* 59(1): 79–97.

Wall, K. (2008) *Leave Policy Models and the Articulation of Work and Family in Europe: A Comparative Perspective*. Paper presented at ISA Research Committee on Family Research Conference, Lisbon, Portugal.

Watson, N., McKie, L., Hughes, B., Hopkins, D. and Gregory, S. (2004) (Inter)dependence, needs and care: the potential for disability and feminist theorists to develop an emancipatory model. *Sociology* 38(2): 531–550.

Webber, M. (1964) The urban place and the non-place urban realm, in M. M. Webber, J. W. Dyckman, D. L. Foley, A. Z. Gutenberg, W. L. C. Wheaton and C. B. Wurster. *Explorations in Urban Structure*. Philadelphia: University of Pennsylvania.

Weeks, J., Heaphy, B. and Donovan, C. (1999) *Same Sex Intimacies: Families of choice and other life experiments*. London: Routledge.

Wellman, B. (1982) *Studying Personal Communities in East York*. Research Paper 128. Toronto: Centre for Urban and Community Studies: University of Toronto.

Wellman, B. (2001) Physical place and cyberplace: the rise of personalised networking. *International Journal of Urban and Regional Research* 25(3): 227.

Wellman, B. and Wortley, S. (1990) Different strokes from different folks: community ties and social support. *The American Journal of Sociology* 96(3): 559–588.

Westwood, S. (1984) *All Day, Every Day: Factory and family in the making of women's lives*. London: Pluto Press.

White, S. (2002) From the politics of poverty to the politics of identity? Child rights and working children in Bangladesh. *Journal of International Development* 14: 725–735.

Williams, F. (2004) *Rethinking Families*. London: Calouste Gulbenkian Foundation.

Williams, G. (1984) The genesis of chronic illness: narrative reconstruction. *Sociology of Health and Illness* 6(2): 175–200.

Williams, S. J. (2001) *Emotions and Social Theory: Corporeal reflections on the (ir) rational*. London: Sage.

Williams, S. (2000) Reason, emotion and embodiment: is 'mental' health a contradiction in terms? *Sociology of Health and Illness* 22: 5.

Willmott, P. (1987) *Friendship Networks and Social Support*. PSI Research Report 666, London.

Wilson, F. (2004) *Organizational Behaviour and Work: A critical introduction*. Oxford: Oxford University Press.

Wolf, D. A. and Longino, C. F. (2005) Our 'increasingly mobile society'? The curious persistence of a false belief. *The Gerontologist* 45(1): 5–11.

Women's Unit of the Cabinet Office (2000) *The Female Forfeit – The Cost of Being a Woman*. London: The Cabinet Office.

Woolcock, M. (2001) The place of social capital in understanding social and economic outcomes. *Canadian Journal of Policy Research* 2(1): 11–17. http://homepages.wmich.edu/~jbiles/woolcock.pdf. Accessed April 7 2009.

Wood, D. and Beck, R. (1990) Do's and don't's: family rules, rooms and their relationships. *Environments Quarterly* 7(1): 2–14.

World Bank (2007) *Migration and Development Brief 3*. Development Prospects Group, Migration and Remittance Team: Remittance Trends 2007. www.worldbank.org. Accessed 28 October 2009.

World Bank Data (2008) *Data on world economies*. www.worldbank.org. Accessed 28 March 2009.

World Bank Statistics Africa (2009) Data on Africa. www.worldbank.org/afr/stats. Accessed 28th March 2009.

World Health Organization (2002) *Impact of AIDS On Older People In Africa: Zimbabwe Case Study*. Geneva: WHO.

World Health Organization (2004) *A Special Health Promotion Project: Health Promoting Schools Initiative*. Geneva: WHO. Available online at: www.afro.who. Accessed 28 October 2009.

World Health Organization (2007) *The World Health Report 2007: A Safer Future. Global Public Health Security in the 21st Century*. Geneva: WHO.

Young, I. M. (2002) Autonomy, Welfare Reform and Meaningful Work, in Feder Kittay, E. and Feder, E. K. (eds) *The Subject of Care: Feminist Perspectives on Dependency*. Lanham, MD: Rowman and Littlefield.

Young, L. (2003) The 'place' of street children in Kampala, Uganda: marginalisation, resistance, and acceptance in the urban environment, *Environment and Planning D* 21(5): 607–628.

Young, L. and Daniel, K. (2003) Affectual trust in the workplace. *International Journal of Human Resource Management* 14(1): 139–155.

Zlotnik, H. (2003) *The Global Dimensions of Female Migration*. Migration Policy Institute. www.migrationinformation.org. Accessed 28 October 2009.

Zontini, E. (2004) *Italian Families and Social Capital: Rituals and the Provision of Care in British-Italian Transnational Families*, Working Paper. London: South Bank University, Families and Social Capital ESRC Research group. http://www.lsbu.ac.uk/families/workingpapers/familieswp6.pdf. Accessed 27 February 2009.

Index

Note: page numbers in **bold** refer to figures and tables.